The Chinese in Vancouver, 1945-80

Contemporary Chinese Studies

This new series, a joint initiative of UBC Press and the UBC Institute of Asian Research, Centre for Chinese Research, seeks to make available the best scholarly work on contemporary China. Future volumes will cover a wide range of subjects related to China, Taiwan, and the overseas Chinese world.

Wing Chung Ng's *The Chinese in Vancouver, 1945-80: The Pursuit of Identity and Power* is the second book in the series. Glen Peterson's *The Power of Words: Literacy and Revolution in South China, 1949-95* was the first.

Editorial Board

Wing Chung Ng

The Chinese in Vancouver, 1945-80: The Pursuit of Identity and Power

UBC Press / Vancouver

Printed in Canada on acid-free paper ∞

ISBN 0-7748-0732-6

Canadian Cataloguing in Publication Data

Ng, Wing Chung, 1961-
   The Chinese in Vancouver, 1945-80

   (Contemporary Chinese studies, ISSN 1206-9523)
   Includes bibliographical references and index.
   ISBN 0-7748-0732-6

   1. Chinese – British Columbia – Vancouver – History. 2. Chinese – British Columbia – Vancouver – Ethnic identity. 3. Chinese Canadians – British Columbia – Vancouver – History.* 4. Chinese Canadians – British Columbia – Vancouver – Ethnic identity.* 5. Vancouver (B.C.) – History. I. Title. II. Series.

FC3847.9C5N5 1999   305.895'1071133   C99-910997-9
F1089.5.V22N5 1999

UBC Press acknowledges the financial support of the Government of Canada through the Book Publishing Industry Development Program (BPIDP) for our publishing activities.

Canadä

We also gratefully acknowledge the ongoing support to our publishing program from the Canada Council for the Arts and the British Columbia Arts Council.

UBC Press
University of British Columbia
6344 Memorial Road
Vancouver, BC V6T 1Z2
(604) 822-5959
Fax: 1-800-668-0821
E-mail: info@ubcpress.ubc.ca
www.ubcpress.ubc.ca

To How Ling

Contents

Maps, Figures, and Tables

Acknowledgments

I want to begin by thanking S.T. So and Eve Au for imbuing in me a love of history while I was a high school student at Ying Wa College in Hong Kong in the late 1970s. At Hong Kong University, W.E. Cheong, Mary Turnbull, and Ming K. Chan initiated me into historical research. Mary, in particular, guided me patiently as I began my study of the Chinese overseas. At the University of British Columbia (UBC), where this work first took shape as a doctoral dissertation, I was fortunate to have Edgar Wickberg as my supervisor. Ed's fine scholarship, his sense of responsibility to the field of learning, and his profound humanity have continued to challenge and inspire me. At UBC I also drew great benefits from the wise counsel and generous support of Alex Woodside, Graham Johnson, and Diana Lary. Bob McDonald was a relentless critic of sloppy scholarship and half-baked ideas. Bernard Wong and Him Mark Lai were gracious hosts when I worked briefly in San Francisco in the summer of 1991, seeking to cultivate some comparative perspectives on the Chinese experience in North America.

The revision of the manuscript began after I joined the history faculty at the University of Texas at San Antonio in 1993. I thank my colleagues Patrick Kelly, David Johnson, and James Schneider for reading my work in progress; many others have generously shared with me their ideas. The year (1996-97) I spent at the National Humanities Center (NHC) as a postdoctoral fellow was immensely beneficial. I am grateful to Lloyd Kramer and members of the seminar on 'Achieved Identities' for many hours of stimulating discussion and the opportunity to present my work. Bob Connor, Kent Mullikin, and the wonderful staff at the NHC all made my time there unforgettable. I also want to thank Vasant Kaiwar, Sucheta Majumdar, Don Nonini, and members of the international migration work group at Duke University for the exchanges at our monthly gatherings. Last but not least, my sojourn in North Carolina allowed me to further my conversation with Arif Dirlik, who, since I was a graduate student, has provided a number of important observations on conceptual issues in my work.

In Vancouver, an important part of my research was conducted at the Special Collections Division of the UBC Library, the Asian Library at UBC, the City of Vancouver Archives, and the Vancouver Public Library. The kind assistance of their librarians and staff is much appreciated. Among the local Chinese, I have received tremendous help from so many individuals and organizations that it would not be possible to thank them one by one here. I managed to conduct forty personal interviews and talked to many others on numerous occasions. A number of organizations kindly gave me access to their publications and internal records, which were absolutely essential to my analysis. Certainly, a lot more can be done to reach out to the members of this ethnic group, and I hope my work will stimulate others to tap broadly and fruitfully into this reservoir of historical memories. In this regard, I am especially hopeful that the recently opened Museum and Archives at the Chinese Cultural Centre, which I visited only briefly in January 1999, will soon develop into a major repository of historical records that will be indispensable for any future study of the Chinese in Canada.

I am glad to have a chance to acknowledge crucial financial support for this work. The full period of my training at UBC (1988-93) was funded generously by a Canadian Commonwealth Scholarship. The University of Texas at San Antonio provided a Faculty Research Award in 1995 and a Faculty Development Grant in 1996. Finally, my year at the NHC was made possible by a postdoctoral fellowship from the Andrew W. Mellon Foundation.

In the final preparation of the book manuscript, Bill Bishel produced the maps and Joanne Poon helped me with the glossary. I am also greatly appreciative of the copyediting by Joanne Richardson and of the sound advice and professional support of Jean Wilson and Holly Keller-Brohman, my editors at UBC Press.

As many scholars have noticed and acknowledged, no less important to us in our scholarly endeavors are the spiritual, emotional, and practical support of our families and friends. I want to thank, above all, my parents and my brother and sister and their families for their understanding and willingness to endure our physical separation. I am exceptionally blessed by my truly loving in-laws. Not to be forgotten is Wing Lock, and I hope the publication of this book will be a celebration of our friendship of over thirty years. In Vancouver, I want to thank Raymond Cheung and many friends at the Chinese Christian Chapel, especially Eve and John Lam, Jackie and Patrick Tung, and Kay and Ka-yin Leung.

Finally, both Cheuk Ming and Stella deserve a special note of thanks for having had to live with this project for as long as they care to remember. My deepest appreciation goes to How Ling, my wife and soulmate, for her love and our shared Christian faith.

Note on Chinese Terms

As a general rule, I render the English names of Chinese persons, publications, and ethnic organizations in their local forms whenever they are known: hence Foon Sien (Wong), not Huang Wenfu; the *Chinese Times*, not *Dahan gongbao*; and the Chinese Cultural Centre, not Zhonghua wenhua zhongxin. I have also decided to follow usages familiar to many English readers, including Sun Yat-sen and Chiang Kai-shek instead of Sun Zhongshan and Jiang Jieshi, respectively. In a few cases, such as my preference for Kuomintang rather than Guomindang and the Wade-Giles spelling of certain individuals affiliated with Taiwan, my choices were based on political sensitivity. All other Chinese names and special terms are given in standard pinyin. As a consolation for such inconsistencies, readers can look up Chinese characters in the glossary at the end of the book.

The Chinese in Vancouver

1
Introduction

On Sunday, 25 April 1993, some 5,000 people voted in one of the most contested elections in the history of Vancouver's Chinatown. The occasion was the election of that city's Chinese Cultural Centre (CCC) board of directors. Fearing trouble, organizers had arranged some private security guards to ensure order in and around the venue, and, in addition, several police officers were on the scene. Just outside the hall, where members cast their ballots, booths were set up by candidates and hundreds of campaign workers.[1] The tense atmosphere surrounding this election was not unexpected. For several months, the CCC had been the subject of a heated public debate and, at times, acrimonious exchanges between two camps. On one side was a group of self-designated 'reformers' seeking to invigorate a community organization that they claimed had been mired in partisan politics and poor management. On the other side stood the incumbents, whose position in the CCC was based mainly on the support of the traditional clan and native place organizations in Chinatown. The latter disputed the criticisms of their leadership and, in turn, accused their 'detractors' of conspiring to mount 'a hostile takeover.'[2]

From its very beginning in 1973, the CCC had been a product of the Canadian government policy of multiculturalism, which encouraged ethnic minorities to preserve and celebrate their cultural heritages with fellow Canadians. The CCC's initial supporters came from all existing generations of immigrants and local-born Chinese, including a majority of Chinatown's well entrenched traditional organizations. Two decades later, however, many of Vancouver's Chinese began questioning whether the CCC, in its current form, still represented the interests and experiences of a rapidly expanding and increasingly diverse Chinese population, many of whom had arrived only recently from Hong Kong, Mainland China, Taiwan, and numerous other places. At the heart of the debate were questions about cultural representation and identity: What should be the content of ethnic Chinese culture in a Canadian context? How should the power to define Chineseness be negotiated? One particularly salient aspect of identity politics in the 1993 election battle was the perceived alignment of the CCC with Mainland China and the office of the Chinese Consulate-General in Vancouver. In the aftermath of the Tiananmen Square incident of 1989, many local supporters of the pro-democracy movement in China (and Hong Kong) demanded that the CCC not be wedded to Beijing and that it be amenable to non-Mainland Chinese cultural models and political ideas.

While this struggle over the CCC and the underlying issue of identity was new to more recent immigrants, long-time Chinese residents of Vancouver may well have realized that it was not the first time that a community organization had been engulfed in such a storm. In the late 1970s, the young CCC itself was involved in a similar 'takeover,' successfully wresting the control of the Chinese Benevolent Association (CBA) from the pro-Taiwan elements in the Kuomintang.[3] Elderly settlers might even have recalled that in 1961-2 the conservative leadership of the CBA had withstood a public challenge from the younger generation of postwar immigrants, who had demanded that it admit representatives from their group.

The Chinese in Vancouver, 1945-80, examines some of these events, but it is important to note that these struggles were the tip of an iceberg. Beneath each confrontation was an ongoing contest – engaged in by several generations of Chinese immigrants and their Canadian-born descendants – over the meaning of being Chinese in Canada. This book traces the beginning of this process of identity formation and contestation to the period right after the Second World War. It unveils a plurality of cultural positions and definitions within this ethnic group and contends that their evolving interactions constituted a discourse on Chineseness over the span of some thirty-five

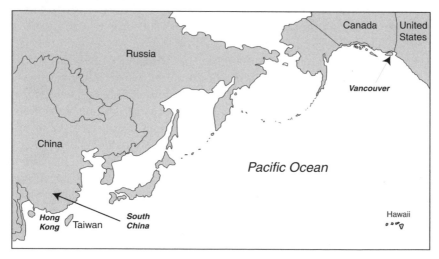

Map 1   Pacific Canada and South China

years. It seeks to explain the differential constructions of Chinese identity within the local context of Vancouver, while attending to the effects of relevant Canadian state policies and the transnational ties of the ethnic Chinese with China and their specific home areas. My primary objective is to help us rethink some deep-seated essentialist notions and to overcome an ahistorical tendency when we talk about ethnic Chinese identities (or, indeed, about any cultural and ethnic identity).

Directly or indirectly, this book has been inspired by a wide variety of scholarly work. One source of inspiration is the anthropological and historical scholarship developed in the 1950s and 1960s, which examined the 'Overseas Chinese' in Southeast Asia.[4] The Cold War atmosphere cast suspicion on the loyalty of the huge population of relatively affluent ethnic Chinese to the indigenous nation-states of this region, and it raised the question of Chinese identity to a new level of academic interest and political urgency. Most of these earlier studies sought to chart the course of ethnic Chinese cultural adaptation and assimilation. Many of them yielded insights into the community structure, leadership, organizational networks, and some salient divisions among the minority Chinese in various Southeast Asian countries. This scholarship was the first to alert me to the possibility of studying dimensions of social organization and cultural life in order to illuminate the more subtle and complex issue of identity, though I realize that it is imperative to eschew the structuralist paradigm and the unilinear logic of assimilation implicit in these earlier works.[5]

Intellectually, *The Chinese in Vancouver, 1945-80*, is more like the new literature on identity and ethnicity that emerged in the 1970s. In the wake of Frederik Barth's trailblazing essay on shifting and permeable ethnic boundaries, scholars have come to stress the situational quality of ethnic identity and its negotiation by individuals, interest groups, and state authorities. The existence of communicable cultural traits and inheritable biological elements is perhaps undeniable, but all these 'primordial' items acquire significance and become part of an identity only in specific contexts. Rather than fixed and stable, ethnic and cultural identities are contingent and malleable. Hence, the most meaningful inquiry does not compose a list of 'heritage items' – such as language, religion, social customs, dietary habits, and so on – in order to see if an identity is present, but, rather, it discerns the historical process within which an identity takes shape and explores how it evolves over time.[6]

This view of identity as a negotiable cultural construct can be applied to the study of individual and collective identities, to the relationship between these two levels of identities, and to their interplay with variables in different arenas of social, economic, and political life. I focus on the construction of identities by generational cohorts among the Vancouver Chinese. These cohorts started with the early migrants, mostly single males, from

Guangdong Province, who arrived in Canada before the exclusion era (1923-47). In the postwar period, these 'old-timers' were joined by a new generation of young immigrants as well as by the small group of Canadian-born Chinese coming of age around this time. Another cohort of local-born youth arrived on the scene by the 1970s, at a time when Canada opened its doors to yet another wave of Chinese immigration. The analysis of generational pattern and distinction is of course germane to immigration history and is by no means unique to the ethnic Chinese.[7] Nonetheless, I go beyond the commonplace emphasis on group differences and mutual estrangement to delineate the process of group interaction and engagement. I show that, although generational cohorts could be internally divided, among the Vancouver Chinese it was primarily the various group articulations as well as the perennial conflicts between the generations that punctuated the history of identity and defined its discursive parameters.[8]

By drawing out the multiplicity of self-definitions and, thereby, the historical agency of the ethnic Chinese, I intend to further a revisionist theme in the relevant Canadian literature. Despite some excellent historical works based on Chinese perspectives over the years,[9] Canadian scholars have developed a long tradition of studying the 'Orientals' in their country so as to shed light on the history of Anglo-Canadian racism, especially in British Columbia. The origins and the manifestations of racism undoubtedly constitute a legitimate subject for scholarly research, but in such studies Chinese people are often portrayed as no more than hapless victims of racial prejudice and discrimination, and Chinese identity is seen as a matter of external imposition.[10] Such a Foucauldian gaze is, indeed, behind an important book on Vancouver's Chinatown written by the Canadian-trained cultural geographer Kay Anderson. Deploying an impressive array of Western social theorists, Anderson argues that 'Chinatown' and 'Chinese' were racial categories constructed by European Canadians through the use of state machinery. The ensuing 'racialization' involved an elaborate process of cultural management by which, through legislation and other forms of government sanction, the host society perpetually defined ethnic Chinese as 'others' and 'outsiders.' Among the Chinese themselves Anderson conveniently finds an absence of initiatives and conscious motivations, except for the internalization of imposed categories and exogenous characterizations, which shows their subjugation to a Western cultural hegemony.[11]

Anderson's theoretical insights are not to be taken lightly, for the asymmetrical relationship between the dominant host and the Chinese minority was too glaring to be ignored. However, her implicit assumption concerning the erasure of Chinese subjectivity is questionable. Her approach overlooks entirely the importance of Chinese agency. Preoccupied with the unyielding domination of the Western mind – an equally idealized

'Occidental' monolithic construct? – even a sympathetic scholar ends up depriving the Chinese people of their voice.[12]

In order to hear a subaltern community speak, I turned to the ethnic Chinese media and public organizational life. Until the end of the period studied (1945-80), when it was overtaken by Toronto, Vancouver had the largest ethnic Chinese population in Canada. Its Chinatown had at least one, and as many as three, Chinese-language dailies, in addition to an English-language biweekly magazine and other smaller and irregular publications. Editorials, news reports, announcements, letters to the editor, and items in the literary supplements were all important outlets for ethnic Chinese voices, allowing us to recapture important events, personalities, and opinions. Even more pivotal to my analysis are the large number of Chinese voluntary associations.[13] Some of them – like the CCC in 1993 or the CBA in the early 1960s and again in the late 1970s – provided an arena in which identity battles broke out. Many others were themselves not sites of contention but, rather, vehicles for the articulation of interests. These included the many youth societies established by the new immigrants in the 1950s and the various organizations emerging in the same period to represent the interests of Canadian-born Chinese. As is shown repeatedly through the first several chapters of this book, these two segments of the Chinese minority clashed over their different cultural orientations and respective propositions for the future of the ethnic group as a whole. Simultaneously, since the cultural claims of these two groups defied and challenged the once dominant position of the old-timers, the elderly settlers resorted to their own traditional organizations in Chinatown, especially the clan and native place associations, to reassert their leadership and influence.

A study of identity and cultural consciousness that focuses on organizational history raises our understanding beyond the level of subjectivities currently so prevalent in cultural and literary studies. This approach allows us to examine the intersection of institutional practices and the power of cultural definition, both of which are especially meaningful given the asymmetrical relationship between the Chinese minority and the dominant host. With ethnic Chinese in Canada being systemically denied access to mainstream resources and opportunities until well after 1945, their myriad voluntary associations constituted a public arena that offered leadership positions, social prestige, mutual support, and a sense of community. These organizations amounted to a self-delineated, albeit circumscribed, social and cultural space for the endeavour of and indulgence in self-definition.

My conceptualization of the subject of Chinese identities in Vancouver is also stimulated by recent interest in diaspora histories and some related work in cultural studies. I understand the reluctance to describe the experience of ethnic Chinese as a diaspora because of its 'inappropriate' and 'unfavourable' reference to the Jews, though I tend to agree with William Safran and, recently, Robin Cohen that the term should not be strictly tied to any historical Jewish archetype.[14] In any case, I invoke the notion of diaspora gingerly to make two analytical points. First of all, Chinese immigration into Vancouver and the rest of Canada was, and still is, part of a larger regional and then global movement of the Chinese population outside of China. To that extent, it is worthwhile to employ some comparative perspectives within this diaspora, juxtaposing and contrasting the experience of the Vancouver Chinese with the divergent or parallel experiences of ethnic Chinese elsewhere. This comparative discussion, which I take up in the last chapter, advances the effort to contextualize and historicize identity construction. This effort, in turn, undercuts the essentialism of an uncritical Chinese cultural paradigm that is quite common in popular journalism and even in some of the scholarly literature on East Asian capitalism (with reference to the success of global Chinese businesses).[15]

More important, following the lead of Stuart Hall and others ruminating on migrant consciousness and cultural hybridity, I see in the critical notion of diaspora identity a discursive strategy. It is a strategy that concerns and prioritizes the perspectives of the transplanted individuals and groups by placing their subjectivity at the centre of the historical stage without unduly emphasizing the hegemonic narratives of either the sending country or the host society.[16] In other words, our project need not be either *e*migration or *im*migration history, viewing the subjects against some supposedly authentic 'Chinese,' 'Canadian,' or any other norms. Migration and settlement constitute an arena of identity construction in and of themselves, and the complex historical and cultural processes therein deserve to be unveiled on their own terms.

This approach is particularly useful in underscoring the evolving consciousness of the ever-shifting relationships of Vancouver's Chinese with China and Canada in the period studied. From the 1940s on, Chinese in Vancouver may have joined most ethnic Chinese communities overseas in shedding the China-oriented and sojourning mentality of the early twentieth century in order to embark on local adaptation and permanent settlement. However, this general shifting from one pole to another hardly begins to capture the dynamics and complexities of Chinese identity construction and contestation.[17] As I will show, the Chinese sense of identity in Canada was continually defined and mediated both by expressions of Old World political affiliations, cultural sentiments, and native place ties and by New World experiences in rejection, alienation, accommodation, and acceptance. Furthermore, each of these variables could play out differently for different groups and at different times, thereby underlying and adding to the intensity of the identity debate. Into the 1970s, when Canadian multiculturalism began to embrace minority ethnicities, Chinese ethnic sentiments and cultural expressions still could not be understood in isolation from their contacts with their place of origin in Hong Kong and South China. Meanwhile, internal divisions and contestation remained salient in the ongoing identity discourse.[18]

Finally, *The Chinese in Vancouver, 1945-80*, dovetails conceptually with a current trend in Chinese studies – a trend that attends to the issue of ethnic and cultural identities, especially in the contexts of internal migration or minority localities. No matter whether it is the Manchus in the Qing period or the Muslims in the People's Republic of China, the Subei people in modern Shanghai or the regional groups that made up the residents of nineteenth-century Hankou, the Hakka scattered throughout many parts of South and Central China or the belligerent speech groups in the coastal provinces of Fujian and Guangdong (and Taiwan), these wide-ranging subjects of investigation have each been framed as a contentious discourse on definitions, meanings, and practices that involves a plurality of voices and forces.[19] Throughout history, behind the façade of cultural sameness and elite or state hegemony, identity politics has been at work. In the same vein, the present study of Chinese in Vancouver furnishes an additional 'off-centre' perspective by extending off-shore our canvas of a composite and multivariate metanarrative of Chineseness.[20]

No closure is really possible for a subject still unfolding, as the 1993 battle over the CCC illustrates. Nevertheless, I conclude my substantive analysis in 1980 so as to include the first decade of Canadian multiculturalism, which is a defining moment in contemporary identity politics for ethnic Chinese in Canada. The year 1980 also appears to be a reasonable cut-off point in view of the drastic growth of the ethnic Chinese population in Vancouver, the proliferation of organizations and the ethnic press, and the rapidly changing local and international environments for Chinese immigration and settlement in Canada which, taken together, have ushered in a different era. Still, the opportunity to offer some historical perspectives on the exciting and breathtaking developments since 1980 is hard to resist, as will be seen in the final chapter, but anything more than that would entail a significant amount of new research and would probably lead to another book. Now, in order to help the reader appreciate the intricacies and magnitude of the changes in the postwar years, let me begin this disclosure of cultural politics by illustrating the evolving contours of identity among Chinese in Vancouver prior to 1945.

2
Early Settlement and the Contours of Identity

Chinese migration to Canada began with the Fraser River gold rush in 1858. The first Chinatown was formed in Victoria by immigrants from Guangdong who had engaged in earlier gold-mining activities in California. Soon afterward, new arrivals came directly from South China to join the group of pioneers. Throughout the 1860s and 1870s, responding to local economic opportunities, pockets of Chinese population appeared in most frontier settlements on Vancouver Island and along (and even beyond) the Fraser River. In the first half of the 1880s, the construction of the Canadian Pacific Railway sent some 17,000 Chinese into western Canada. Though a substantial portion of the railroad workers followed the footsteps of the gold miners and returned to their native country, the Chinese population in the province of British Columbia increased from about 4,000 in 1880 to more than 10,000 in 1884.[1]

At that point, in Burrard Inlet there were reportedly 114 Chinese, among whom were a handful of merchants and their store employees, some thirty cooks and laundrymen, and a group of people who worked at the Hastings sawmill.[2] In 1885, it was announced that the Canadian Pacific Railway would extend its western terminus to this area, where the City of Vancouver was to be incorporated the following year. There, a small settlement of Chinese sprang up almost immediately on a piece of 'mud flat' north of False Creek, located on the southern fringe of the emerging city centre. This turned out to be the beginning of an ethnic neighbourhood that was to grow into the largest concentration of Chinese population in Canada by the first decade of the twentieth century. This background chapter looks briefly at this settlement prior to 1945, with particular reference to its demographic features, its immigrant organizations, and its evolving sense of cultural identity and community.

The first sixty years of ethnic Chinese presence in Vancouver can be roughly divided into three stages. During the first stage (1884-1911), the number of Chinese increased to more than 3,500. The exact figure is hard to determine because Chinese immigrants were very transient: a large number of them returned to China and a number of them sought illegal entrance to the United States.[3] The problem is compounded by local mobility, as some Chinese were engaged in seasonal occupations like lumbering and salmon canning outside the city. Nonetheless, the physical expansion of Chinatown was unmistakable evidence of the growing presence of the Chinese. Except for those whose occupations (e.g., laundry, household service, and farming) required them to live elsewhere, the large majority of the Chinese population chose their neighbourhood because it was convenient, comfortable, and offered them protection from racist violence. By 1911, Vancouver's Chinatown had come to encompass several blocks of buildings, from Canton and Shanghai Alleys west of Carrall Street, stretching eastward along both sides of Pender Street to Main Street (see Map 2).

At the beginning of the twentieth century, the Chinese population in Vancouver was comprised overwhelmingly of adult males. Overseas migration from South China was mainly a male enterprise, and Canadian racial antipathy towards ethnic Chinese discouraged these immigrants from bringing their families. An additional burden was, of course, the head tax, which the federal government first imposed on the Chinese in 1885. Initially $50, the amount was raised to $100 in 1901 and to $500 in 1903. Whatever the reasons behind the preponderance of males among the Chinese immigrants, Vancouver's 1901 Chinese population of 2,000 contained fewer than sixty women and children. Ten years later, Chinese women were still outnumbered by twenty-eight to one. Needless to say, most of these women and minors belonged to the few merchant families.[4]

Affluent merchants not only had a better chance to enjoy the privilege of family life in early Chinatown, but they also came to assume leadership in this small immigrant settlement. In the second half of the 1890s, two local merchants societies were formed and were quickly amalgamated into the Chinese Board of Trade. More imposing was, perhaps, the CBA, set up around the same time to represent all local Chinese and similarly led by merchants. The early history of the Board of Trade and the CBA remains obscure, but it seems that both organizations were intended to protect Chinese business interests and livelihoods against unsympathetic Canadian officials and a generally hostile environment.[5] These merchant initiatives must have received approval, if not direct assistance, from the Chinese government. China had been weakened by internal rebellions and foreign encroachment for much of the nineteenth century. The ruling Qing dynasty now sought to cultivate the loyalty of the Chinese merchants in the treaty-ports as well as in foreign countries to support its modernization programs. One consequence of this state promotion was the formation of Chinese chambers of commerce and the institutionalization of merchant leadership in many overseas Chinese settlements.[6]

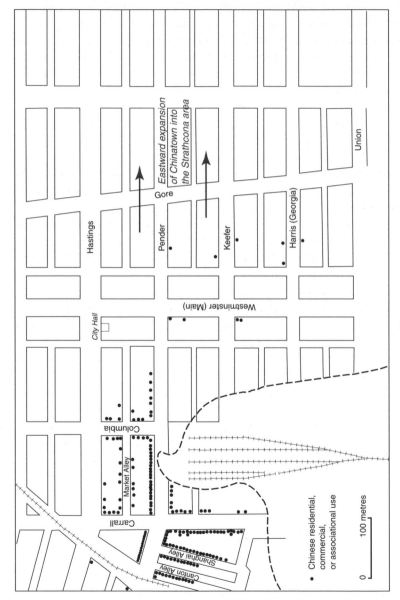

Map 2 Vancouver's Chinatown in the early twentieth century

Source: Based on *Henderson's British Columbia Directory 1910*, as adopted by Kay Anderson, *Vancouver's Chinatown:*
Racial Discourse in Canada, 1875-1990 (Montreal and Kingston: McGill-Queen's University Press, 1991), 76-77, 125.

While Chinese merchants could claim to lead, they were not the only ones to get organized. The first formal Chinese organization in Vancouver was the Chee Kung Tong, which officially opened in 1892. This fraternity had been established earlier among Chinese gold miners and labourers in settlements along the Fraser River. Drawing from the tradition of brotherhood and secret societies prevalent in the volatile and frontier part of coastal South China, the Chee Kung Tong exalted group loyalty, mutual trust, and other forms of virtuous behaviour. The organization appealed greatly to single migrant workers, shopkeepers, and small merchants, thereby entrenching itself as a very influential group in Vancouver's Chinatown.[7] Additionally, based on clan ties or common home county origins, ordinary workers often set up 'rooming houses' (*fang* or *fangkou*) for communal housing, mutual assistance, and a social life.[8]

Ethnic Chinese were noticeably concerned about the fate of their ancestral country during this period of traumatic political change in China. The defeat of China at the hands of Japan in 1895, the abortive constitutional reform movement of the summer of 1898, the outbreak of the Boxer Uprisings in 1900, and the unfolding of the revolutionary movement to topple the dynasty could not but draw the attention of Vancouver's Chinese.[9] Their interest in Old World politics was undoubtedly augmented by Canada's conscious rejection of them and by their being virtually confined to the ghetto. They confronted discriminatory legislation and occasional mob violence, such as the anti-Chinese riot of 1887 and another assault on their district (as well as on the neighbouring Japanese settlement) in 1907.[10] Believing that a stronger China would improve Canada's treatment of them, the Chinese in Vancouver entertained almost any proposal coming their way. They were excited by the visits of Qing officials (e.g., the brief stay of Li Hongzhang in 1896), but they were no less intrigued by the solicitations of exiled reformers and revolutionary émigrés. Around 1899 some wealthy merchants set up the Empire Reform Association (Bao huang hui) in Chinatown to support Kang Youwei and Liang Qichao in their attempt to turn China into a constitutional monarchy. The Chee Kung Tong, interestingly, sided with Sun Yat-sen and his revolutionary followers after a brief flirtation with the reformers. Its support came not only in the form of financial donations, but also in the form of some local members returning to China to plot insurrections. At the same time, a newspaper battle broke out in Chinatown, involving the reformers' *Daily News* (*Rixin bao*), the revolutionaries' *Chinese-English Daily News* (*Huaying ribao*), and the Chee Kung Tong's *Chinese Times* (*Dahan bao*; later *Dahan gongbao*). Such intense interest in Old World politics marked the beginning of 'sojourning Chinese' (*huaqiao*) nationalism, which was discernible throughout the Chinese diaspora of that era.[11]

In the second stage (1911-23) of Chinese presence in Vancouver the Chinese population almost doubled. Because of a high level of immigration in 1911-14, and another brief influx in the aftermath of the First World War, the number of Chinese reached 6,500 in 1921. More important to the long-term development of this minority were the improvement in the sex ratio and the increasing number of immigrant children, plus a few who were local-born. The 1921 census indicates close to 600 Chinese women in Vancouver; that is, a ratio of about ten Chinese men to every Chinese female. At the same time more than 500 Chinese children were attending local public schools. Indeed, two years earlier, a missionary report noted that there were 210 Chinese families in the city, and 7 percent of the Chinese were Canadian-born.[12] Thus, after a quarter century of settlement in Vancouver, the Chinese finally and gradually proceeded to the stage of family formation and the raising of a second generation.

Now, the eastern boundary of Chinatown extended all the way past Gore Street into the Strathcona area. No less impressive was the expansion of the inventory of Chinese organizations. Reflecting the rise of population and the desire to better organize for mutual help and to gain influence within the ethnic group, formal native place societies and surname associations sprang up in large numbers. By 1923 almost forty of them were known to exist in Chinatown.[13]

The need for protection against Canadian discrimination was one reason behind the proliferation of Chinese organizations during this period. For instance, some trade associations and labour unions emerged briefly to protest against various forms of business restriction or ill treatment in the workplace.[14] Meanwhile, Old World politics after the downfall of the Qing in 1912 continued to generate interest and conflict among Vancouver Chinese. Several reading rooms were set up, based on home locality and surname ties, to make available newspapers and political literature from China. The major political division was now between the Chee Kung Tong, which started to call itself the Chinese Freemasons in 1920, and the Kuomintang, which was organized by the supporters of Sun Yat-sen. Because the Freemasons believed Sun had reneged on his promise to share power after the initial success of the republican revolution, they treated him and his followers as political opponents. Locally, the Freemasons considered the Kuomintang as a challenge to their established position in Chinatown.[15]

As for the various native district and clan associations, it is interesting to see how quickly they were accepted and naturalized as underlying units in the formal social structure of this immigrant group. Basically all Chinese migrants in Canada were natives of Guangdong, notably from the Pearl River Delta region of Siyi (the 'four counties,' or districts, of Taishan, Xinhui, Kaiping, and Enping), Sanyi (the 'three counties' of Nanhai, Panyu, and Shunde), and the nearby county of Zhongshan (see Map 3). These more

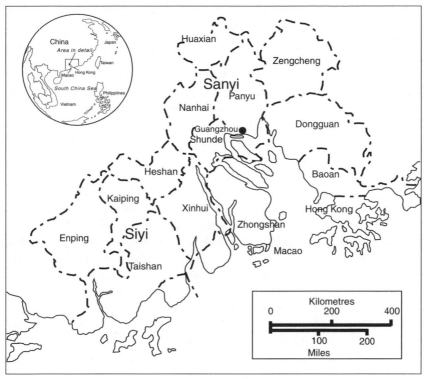

Map 3   Pearl River Delta region in Guangdong

narrowly defined regional identities, together with the strong tradition of lineage organization in South China, became the most immediate and valuable resources for helping the migrants adapt to a foreign land.[16]

Many Chinese immigrants relied on their district societies and surname associations for boarding, introduction to employment, and a social life that gave them a sense of belonging and security. These organizations also kept them in touch with the native place by serving as a point of contact (for incoming and outgoing mails) and, in some cases, by coordinating membership investment in public projects at home. General recognition of the importance of these traditional organizations came quickly in 1918 when the CBA formally adopted a system of indirect election. Under the new regulations, the native place organizations would be represented in the executive committee of the CBA according to a formula that reflected the current distribution of different groups in the local Chinese population. Since these native place associations had overlapping memberships with the surname societies, a rather crude but idealized segmentary structure emerged in which the CBA, as an umbrella organization, could claim legitimacy by 'representing all Chinese.'[17] This overall organizational arrangement epitomized a paradox whereby subethnicities among the Chinese were at once recognized and transcended as a result of a desire for larger unity and community.

Canada's Chinese Immigration Act, 1923, marked the beginning of a third stage in the early history of the Chinese in Vancouver. The ensuing exclusion retarded for the next twenty-four years the smooth demographic transition of this minority into a more balanced and stable population of settlers. New immigration, which had brought in more Chinese women and children since the second decade of the twentieth century, was virtually terminated.[18] This draconian legislation and, later, the devastating effects of the Great Depression led to a drastic outflow of Chinese from the country back to China. Vancouver's Chinese population suffered no immediate decline. The census of 1931 in fact reported more than 13,000 Chinese in the city, which reflected the relocation of Chinese from interior British Columbia to avail themselves of the aggregate ethnic resources in this largest Canadian Chinatown.[19] By the early 1940s, however, the number of Chinese had plummeted to a mere 7,000. This dwindling Chinese population consisted largely of adult immigrants, in their thirties or older, who continued their bachelor lives in Canada without their families. On 15 October 1941, the *Province*, a local English-language daily, suggested that Vancouver's Chinese faced the grim prospect of 'racial extinction' because deaths among them were almost twice as common as births.[20]

Despite the adversities, there were signs of vitality in the activities of Chinese organizations. The difficulties may just have spurred the Chinese to intensify their collective endeavours to fend for themselves. While the economic downturn and the departure of many Chinese paralyzed some associations, new ones were formed. Others consolidated two or more existing bodies with the same surname into a single structure. A larger number even reorganized themselves into the Canadian headquarters of their associations, reflecting a new sense of nationwide connection and Vancouver's importance in terms of the relative size of its Chinese population and its convenient Pacific Rim location. Equally intriguing was the emergence of almost a dozen Chinese-language schools and some youth-oriented musical and recreational societies in Chinatown.[21]

Chinese-language schools were nothing new in Vancouver. The first one had been set up by the Empire Reform Association at the beginning of the twentieth century, and another, the Chinese Public School (which still exists), was founded by the CBA in 1917. The exclusion period added considerably to the anxieties and concerns of the immigrant Chinese, leading to a crusade for cultural maintenance. In the eyes of the immigrants, children who had come to Canada and their local-born counterparts all needed to be taught the Chinese language and other cultural subjects because they were vulnerable to deculturation. Moreover, opportunities for ethnic Chinese in the larger society were so limited that these youngsters would need Chinese language and cultural skills either to work in Chinatown or in China, should they wish to return.[22]

Also fuelling such cultural sentiment, and the general upsurge in organizational activities of this period, were events in China. Despite a promising beginning the republican revolution was soon derailed by political opportunism, and China fell into the hands of the warlords. The ensuing political chaos apparently came to an end in 1927, when the Kuomintang arrived in power amidst rising Chinese nationalism and popular outrage against foreign imperialism. The national unification claimed by the new Nanjing government might have been nominal, but it was probably the finest moment in China since the end of imperial rule. Under Chiang Kai-shek, Sun Yat-sen's successor, the Kuomintang's promise of modernity and national dignity aroused much excitement among Chinese at home and abroad.

In Vancouver, Chinese nationalism was definitely on the rise. The local Kuomintang, now representing the Chinese government in power, claimed more influence in Chinatown than ever. Kuomintang supporters sought to promote Chinese education and other patriotic activities, even if they were not always successful in gaining full control. Consider the almost ubiquitous efforts to contribute to relief work in China and, specifically, in the immigrants' native areas. Chinatown's organizations were all actively involved in these undertakings, but community-wide cooperation was often pursued on an ad hoc basis among the participating groups. After the Sino-Japanese War broke out in 1937, these kind of China-bound activities and commitments quickly reached an all-time high.[23]

Even at the height of the so-called 'national salvation movement' to help China in its battle against Japanese invasion, Vancouver's Chinatown was still plagued by bad feeling between the Freemasons and the Kuomintang, other group rivalries based on clanship or native place affiliations, and recurrent leadership and personality clashes. Nevertheless, since the late nineteenth century two sets of conditions had contributed to a general outlook that transcended these divisions. On the one hand, some underlying commonalities, including family ties in South China, parochial native place feeling, enduring cultural sentiments, concerns for Old World politics, and rising Chinese nationalism, appealed to this generation of male immigrants and shaped their Chinese consciousness. On the other hand, Canadian society, by legislation and convention, offered these immigrants no sense of acceptance. The same rejection defined the experience of the small number of young Canadian-born Chinese, who were confined to the Chinese ethnic group in their upbringing, social life, and careers right up to the eve of the Pacific War.

Among ethnic Chinese, this sense of Chineseness intertwined with a pervasive feeling of community. For that generation of immigrant settlers and their junior local-born descendants, community could be readily identified with their fairly compact ethnic neighbourhood, in which most of them worked and resided. No less important was the intense articulation of community feeling in the male-dominated traditional organizations, which exalted the value of mutual assistance, domestic harmony, and, ultimately, ethnic solidarity. Admittedly, these organizations were vehicles of internal competitions and rivalries, but they were also the principal locus, where the powerful rhetoric of community provided the Chinese with a sense of belonging, a realm of public responsibility and leadership, and a common cultural identity.[24]

However cherished by the first generation of Chinese immigrants, this prevailing sense of Chineseness and community was not a cultural given, as the changing historical context after the Second World War was to dismantle this overall consensus and replace it with different identity constructs. The result was an unprecedented intramural debate – a battle over the power of definition and the meaning of being Chinese.

3
Renewed Immigration and Cultural Redefinition

At the end of the Second World War, the Chinese in Canada were about to enter a new era. The mood of the time was quite extraordinary. With the members of the larger society, ethnic Chinese shared the enormous joy of victory over the Axis Powers. In particular, the defeat of imperial Japan, whose invading armies had been on Chinese soil for years, generated tremendous relief and exhilaration in all Canadian Chinatowns. Additionally, this was a moment of great expectation, as it was believed that the low status of the Chinese in Canadian society would soon be improved and the ill-treatment of the Chinese by the Canadian government would be rectified. A major item of Chinese grievance was, of course, the highly prohibitive Immigration Act, 1923. Immediately after the Second World War, the movement seeking its repeal gathered momentum in the Toronto-Montreal-Ottawa area, with the support of sympathetic mainstream organizations and the media. Finally, in May 1947, the act was repealed by the Canadian Parliament, reopening the door of immigration to the Chinese people after almost a quarter century of virtual exclusion.[1]

Interestingly, most scholars have argued that the significance of this historic accomplishment was more symbolic than real. They point out that Canadian immigration policy towards the Chinese continued to be restrictive for another twenty years. Graham Johnson vividly portrays what the Chinese got in 1947 as 'half a loaf.'[2] Coming under the Order-in-Council P.C. 2115, Chinese, like other Asians, could only sponsor the immigration of their wives and children under eighteen years of age. There were extra concessions in the following years, such as, in 1950, the raising of the age limit for children to twenty-one and, until 1955, the actual admission of those up to twenty-five years old on compassionate grounds. Also, in 1955 parents were included for the first time in the admissible categories, and, two years later, the right of immigration sponsorship was extended from the citizens to the landed immigrants. Still, as Peter Li has argued, Chinese compared most unfavourably with immigrants from across the Atlantic, who were accorded far more generous treatment during the same period. Chinese did not attain full equality in immigration matters until 1967, when a universal points-system was implemented to screen all applicants without any reference to their racial and ethnic background. Only then did a sizable number of Chinese begin to arrive.[3]

The restrictive nature of Canadian immigration policy towards the Chinese between 1947 and 1967 is indisputable, and the tendency among scholars to gloss over this period of Chinese immigration history is unfortunate. No major attempt has been made to address the nature of Chinese immigration during those twenty years at either the national or the local level. This period is simply taken as a transitional stage between the exclusion era and the liberalization era. Needless to say, Chinese immigrants who came over during that time are seldom recognized as a distinctive group with a discernible impact on the historical scene.[4]

This chapter seeks to revisit this period of Chinese immigration. Following a general sketch of the size and composition of what I will attempt to show as a major influx, I will focus on the social and cultural ramifications of this renewed immigration. The fact is, despite the perceived institutional completeness of the ethnic neighbourhood, Chinatown and its many organizations did not meet the various needs of some newcomers. Before long, young new immigrants began to venture into the arena of Chinese organizations in a quest for public recognition and social space. In the process, they criticized the older Chinese settlers, their cultural norms, and their social practices. They also expounded their own ideas of cultural identity and espoused new visions of community for the ethnic group.

The Replenishment of a Minority
The enforcement of the Chinese Immigration Act, 1923, was both humiliating and devastating for the ethnic Chinese. A most tangible outcome was the significant decline of the Chinese population in Canada. Between the early 1930s and the end of the Second World War, the number of Chinese shrank from more than 46,000 to around 30,000. In the same period, the Chinese population in Vancouver was reduced even more drastically, from 13,000 to about 7,000.[5] Table 1 shows the age and sex distribution of the Vancouver Chinese in 1951, when this minority group was slowly recovering from the effects of exclusion but still clearly bearing the imprint of that earlier period. Both age and gender distributions were highly skewed, with over half of this population made up of adults forty-five years old or older; more than 92 percent of this group were men. Actually, one in every three Chinese in this city was an elderly man who was at least in his late fifties. It is not difficult to imagine that, only a couple of years earlier, this had been a dwindling and aging Chinese settlement with a large majority of above middle-age males, relatively few families, and a small local-born

Table 1

Age and sex distribution of Chinese population in Vancouver, 1951

Age groups	Males		Females		Total	
	No.	%	No.	%	No.	%
0-9	467	5.35	474	5.43	941	10.78
10-19	755	8.65	432	4.95	1,187	13.60
20-34	603	6.91	636	7.28	1,239	14.19
35-44	556	6.37	316	3.62	872	9.99
45-54	938	10.74	186	2.13	1,124	12.87
55-64	1,605	18.38	98	1.12	1,703	19.50
65 & above	1,600	18.33	63	0.72	1,663	19.05
Total	6,524	74.73	2,205	25.25	8,729	99.98

Source: Census of Canada, 1951, 6-30.

generation. It is in light of these demographic features that the impact of renewed immigration can be properly assessed.

Based on immigration records, Table 2 indicates that more than 14,000 Chinese entered Canada between 1946 and 1955. By 1960, another 10,000 had landed. In the following decade, some 43,000 Chinese arrived in this country. The same source also provides the number of Chinese immigrants arriving in British Columbia, but further disaggregation of data is not available. The only official statistics on Chinese immigration in Vancouver are given in the census of 1951, which reported over 700 Chinese arriving in the city between 1946 and May 1951; that is, about 55 percent of the provincial intake of Chinese migrants during that period.[6] Since many smaller Chinese settlements on Vancouver Island and in the interior of British Columbia were withering away around that time, it is conceivable that Vancouver would draw an even larger proportion in the following years.[7] Based on this projection, it is estimated that there were approximately 4,600 and 10,000 new Chinese arrivals in Vancouver in the decades 1951-60 and 1961-70, respectively, as is indicated in Table 3.

If these estimates are correct, then Chinese immigration after 1947 was certainly sizable relative to the existing population. Again, from Table 3, it can be calculated that in 1951 about 8 percent of the 8,700 Vancouver residents of Chinese descent had arrived since the end of the Second World War. The proportion increased to one-third in 1961; by 1971, when the Chinese population reached 30,000, over half of its members were postwar immigrants.

Since Canadian policy up to 1962 limited Chinese immigration to only a few categories of applicants, it is possible to use national-level statistics to identify the various components of this population movement and their relative distribution. Up to 1955, entrants were restricted to spouses and unmarried minor children. Table 4 shows that for Canada as a whole, these two groups accounted for about 90 percent of Chinese immigration in 1950 (and the rest were presumably re-entries of previous migrants and students). The declining percentage of children in 1951-56 is misleading because the figures do not include those between eighteen and twenty-five who were

Table 2

Number of Chinese immigrants entering Canada and British Columbia, 1946-70

Year	Canada	British Columbia
1946-47	7	4
1947-48	24	12
1948-49	111	59
1949-50	1,028	367
1950-51	2,178	808
1951-52	2,745	1,002
1952-53	1,961	682
1953-54	2,028	657
1954-55	1,950	644
1955-56	2,575	?
1956	2,093	799
1957	1,662	601
1958	2,615	993
1959	2,561	822
1960	1,370	461
1961	861	274
1962	670	175
1963	1,187	405
1964	2,674	810
1965	4,352	1,310
1966	5,178	1,676
1967	6,409	2,413
1968	8,382	3,070
1969	8,272	2,617
1970	5,377	1,588

Note: From 1946 to 1961, the figures represent the numbers of immigrants of Chinese ethnic origin, with ethnicity being self-reported at the point of entry. From 1962 onward, they indicate the numbers of immigrants whose country of last permanent residence was China, Hong Kong, or Taiwan.
Sources: Immigration Branch, Department of Mines and Resources, *Annual Reports* 1946-49; Department of Citizenship and Immigration, *Annual Reports,* 1949-56; and *Immigration Statistics,* 1956-70.

Table 3

Estimate of postwar Chinese immigrants arriving in Vancouver, 1946-70, and total Chinese population in Vancouver during census years

Year	Chinese entering BC	Proportion settling in Vancouver		Total no. of Chinese in Vancouver	
		%	No.	No.	Year
1946-51	1,250	55	700	8,729	1951
1951-55	3,724	60	2,250		
1956-60	3,676	65	2,400	15,223	1961
1961-65	2,974	70	2,100		
1966-70	11,364	70	8,000	30,640	1971

Sources: See Table 2 and *Census of Canada*, 1951-71.

admitted on compassionate grounds. The Chinese must have made the best use of this concession, and this particular cohort of young adults could be as large as some 40 percent of the total number of arrivals in the early 1950s (note the last column of Table 4).[8]

The older settlers also sent for their spouses. In the early 1950s, wives of old-timers made up about one-quarter of the new immigrants.[9] For several years after 1956, they actually formed a majority, though by then this group would include young wives whose husbands were themselves post-1947 arrivals. Finally, immigrant parents were admitted beginning in 1955, and Canada began to accept Chinese as independent immigrants in 1962. These last two groups contributed to the steady expansion of the 'Remainder' category in Table 4.

While useful, these figures alone hardly convey the initial exhilaration in Vancouver's Chinatown over this new wave of immigration. In the late 1940s and early 1950s, many native place and clan associations hosted receptions for their members to formally announce the arrival of spouses and children.[10] Understandably, these events gave the elderly immigrants great satisfaction, for they amounted to a public vindication of their hard work and years of sojourn. Moreover, family reunion (even if it was only partial, for not every member in a family was eligible) could not have come at a better time. Peace in China was shattered by the outbreak of civil war between the Kuomintang-controlled Nationalist government and the Chinese Communist Party. With the communist victory in 1949, many elderly Chinese could only hope to apply for their remaining families to join them in Canada.

Renewed immigration thus provided the Chinese with some relief from their 'bachelor life.' For the ethnic group as a whole, the coming of young adults and children helped to rejuvenate an aging population, while the arrival of wives and daughters had a balancing effect on the sex distribution.

Table 4

Number and percentage of dependent children (under 18) and wives among Chinese immigrants entering Canada, 1946-67

Year	Children		Wives		Remainder
	No.	%	No.	%	%
1946-47	4	57.14	3	42.86	0.00
1947-48	4	16.66	19	79.16	4.18
1948-49	21	18.91	79	71.17	9.92
1949-50	617	60.01	329	31.90	8.09
1950-51	1,318	60.51	556	25.52	13.97
1951-52	969	35.30	569	20.72	43.98
1952-53	445	22.69	450	22.94	54.37
1953-54	437	21.54	554	27.31	51.15
1954-55	431	22.10	607	31.12	46.78
1955-56	449	17.43	737	28.62	53.95
1956	385	18.39	773	36.93	44.68
1957	304	18.29	913	54.93	26.78
1958	681	26.04	1,439	55.02	18.94
1959	742	28.97	1,243	48.53	22.50
1960	331	24.16	744	54.30	21.54
1961	156	18.11	494	57.37	24.52
1962	130	19.40	240	35.82	44.78
1963	294	24.76	428	36.05	39.19
1964	984	36.79	737	27.56	35.65
1965	1,602	36.81	970	22.28	40.91
1966	1,161	22.42	862	16.64	60.94
1967	1,796	28.05	1,254	19.56	52.39

Source: See Table 2.

Though statistical data on Vancouver are unavailable, these trends are unmistakable at the national level, as is indicated in Table 5. A younger population with an improving sex ratio; more settled, intact families; and the local reproduction of a second generation all augured well for the future of this minority – more so than at any time since the beginning of Chinese settlement in Vancouver eighty years ago.[11]

There were signs of rejuvenation in and around Chinatown in the mid-1950s. According to a news report, the number of Chinese grocery stores had increased from eight to twenty-four as a result of a larger ethnic clientele. These firms and other Chinatown businesses also benefited from the cheap labour provided by the new immigrants. The same report indicates that other ethnic institutions were similarly enjoying a period of growth: the Chinese press was blessed with a higher volume of circulation and the Chinese-language schools with larger enrolment.[12] Even the handful of

Table 5

Age and sex distribution of Chinese population in Canada, 1951 and 1961 (as percentage)

Age	1951			1961		
	Male	Female	Total	Male	Female	Total
0-9	5.50	5.09	10.59	11.90	10.91	22.81
10-19	9.39	4.17	13.56	5.97	4.38	10.35
20-34	6.72	5.55	12.27	17.30	10.92	28.22
35-44	7.74	3.10	10.84	3.08	3.23	6.31
45-54	12.86	1.80	14.66	4.43	4.13	8.56
55-64	21.00	0.94	21.94	6.20	2.85	9.05
65 & above	15.67	0.43	16.10	13.08	1.59	14.67
Total	78.88	21.08	99.96	61.96	38.01	99.97

Source: Census of Canada, 1951 and 1961.

Chinese Christian churches experienced modest growth, especially if they were able to offer some social services – like English evening classes or a youth dormitory – to the newcomers.[13] At the same time, Foon Sien Wong, a community leader and a recognized CBA spokesman, observed an increase in the ownership of Chinese residential properties in the city, particularly in the adjacent Strathcona area, even though some established Chinese families had taken advantage of the new opportunity to move out of that neighbourhood and to seek a better living environment elsewhere.[14]

These developments are not to be dismissed. However, what has not been noticed, even though it is no less discernible, is that by the mid-1950s there were tensions and bad feelings between the two generations of immigrants in many corners of Chinatown.

A Glimpse into a Gathering Storm: The Boarding Houses

Though the older settlers and their traditional organizations continued to celebrate the coming of spouses and daughters through the 1950s, it was the several thousand young men in the current influx who drew the most public attention in Chinatown. Some extant writings suggest that the old-timers saw in these youngsters their own previous images – young men who had left home and come to Canada in search of a better life. They wished them well, of course, but they also insisted that, just as had allegedly been the case for them, the newcomers should win a good future by hard work, frugality, and perseverance. The older generation further expected respect and submission from these 'youth from the ancestral country' (*zuguo qingnian*), perhaps through participation as junior members in the native place and surname associations.[15]

The above turned out to be merely wishful thinking. At first, the young newcomers accommodated these expectations, but they soon made known their objection to, and repudiation of, the existing norms and practices in Chinatown. The result was considerable ambivalence and even tension between the two generations, as can be glimpsed in the postwar history of the Chinese boarding houses.

Since the beginning of Chinese settlement in Vancouver, the boarding houses had served as lodging facilities and as an important nexus in the lives of single migrants.[16] Referred to in English sources as 'Chinese bachelor houses,' their exact number is not known, though they were likely to have been all over Chinatown by the late 1920s. Some were run by the district and surname associations for their members; a larger number were set up by fellow districtmen and clansmen and had some sort of affiliation with the associations.

With the increase in family households after 1947, the demise of boarding houses seems to have been inevitable. However, there is evidence of some new immigrants taking up residence in these lodging facilities, probably because their sponsoring relatives were boarders themselves. According to the bookkeeping records of Ing Suey Sun Tong, one of the smaller surname associations in Chinatown, a majority of its boarders during 1945-55 were elderly Chinese who had been living there for at least the past decade. Close to one-half of the occupants, however, had unfamiliar names and were, presumably, recent arrivals.[17] In the following year, 1956, while surveying the Chinatown area in preparation for urban redevelopment, city planners discovered that 80 percent of the 150 Chinese bachelor houses in the neighbourhood had young men among their tenants.[18]

Interestingly, other findings in these two sources belie the interpretation that the situation was simply a case of ethnic succession by a new generation of immigrants. The new boarders at Ing Suey Sun Tong all had a much shorter period of tenancy than had the previous occupants. Take 1955, the last year of the records, as an illustration: among the twenty-two renters, seven had been living in the Tong for almost twenty years, ten were totally new to the facility, and only five had been there from two to four years. Evidently, many other postwar arrivals who had once resided in the Tong were gone, and this suggests a short period of tenancy.[19] Consider also the following classification of Chinese bachelor houses devised by city officials in their 1956 survey. First of all, one-fifth of the boarding houses were occupied exclusively by elderly Chinese, and these were associated with the highest-density occupancy, the cheapest rent, and the poorest housing and sanitary conditions. An unspecified number housed both elderly and young Chinese, usually in slightly better facilities. The last was a noticeable group in which 'young working men' shared a house in what officials considered a less overcrowded and more agreeable environment.[20]

The picture becomes clearer when we take into account some public criticism levelled by the new immigrants at the boarding houses around that time. In the Chinese press, young essayists castigated the boarding house as 'a deplorable institution' that perpetuated appalling living conditions. These critics indicated that they were ready to break away and design their own lives.[21] As I will argue below, the latent tensions and, at times, open conflicts between the two generations were more than a matter of different expectations and lifestyles. For the newcomers, it was a struggle for social space and autonomy. Above all, it was a contest for the power to redefine Chinese culture and the meaning of community.

Struggle for Recreation: The Auxiliary Youth Organizations
It is important to remember the relative homogeneity of the Chinese minority on the eve of renewed immigration, when families were few and the juvenile cohort tiny. The elderly immigrants in charge of the existing organizations were certainly unaccustomed to serving the needs of teenagers and young adults in their twenties. In the late 1940s, amenities for young people in Chinatown were scarce indeed. Back in 1938, the Vancouver YWCA had formed a Chinese department and, in 1943, it opened a centre on Pender Street with the support of the Chinese United Church. The patrons of the Pender Y, as the facility was called, were mainly English-speaking youngsters or school-age children, not the Chinese-speaking immigrant youth.[22] Also in the late 1930s and early 1940s, the Chinese Freemasons and the two Wong associations had set up athletic societies for the small group of Canadian-born Chinese who had reached their adolescence. The idea then was to cultivate the latter's patriotic sentiments and to drum up their support for the national salvation movement.[23] When maturing local-born Chinese began to organize on their own during and after the Second World War, these youth auxiliaries withered until they existed in little more than name only.

This was the background of a writing contest organized by the *Chinese Voice (Qiaosheng)*, one of the Chinatown dailies, in 1955. Readers were invited to submit essays on the topic 'How to improve recreational facilities in our community,' and the event naturally touched a chord among the immigrant youth. The two winning entries were almost identical. They lamented the problem of gambling prevalent among the elderly Chinese and considered the gambling parlours disgraceful to the neighbourhood. For the new generation of Chinese youth arriving in Canada since 1947, the authors argued that sports clubs, musical societies, literary groups, drama clubs, libraries, and theatres were much more desirable options.[24]

These were surely not empty words, for the immigrant youth had joined and revived a number of the dormant societies in the preceding years, including the Freemasons Athletic Society and the (Wong) Hon Hsing.

Also revitalized were two theatrical and musical groups with similar organizational affiliations: the Jin Wah Sing of the Freemasons and the Ching Won of the Kuomintang. Of these four, the case of Jin Wah Sing is best documented.

The name of Jin Wah Sing literally means 'raise the Chinese voice.' Jin Wah Sing was a theatrical troupe organized by the Chinese Freemasons in 1934 during the time of the Great Depression. The original idea was to raise relief funds through opera performances, but the troupe went on to enjoy success for over a decade, especially during the Chinese national salvation movement. Only the departure of many members for China after 1945 precipitated its decline. Then, in 1954, several dozen young immigrants interested in Cantonese opera joined and reactivated the organization. Jin Wah Sing quickly regained its vitality, providing training in Chinese opera and musical instruments to its members and staging occasional performances. Wittingly or unwittingly, it also became a recruiting ground for the Chinese Freemasons.[25]

This example suggests that some young newcomers did consider the traditional associations to be valuable and feasible venues for the organization of recreational and social activities. Likewise, the older generation in control of the Chinese Freemasons and a few other associations must have seen the wisdom of recycling otherwise dormant facilities in order to bring immigrant youth into the orbit of their organizations. Unfortunately, these successful cases were few and far between.

First of all, out of concern for their own autonomy, many immigrant youth did not approve of the above arrangement. The subsequent development of Jin Wah Sing actually illustrates this point. Since its revival, Jin Wah Sing's membership was troubled by its affiliation with the Chinese Freemasons. This perceived dependence upon the Freemasons must have been aggravating, as the society defended its autonomy in its anniversary declaration of 1957. This public announcement insisted that Jin Wah Sing was a non-partisan group, financially independent and free from any outside interference.[26] The statement obviously did not resolve the problem and, in 1961, a disenchanted group broke away to form the Ngai Lum Musical Society. Fortunately for Jin Wah Sing, because of the commitment of those who remained, the secession seems not to have crippled it.[27]

As for the old-timers and their organizations, the large majority were not interested in meeting the demand of the newcomers for resources and support. Table 6 gives a list of youth corps set up in the clan and district associations in the 1950s, supposedly for the promotion of youth activities. Some of them, such as the one formed by the Lee Clan Association in 1951, never got off the ground, and others were short-lived.[28] Critics on both sides were quick to point a finger at one another. The old settlers accused the youngsters of squandering public money and indulging in what they

Table 6

List of youth corps established by traditional
associations in Vancouver's Chinatown in the
1950s

Year	Organizations
1951	Lee Clan Association HQs
1952	Yee Fung Toy Tong HQs
1952	Lung Kong Kung So HQs
1952	Yue San Association HQs
1952	Kong Chow District Association HQs
1952	Shon Yee Benevolent Association HQs
1953	Sue Yuen Tong HQs
1955	Chan Wing Chun Tong HQs
1958	Yin Ping District Association HQs

HQs = National Headquarters
Sources: *Chinese Times* and *Chinese Voice*, 1951-58.

considered to be meaningless recreational activities. In return, the immigrant youth took the elderly Chinese to task for their intention to control
and dominate the younger generation. Many a youth corps thus ended up
being a scene of contention and frustration.[29]

To a large extent, the records of the youth corps epitomize the differences
between the two generations of Chinese immigrants. Despite the fact that
basically all young newcomers (entering the country between 1947 and
1962) arrived as dependents of the older settlers, the cultural, emotional,
and generational gaps between them were considerable. Compared to the
old-timers, the immigrant youth usually had a better Chinese education,
more urban experience in China and Hong Kong prior to their arrival, and
higher expectations concerning their futures in Canada.[30] They had heard
about racial discrimination from afar, but their educational backgrounds
and youthful idealism made them less willing than the preceding generation to accept cultural disability and isolation in the host society. Especially
for those whose age and other personal circumstances did not permit further schooling after arriving, they resented the perceived confinement to
the ethnic labour market, which offered low salaries and poor prospects.
Their original anticipation about the ample opportunities in the New World
quickly gave way to profound disillusionment.[31]

During the mid-1950s, the new immigrant youth emerged as the severest
internal critics of the existing Chinese minority. Their criticisms of the boarding houses, the vice of gambling, and the dearth of proper entertainment
have been mentioned. Other established institutions and practices in
Chinatown were not spared. In their writings, the young Chinese castigated
the traditional associations as 'mere formalism,' the community leaders as

'power-seekers,' and the consular officials and visiting dignitaries from the Kuomintang government (withdrawn to Taiwan after 1949) as 'unconscionable.'[32] They decried the patriarchal authority of the elderly Chinese, the incessant demand for respect, and the intolerance of different lifestyles.[33] Overall, as one young Chinese attempted to generalize, the problem was manifestly 'the cultural backwardness of the overseas Chinese' (*Huaqiao wenhua de luohou*).[34]

The agonized immigrant youth had few sympathizers outside their group. One of them was the Chinese-language newspaper *Chinese Voice*. Considering itself a channel for non-partisan opinions in Chinatown, unencumbered by any existing divisions and rivalries, the daily had adopted a relatively sympathetic stance towards the views of the young newcomers since its launching in November 1953. Its literary supplement, in particular, was the most popular venue for the views of Chinese youth.[35]

Among those who sympathized with the Chinese youth was an interesting personality, Father Peter Chow, who himself arrived in Vancouver in December 1953 as a newcomer. Originally a Roman Catholic priest from Hong Kong, Father Chow just finished his doctorate of Canon Law in Rome and was assigned at once to work at the Chinese Catholic Mission in Vancouver (which was soon renamed the Chinese Catholic Centre). His observations on this generational conflict are quite revealing. He attributed the problem to the lack of 'acquired intimacy' (*houtian de qinshan'gan*), which was caused by prolonged separation between the sojourning father and his children at home. Initially, Father Chow saw himself as a mediator, and he urged the youth to be patient and forbearing. His writings from this period suggest that he shared the critical spirit of his immigrant peers. In one passage, written in early 1956, he described the old-timers as too obsessed with money-making. 'Work would never be too much whereas recreation should be kept to the minimum'; that seemed to him to be an adage of the older generation. In the eyes, and to the dismay, of Father Chow, the older immigrants' own passion for gambling had turned Majong and Tiankou – two favourite Chinese games – into 'cultural heirlooms.'[36]

Such sympathy towards the young newcomers was uncommon, and the reaction of the majority of older settlers was that of alienation and outrage. Having toiled for years and finally obtaining the means to send for their families, any attack by the younger generation was the last thing the elderly Chinese would have expected. For instance, Foon Sien Wong, the chief executive of the CBA in the 1950s, noted that the elderly Chinese were most disgusted by the youth's extravagant spending habits and their fondness for entertainment.[37] In the *Chinese Times*, another commentator hinted alarmingly that the newcomers' reluctance to provide cheap labour would harm business interests in Chinatown.[38] Since this was the time of the Cold War and a few newcomers seemed to be sympathetic to the communist regime in Mainland China, it became popular for the older settlers – particularly those who were Kuomintang supporters – to vent their disappointment and bitterness by labelling those 'incorrigible' youngsters as 'Commie kids' (*gongchan zai*).[39]

Under these circumstances, the reluctance of most traditional associations to underwrite youth activities is understandable. Between 1954 and 1958, the Yin Ping District Association frustrated several attempts to set up a youth corps. The explanation, given in news reports and in its official publication, was an intergenerational conflict over money and the use of limited floor space. For reasons that are still not clear, the youth corps was finally set up, but there must be many other cases, as in the Mah Society, in which similar opposition prevailed.[40] Youth corps were considered potentially troublesome, so, once they were formed, they had to be closely monitored. Hence the Kong Chow District Association revised the bylaws of its youth corps in early 1954 when the latter was barely two years old. The amendments imposed mandatory membership, requiring all youth corps participants to first sign up with the district association, and it stipulated the categorical subordination of the corps to the larger native place organization.[41] With the viability of the youth auxiliaries so quickly undermined by mutual dislike, suspicion, and antagonism, the stage was set for a new kind of youth organization.

Contest for Chineseness: Autonomous Youth Societies
Given the inadequacy of recreational facilities for young people in Chinatown and the limited access to mainstream resources due to language and other barriers, it is not surprising that young immigrants organized independently among themselves. Indeed, so many youth societies mushroomed in this way in Chinatown from the mid-1950s that tracking their number is difficult. Table 7 shows a list of those that left traces of their activities in the Chinese press.

From the very beginning, the most distinctive feature of these new youth organizations was their assertion of autonomy outside the parameters of the traditional associations. As the latter claimed to provide leadership and define issues of community interest, the endeavour of the immigrant youth was daring, to say the least. Bearing the burden of defiance, the youth societies had to confront a suspicious and forbidding environment. They had to survive solely on the limited resources of their young members. These disadvantages explain why many of them enjoyed only an ephemeral existence. They sprang up to organize, or to take part in, certain social, cultural, and sports events, but they all suffered from a lack of financial support and organizational experience.

However, these disadvantages could also be considered strengths. Independent societies usually had several dozen members, most of whom appear

Table 7

Partial list of autonomous Chinese youth societies in Vancouver in the postwar period

Name	First report/Founding date
Qiao Ying Qingnian She (G)	13 August 1952
Qun Qing She (G)	27 May 1954
Qingnian Lianyi Hui (G) [Chinese Youth Association]	31 May 1954/19 May 1954
Hua Cui Wenyi Xuehui (L) [Chinese Literary Society]	11 February 1955
Xian Qu Wenyu She (G)	17 September 1955
Chen Zhong She (G)	9 December 1955
Bo Yi Ju She (D)	18 February 1956/1955
Qing Hua She (L)	14 April 1956
Wen Yu Zhi Yao She (G)	26 May 1956
Qing Lian Wen Lian She (L)	22 June 1956
Hai Feng Hui (G) [Hai Fung Club]	16 October 1959/1956
Qing Yun Cao Tang Shi She (L)	16 November 1961
Yun Qing Hui (G)	8 January 1965/1963-64

Note: English names are provided in square brackets if known; also G = General, L = Literary, D = Drama.
Sources: Chinese Voice and *Chinese Times*.

to have been relatively better educated than their peers in the youth corps. By the 1960s, among their better known activists were university students and young professionals.[42] As for their asserted autonomy, such defiance of the elderly Chinese afforded these youngsters the freedom and space to develop and expound their own ideas about life, culture, identity, and community. Accordingly, they were able to explore wide-ranging and nonconformist interests, unlike those youth involved in the auxiliaries, most of whom were confined to recreational activities in traditional Chinese music, martial arts, and sports.

If the list of youth societies in Table 7 is representative, then it seems that most of them came into being around the mid-1950s; that is, after the bulk of young male adults in their late teens and early twenties had arrived, after they had begun to openly criticize the older generation, and after the experiment of youth auxiliaries in the traditional organizations had failed (see Table 6). One of the independent societies called itself a drama club and four were literary societies, but the large majority were of a more general type that sought to promote cultural and social activities.

On the whole, information on these individual societies is limited. The case of the Hai Fung Club is exceptional – a result of its relatively long existence and its impact on other youth organizations. Founded in late 1956

Table 8

Summary of Hai Fung Club's major activities, 1959-68

Year	Events
1959	Its literary group started a weekly column, 'Qingnian tiandi' (The World of the Youth) in the *Chinese Voice*.
1960	Began to organize the first annual table tennis tournament in Chinatown (open to non-Chinese); The competition was held seven more times in the following years.
1960	Held the first Cantonese Speech Festival
1960	Held the first Chinese Students Chess Competition (five times)
1960	Set up a junior section in the club to enrol members in their early teens
1961	Co-sponsored an open Chinese chess tournament with the Hon Hsing Athletic Society
1961-62	Held a series of public lectures on some interesting academic and cultural topics
1963	Sponsored the first British Columbia Overseas Chinese Art Exhibition .
1964	Began to provide free lessons on English language, citizenship, table tennis, and swimming
1964	Organized a Chinese volleyball tournament
1965	Held the second art exhibition
1965	Jointly organized the Chinese Basketball League, which lasted until the early 1970s

Note: There were also a couple of public concerts, the timing of which cannot be ascertained.
Sources: Chinese Voice and *Haifeng hui jinian kan.*

and lasting well into the 1970s, the Hai Fung Club was committed to providing what it called 'a higher form of entertainment' (*gaodeng yule*) for its members. It believed that proper entertainment would nourish individual character and, collectively, would create a healthier Chinese society.[43] Inside its Chinatown clubhouse were a small library, an exercise room, a music studio, a darkroom, and other rudimentary facilities. Membership activities were organized on different subjects, including literature, music, photography, painting, table tennis, and so on.[44]

A turning point in the history of the Hai Fung Club came in late 1959 during the celebration of its third anniversary. The club decided not to concentrate on membership welfare any more but, rather, to venture beyond the clubhouse to influence the Chinese public. This resulted in a discernible reorientation by which the Hai Fung Club sought to live up to its name as 'the vanguard of the overseas Chinese' (*haiwai huaqiao zhi xianfeng*).[45]

The Hai Fung Club's impressive program of activities in the following years testifies to its vibrancy. A partial summary of its functions in Table 8 indicates a broad range of cultural and sporting events. In addition to

Figure 1 Lion Dance performed by the Hon Hsing
Athletic Club, 1964

recreation, many of its activities were educational in intent. For example, included in its public lecture series was a talk concerning the use of libraries. The speaker was the first Chinese librarian (Ms. Tung King Ng) at the Asian Library, which is located at the University of British Columbia.[46] Evidently, the Hai Fung Club had outgrown its first phase of existence, during which it held only in-house events, and had entered an ambitious second phase that addressed a larger Chinese audience. By inviting public participation, the club not only made known its agendas but sought to unleash social and cultural change.

The efforts of the Hai Fung Club in spearheading these multifarious events had an immediate impact on that generation of immigrant youth. Other autonomous societies and even some youth auxiliaries were influenced by its example, though none of its contemporaries was able to match the scope and intensity of its activities. A case in point was Hon Hsing, whose several

Figure 2   Hon Hsing and Freemasons Athletic Society basketball teams, 1964

key leaders in the early 1960s were concurrently Hai Fung members. According to its own published history, Hon Hsing underwent a reform at that time that resulted in the expansion of a Chinese music department as well as the setting up of a small library, a drama department, and a very popular lion-dance troupe. In cooperation with the Hai Fung Club, it organized the first open Chinese chess competition in 1961 and a volleyball tournament in 1962.[47] Another memorable sporting event of this period was a basketball tournament held by the Yin Ping Youth Corps in 1964. The game generated such enthusiasm that the Chinese Basketball League was formed in its aftermath, with the Hai Fung Club again playing a leading role.[48]

This series of events in the early 1960s was epochal in marking the full entrance of the post-1947 generation of immigrant youth into the organizational arena of public life. With the Hai Fung Club as the torchbearer, this younger generation of Chinese immigrants refused to remain on the sidelines; instead, its independent societies delineated a sphere of public activities and presented a challenge to the older generation over the definition of Chinese identity and community.

At the basic level, the existing formulation of cultural identity and community was unacceptable to the immigrant youth because it was associated exclusively with the older generation of settlers and their associations. Refusing to be marginalized, the newcomers and their autonomous youth societies forced their way into the limelight and contended that they, too, were entitled to public resources, space, and leadership positions within the ethnic group.[49]

More specifically, the old definition of identity and community was objectionable to the young newcomers because of its underlying parochialism. The traditional Chinatown organizations were mostly formed on the bases of specific native place identities and clanship ties. As Wong Sang, the founder of the Hai Fung Club, argued in an article on the historical roles of the surname organizations, the webs of parochial relationships were beneficial only to small groups and were antithetical to any broader conception of unity.[50] Such antipathy towards entrenched parochial institutions accounted for the young immigrants rejecting the youth auxiliaries because they believed that joining them would mean being coopted into an anachronistic structure. To register their opposition, an open membership accessible to all interested Chinese youth, regardless of clan or region of ancestry, was de rigueur for the autonomous youth societies.[51]

Another bone of contention was the perceived cultural conservatism, or backwardness, of the older generation. The latter's insistence on internal harmony and filial piety and its idea of preserving heritage were all problematic in the eyes of the newcomers. For one thing, the youngsters viewed such utterances by the older settlers as instruments of control. For another, their own ideas about contemporary Chinese culture were different. Having been exposed in various degrees to modern Chinese education in China or Hong Kong prior to departing, they were self-conscious about their sophistication and their ability to redefine the content of Chinese culture among the migrants overseas. Some of them took pride in their literary creation. They formed writers groups or literary clubs, started modest collections of books and literature, and circulated their own works.[52] With an inflated cultural pride vis-à-vis the existing Chinese minority, they even claimed to champion a spirit of cultural renaissance. Following the tradition of the much celebrated May Fourth New Cultural Movement in China during the period 1915-25, they referred to their brief discussions on Chinese poems and drama in the literary supplements of the *Chinese Voice* in the mid-1950s as 'movement' (*yundong*).[53]

Moreover, the immigrant youth were generally more prepared than the preceding generation of settlers to adapt to local Canadian and modern Chinese cultural forms. The programs of the Hai Fung Club vividly show their enthusiasm and confidence in promoting Western artistic activities and sporting events. Rather than encouraging them to cling to the archaic and passive language of cultural persistence, their sensitivity to the foreign cultural environment propelled them along the road of acculturation.[54] Of course, along with their own cultural background, the timing of their arrival in Canada (when overt discrimination against Chinese people was receding) also explains their ability to make changes.

Lastly, interwoven with this enterprise was the shared aspiration among the majority of the immigrant youth for an apolitical and non-partisan expression of Chinese cultural identity. Initially, this was largely a reaction against the lingering conflicts among the old-timers over Old World politics and leadership rivalries in Chinatown. It also seems to have been the newcomers' defence against the accusation that they were communist sympathizers. By the late 1950s, this attitude had given rise to a stronger belief in the virtuosity of a Chinese identity unblemished by political affiliations, religious divisions, and partisan interests. The first public announcements of many youth societies often consisted of a ceremonious denial of any interest in Chinese politics.[55]

Lest this categorical refusal to get entangled in Old World politics be taken as the only common tenet of the youth societies, the Chinese Youth Association should be mentioned as a notable exception. Members of this society considered Chinese politics not simply to be relevant, but, in fact, to be a key component in a viable Chinese identity. From its inception in 1954 to its dissolution in the early 1980s, the Chinese Youth Association displayed a leftist ideological orientation and supported the People's Republic of China. The latter, it insisted, had laid a new foundation for a modern Chinese national pride, which the overseas Chinese could ill afford to put aside. To propagate the accomplishments of the new regime, the association often sponsored movies from Mainland China. It started a Chinese-language biweekly newspaper, *Da Zhong Bao* (lit. the masses), as its mouthpiece. It further established close ties with Vancouver's Canada-China Friendship Association, formed in 1964 mainly by non-Chinese local sympathizers of the People's Republic of China.[56]

It would not be surprising if this political maverick attracted admirers among the ethnic Chinese, but, more often, it had to confront hostility and ostracism. According to its former members, active participants through the 1960s numbered only a few dozen; the clubhouse was once ransacked and set on fire, and its functions were occasionally interrupted by the police.[57]

If the bold agenda of the radical Chinese Youth Association was treated with intolerance by the older generation of Chinese settlers, then the new visions of identity and community put forward by other independent youth societies also generated negative reactions. Chapter 5 discusses how the elderly Chinese answered their young critics and asserted their cultural claims through the traditional organizations. In the meantime, a snapshot of a brief acrimonious exchange should give a sense of the debate.

The occasion was the British Columbia Overseas Chinese Art Exhibition organized by the Hai Fung Club in 1963. To promote the event, Wong Sang published a short essay in the *Chinese Voice*, in which he suggested that this meaningful undertaking would mark a departure from the backward state of Chinese culture in Vancouver.[58] This comment prompted an immediate and acerbic response from Father Chow, who, as the reader will recall, had once been quite sympathetic to the views of the immigrant youth. By this time, however, he was better known for his doctrinaire anti-communism and was identified with the conservative establishment. In a lengthy article printed in the local Kuomintang party press, the *New Republic* (*Xin minguo bao*), Father Chow retorted that the present condition of overseas Chinese culture was not as unworthy as Wong had portrayed. 'Only a believer in materialistic communism could say such utter nonsense,' he concluded, 'and we better keep an eye on this person!'[59]

Undaunted by such criticisms, if not threats, the Hai Fung Club mustered its strength for a spirited defence. In a rejoinder published in the *Chinese Times* the following week, Wong Sang started off by accusing his critic of seeking to 'monopolize [the definition of] overseas Chinese culture' (*longduan huaqiao wenhua*). As he went on to explain:

> In describing the current state of Chinese culture in our community as reasonably advanced, Father Chow has discouraged us from working harder and making further progress. Such being the case, those self-claimed leaders among us will be leaders forever ...
>
> As for myself, I have never made any claim for leadership in Chinese culture. Neither am I a communist as Father Chow insinuated ... By recklessly putting red labels on the others, he tried to generate unnecessary misunderstanding and hatred among the Chinese in order to spoil this meaningful event – the Art Exhibition.[60]

Later that month, the literary group of the Hai Fung Club published an essay entitled 'The New Pharisee.' The protagonist was accused of being a 'hypocrite' who misused public charities for personal interests; he was against open-mindedness and social progress; he was absolutely intolerant of people not sharing his opinions.[61] The target was clearly Father Chow. No less apparent was the resolve of the Hai Fung Club to defend its rights to speak differently on Chinese culture.

To conclude, the wave of renewed Chinese immigration into Canada after the repeal of the highly restrictive Immigration Act in 1947 was instrumental in replenishing a dwindling Chinese minority. However, the process of replenishment was punctuated by the open conflict between the older generation of Chinese settlers and the new arrivals, particularly the young men who made up a sizable and visible portion of this inflow.

The foregoing analysis has concentrated on the initiatives and perspectives of the immigrant youth. Their encounter with the elderly generation over the brief development of youth auxiliaries in the traditional organizations was an unpleasant one. With only a few exceptions, that experiment failed because of growing mutual dislike and antagonism. The search for autonomy and a desirable form of social and cultural life among the immigrant youth led to the formation of their own independent societies.

Many autonomous youth societies were short-lived, but a few, such as the Hai Fung Club and the Chinese Youth Association, enjoyed a fairly long period of existence. Their activism represented a competitive claim on social space, resources, and power within the ethnic group. Indeed, their agendas spoke constructively of new visions of Chinese identity and community, thus altering a discourse of power and culture that had been in place for decades among the immigrant Chinese.

4
Local-Born Chinese and the Challenge to an Immigrant Discourse

In the first book-length study of the Chinese in Canada, published in 1967, the author, David T.H. Lee, who belonged to the generation of postwar new immigrants, attempted to define the group of local-born Chinese, the *tusheng huayi*, or simply *tusheng*, in the following unforgettable passage:

> By *tusheng huayi* we mean those ethnic Chinese who have received only English education and do not have a Chinese mind. This group includes those who were born locally and those who came from the ancestral country to Canada as minors and are English-educated ...
>
> Local-born Chinese usually [mis]take things in Chinatown as representative of Chinese culture. They consider the lion dance, traditional opera, and martial arts our cultural heirlooms, without which Chinese civilization would be devoid of merit. They think Chinese culture is despicable and China is no more than just a huge country. Hence they suffer badly from an inferiority complex ...
>
> Among Chinese people, the local-born often claim to be Canadians ... Yet westerners have little respect for them and continue to call them Chinese. Since their [way of] thinking has been westernized, they mix with westerners in their social life and have lost touch with the Chinese. Their contact with [our] community has also been attenuated as a result of their poor command of Chinese language. So, it is hard to expect them to support charitable undertakings or participate in organizations within the community, not to mention contributing to relief work for the homeland or the national salvation movement [of anti-communism based in Taiwan]. Nevertheless, they are more than enthusiastic about some recreational events in Chinatown. Whenever there are parades and dancing parties, or when some beautiful [Chinese] ladies from elsewhere visit Vancouver['s Chinatown], they are the first ones to show up at the special functions. Probably they are influenced by western utilitarianism.[1]

According to David Lee, then, the cultural deficiency of the *tusheng* was a reflection of the larger problem with the existing shallow and distorted 'Chinatown culture,' but the local-born Chinese themselves were undoubtedly to be blamed. Most despicable to Lee was the *tusheng*'s attempt to behave and pass as Canadians. He was quick to point out, with much delight, that such pretension had gotten them nowhere in the host society.

Such derisive attitudes towards the local-born were anything but new among the immigrant Chinese. Ever since a small number of *tusheng* children appeared at the beginning of the twentieth century, the immigrants had shown a grave concern for the susceptibility of these youngsters to deculturation. In Vancouver, the first Chinese-language schools were set up to preserve their Chinese cultural skills and national sentiments as they grew up in a foreign country. Up to the outbreak of the Sino-Japanese War in 1937, it was common for the affluent merchant families and even more modest shopkeeper households to send their children back to China for a native education. In the eyes of the early immigrants, the Chineseness of the *tusheng* was fragile and vulnerable; they occupied only a marginal position in a community defined by and for the immigrant Chinese.[2]

In Vancouver, this prejudice against the *tusheng* was to intensify in the hands of the post-1947 immigrants from South China, but by then the other side of the equation had begun to change too. Previously, the local-born segment of the Chinese population had been small and junior in comparison with the immigrants. The balance shifted in the postwar period, as the maturing Canadian-born acquired both visibility and autonomy within the ethnic group. In the public arena of ethnic organizations and media, the *tusheng* developed the ability of self-definition. No longer did they remain a subject of concern and disparagement for other Chinese.

The rise of the *tusheng* was predicated on two general conditions. The first was demographic, including the growing size and increasing age of their population. The other was the gradually increasing openness of the host society since the Second World War, with job opportunities, social life, and cultural options beyond Chinatown becoming more accessible to the ethnic Chinese. Ideally, some quantitative data on age distribution, occupational mobility, residential patterns, and the like would allow us to pursue an analysis on the momentum and direction of these changes, but this information on the *tusheng* does not exist, either locally or nationally.[3]

Fortunately, the limited quantitative data are more than compensated for by the rich records on the activities of the local-born Chinese. These materials contain abundant evidence of intramural contests, suggesting that important dimensions of *tusheng* identity first took shape when the local-born sought to reposition themselves vis-à-vis both the elderly settlers and the newcomers. Often enough, the *tusheng* Chinese disclosed a strong sense of cultural distinctiveness in their debates on issues of identity and community with the two generations of immigrants. The evolving interaction was punctuated by mutual prejudice and cultural assaults between the local-born Chinese and the other two groups.

Tusheng Population and Organizations

Let us begin with a sketch on the *tusheng* population in Vancouver. Due to the lack of precise local data, I will use national-level statistics as my first reference. Table 9 shows that the percentage of local-born within the total Chinese population in Canada increased steadily during the first half and well into the second half of the twentieth century. Between 1941 and 1961, the proportion actually doubled, so that by the latter census year as many as two-fifths of the Chinese were registered as having been born in Canada. Thereafter, the sizable influx of new immigrants reversed this upward trend.

The situation in Vancouver roughly corresponded with the national pattern. The census of 1951 shows 3,200 native-born Chinese in the city, which was about 37 percent of the Chinese minority.[4] This was higher than the national average of 31 percent at that time. Comparable local data for 1961 and 1971 are unavailable, but the 1981 census reports that 27 percent of the Chinese in Metropolitan Vancouver were Canadian-born, which was again above the national average.[5] The higher percentage of *tusheng* in the Vancouver area is not difficult to explain. First, the relatively large size of its Chinese settlement made family formation possible earlier there than among other Chinese populations in the country. Second, Vancouver is known to have attracted some local-born Chinese from the older and shrinking

Table 9

Native-born Chinese within the total Chinese population in Canada, 1901-81

Year	Total Chinese population	Native-born	
		%	No.
1901	17,312	–	–
1911	27,831	3	635
1921	39,587	7	2,771
1931	46,519	12	5,582
1941	34,627	20	6,925
1951	32,528	31	10,084
1961	58,197	40	14,549
1971	118,815	38	45,150
1981	289,245	25	72,311

Source: Census of Canada, 1901-81, in Peter Li, The Chinese of Canada (Toronto: Oxford University Press, 1988), 61.

Table 10

Estimate of the percentages of the three different groups in Vancouver's Chinese population, 1951-71

Groups	1951	1961	1971
Early generation of immigrants	55	23	9
Post-1947 newcomers	8	33	50
Local-born Chinese	37	44	41

Sources: Census of Canada 1951-71. For the proportion of the post-1947 immigrants, see the discussion in Chapter 3, especially Table 3. The percentages of local-born are based on an adjustment of the national average.

Chinatown in nearby Victoria.[6] Whatever the reason, my estimate, as given in Table 10, is that about two out of five Chinese residents in Vancouver during the period 1951-71 were Canadian-born.

Although the age distribution of the *tusheng* Chinese is not known, the first significant batch of Canadian-born youth and adults became active within the Chinese minority around the Second World War. They were born in the 1920s or earlier and were referred to as the first generation of local-born Chinese. Sharing with this group a comparable childhood and similar cultural traits were an indeterminable number of Chinese who had come to Canada at an early age before 1923 and stayed. I agree with David Lee and Edgar Wickberg that the latter should be considered part of this first generation of local-born.[7]

Just as the *tusheng* component was growing in size and arriving at maturity, the federal government provided a catalyst for the transition of a fledgling Canadian-born Chinese identity into a more coherent and assertive form. At the last stage of the Pacific War, about 500 local-born Chinese, half of them from British Columbia, were inducted into the Canadian armed forces. Up to this point, the *tusheng* Chinese in British Columbia held only second-class citizenship. In spite of their status as British subjects by birth, they enjoyed no franchise at any level of state elections and, accordingly, were denied access to government employment and certain choice professions. They were exposed to Canadian culture through public education and the mass media, but they were deprived of substantial contact with mainstream society. Being equally victims of discriminatory legislation and popular racism, they could well be bracketed with the rest of the ethnic group as uniformly 'Chinese.'

Against this background, the draft order in the summer of 1944 had the dramatic effect of singling out the *tusheng* from the Chinese population as a special category.[8] The initial responses of the local-born Chinese were mixed. Some of them resented being called up to fight for a country that denied their rights as citizens. However, the majority wished to seize this chance to demonstrate loyalty to Canada and planned to demand full citizenship later. Indeed, no sooner had enlistment begun than a few local-born took action to seek redress for their inferior constitutional status by setting up the Chinese Canadian Association in Vancouver. The following February they petitioned the government of British Columbia 'for the granting of franchise to all Canadians of Chinese descent in the province.' The document deplored the range of political and economic disabilities imposed on the Canadian-born Chinese. It referred with pride to the progress the local-born had made in acculturation and assimilation as well as to the manifold contributions they had rendered to Canada's war efforts. It argued passionately that 'since they [the Canadian-born Chinese] bear, and bear gladly, full citizenship responsibilities, they should be entitled to all citizen rights.'[9]

The petition yielded no immediate result. So, at the end of the war, the returning Chinese soldiers organized themselves into the Army, Navy, and Air Force Veterans of Canada, Unit 280, with its headquarters in Vancouver, to continue the lobbying effort. With their records of wartime enlistment, and the support of public opinion, the Chinese in British Columbia finally won their franchise in provincial and federal elections in 1947. By obtaining the municipal ballot two years later, they completed their enfranchisement.[10] Given the important role military service had played in achieving this cherished objective, one might expect that the Chinese Veterans organization would flourish. Compared to the memberships of most existing associations in Chinatown, the membership of the Veterans organization was young and fresh with esprit de corps, and its image commanded respect both inside and outside the ethnic group. Surprisingly, Unit 280 seems to have lost its raison d'être after the successful conclusion of the campaign for enfranchisement and, in the following decade, became a low-key social club on Pender Street.[11]

Under some energetic leadership in the early 1960s, a rebound finally came. There is good indication that the Veterans organization was being used by some local-born Chinese as a vehicle to participate in Canadian electoral politics, something I will address in a later chapter. What seems particularly interesting is the earnest attempt at that point to refurbish the Veterans' collective image and to elevate the pride of the *tusheng* vis-à-vis the immigrant Chinese. The first public event marking the revival of the Veterans organization was the commemoration of its fourteenth anniversary in early 1961. Typical of anniversary celebrations by Chinatown organizations, the Veterans organization issued public statements in the Chinese press, organized a parade, and held a banquet that was attended by its members and their families, leaders from other Chinese associations, and representatives of all three levels of the Canadian government. The first statement the Veterans issued was noteworthy. Not only did they claim to be the 'heroes of Canada,' they said that their wartime service had won important 'trophies' for 'all ethnic Chinese,' including the end of exclusion, full enfranchisement, and access to government employment. These privileges, the Chinese Veterans reminded the readers, 'were beyond our reach before the war.'[12]

In the late 1940s, the local-born Chinese had used the status of Veterans to advance their claim for full citizenship. After the lapse of a decade, they deployed the same symbol to gain cultural and psychological advantages over the other Chinese. They now asserted themselves as heroes who had ushered in all the historic changes in favour of the Chinese. What triggered their assertion in 1961 is not clear. Nevertheless, from the 1950s on, the local-born often presented themselves publicly as trailblazers who were helping ethnic Chinese to enter a more hospitable Canada. The early history of another *tusheng* organization, the Chinatown Lions Club, clearly illustrates this point.

Compared to the Chinese Veterans organization, the Chinatown Lions Club brings to our attention some important socioeconomic and cultural changes unfolding among the Vancouver Chinese. Chartered in January 1954, it was the second major Canadian-born Chinese organization founded in the postwar period. Its members were all of professional and business backgrounds. Heading the list of its twenty-six charter members was George D. Wong, a McGill graduate and the first ethnic Chinese manager employed by a Canadian bank. Another active member was Andrew Lam, the first native-born Chinese pastor in Canada, who, in 1941, commenced his ministry at the local Chinese Anglican Church.[13] These individuals were among the earliest beneficiaries of the breakdown of discriminatory barriers against

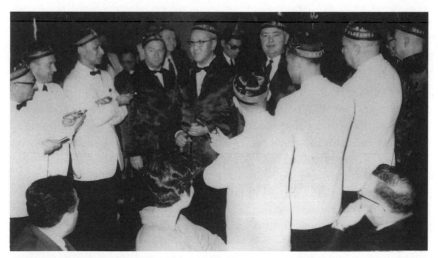

Figure 3 George D. Wong inducted as gong banger of the Chinatown Lions Club, 1968

Figure 4   Gavel presented to Chinatown Lions Club president Hin-Fong Yip in appreciation of the contributions made to Mount St. Joseph Hospital, 1971

the social and economic mobility of the Chinese. An increasing number of *tusheng* of their generation began to get jobs outside the traditional ethnic economy and to enter professions that had once been inaccessible. Needless to say, this elevated the social and economic profile of the local-born within the minority. It further raised the possibility of substantial interaction with non-Chinese. Western organizational styles, middle-class behavioural norms, and other cultural paraphernalia from mainstream society all became available. The prestigious Lions international organization and its example of high-profile public service was compatible with the Chinese idea of public charity and leadership that had been institutionalized by the traditional associations of the immigrants, and it readily became a cherished alternative for the up-and-coming Canadian-born Chinese elite.

The Chinatown Lions Club was able to maintain a better symmetry between organizational vitality and ideological claims than was the Veterans organization. From the very beginning, by following the Lions' code of ethics and organizational precepts, it acted as a progressive, non-traditional style society. Its ethnic membership notwithstanding, non-Chinese were eligible to become full members and even to hold the club presidency. Conscious of its ties beyond the ethnic group, in less than ten years the club campaigned vigorously and successfully to promote George Wong, its charter president, to the top position of the Lions international directorship.[14]

Contrary to what David Lee has insisted in his book, this cosmopolitan orientation of the Chinatown Lions Club did not drain away its sense of Chineseness. Like the Veterans, the Lions Club keenly positioned itself between the ethnic group and the larger society. Through the choice of its name, it anchored its image to the ethnic neighbourhood. The bulk of its charitable undertakings were also targeted at ethnic Chinese. Good examples included Mount Saint Joseph Hospital and the Home for the Aged on Campbell Avenue, both of which treated primarily Chinese patients. Furthermore, some of the Chinatown Lions Club's public functions, such as its 1958 sponsorship of the first local performance of traditional Chinese opera in the English language, sought to present various aspects of Chinese culture to a Canadian audience.[15] Clearly, these Canadian-born Chinese were not just celebrating their own social and economic advancement into the mainstream middle class. Their roles as charity benefactors and cultural brokers redefined their relationship with the ethnic community. As cultural performances – in anthropological parlance – their activities in the Chinatown Lions Club invalidate David Lee's formulation of local-born identity as a zero-sum game.[16]

The Chinese Veterans and the Chinatown Lions were certainly the best known organizations of the first generation of Canadian-born Chinese, but lesser examples are not lacking. For instance, the Chinese Golf Club was set up as early as 1950. It was probably the precursor of the Lions, for many of its members later joined the Lions Club.[17] In 1965, a lodge of the Benevolent and Protective Order of Elks of Canada was formed by a few dozen local-born Chinese in such white-collar occupations as insurance and real estate. Similar to the Lions, but in a less flamboyant fashion, the Chinese Elks engaged in public charities and organized regular social events.[18] During the same period, some local-born Chinese climbed to leadership positions in the ethnic churches, mediating between mostly Chinese-speaking pastors, their congregations, and the local delegates from the Canadian home mission authorities. Besides personal faith, their English educations, language skills, professional accomplishments, and middle-class backgrounds were plausible attributes of their new status.[19]

Also from the 1950s, a younger generation of *tusheng*, made up of those born in the 1930s and 1940s, began to organize as teenagers and young adults. One such organization was the Chinese Varsity Club on the University of British Columbia (UBC) campus. Although the club claims to this day to have been founded early this century for Chinese who had been excluded from other student bodies, very few Chinese students had attended UBC before the Second World War. Only eleven of them had reportedly graduated by the mid-1930s.[20] The growth of the Varsity Club into a centre of native-born Chinese student activities did not occur until the 1950s. In 1958, the official number of Chinese students at UBC was 230. Meanwhile, with membership expanding from fifty in 1955 to almost 200 in the following ten years, the Varsity Club was able to organize in-house social events around the academic year.[21]

Back in Chinatown, the junior *tusheng* searched appropriate venues for sports and other social and recreational activities, not unlike the immigrant youth mentioned earlier. In this respect, the young immigrants and *tusheng* Chinese were similar in that they both rejected the traditional organizations because of generational and cultural differences with the controlling elderly Chinese. One might expect that this common orientation – interest in sports and recreational activities apart from the established circle of Chinatown associations – would provide some sort of a meeting ground for the two groups. The ensuing interaction could (and, in a few cases, did) generate some mutual understanding and personal friendship, but, by and large, both sides seem not to have been eager to pursue this opportunity, and they remained far apart.

For the young local-born, Chinese Christian churches offered some attraction in the form of youth fellowship groups and boy scout teams.[22] The most popular recreational facilities by far were provided by the Pender Y. The YWCA opened its Chinatown centre in 1943 and then expanded it in 1952. Even though it was officially named the 'International Y' in 1950, close to 80 percent of its several hundred young patrons were Chinese. Among them must have been some new immigrants, but the large majority were English-speaking local-born youth. Indeed, some *tusheng* youth societies, such as the Chinese Bowling Club and the Chinese Athletic Club, used the premises regularly for their meetings. During the mid-1950s, these affiliated societies mushroomed at such a speed that the Pender Y convened an inter-club council to coordinate their activities.[23]

In retrospect, the engagement of both the junior and the more mature local-born Chinese in institution building was surely a function of their coming of age in the postwar period. No longer the appendage of an immigrant minority, they now formed a critical mass and had the means to establish their own organizations. This was especially the case for the older cohort among the *tusheng*, who were understandably more capable than the junior ones of articulating their interests. Their Veterans organization and the Chinatown Lions Club were strong vehicles of cultural expression, and their efficacy was considerably augmented after 1953 by the English-language magazine, *Chinatown News*, the first successful publication of the local-born Chinese.[24]

'We, Canadians of Chinese Ancestry': A Local-Born Chinese Voice

It is no exaggeration to say that any discussion of the Canadian-born Chinese during the postwar period would be incomplete without paying attention to the role of the *Chinatown News*. Two *tusheng* publications had appeared previously in Vancouver – the *Chinese News Weekly* in 1936 and the *New Citizen* in 1949 – but both were short-lived.[25] The *Chinatown News* was the first to last (all the way to early 1995). This Vancouver-based biweekly was run by its founding editor, Roy Mah, who was a member of the Chinese Veterans organization and belonged to the first generation of *tusheng*. The publication claimed to represent the interests of the local-born, English-speaking Chinese. Obviously, not every native-born subscribed to its point of view; the editorial opinions reflected Mah's background.[26] Nevertheless, the *Chinatown News* reported extensively on the activities of both the older and junior Canadian-born, which were seldom covered by the Chinese-language press, let alone the mainstream media. Instrumental in reclaiming an otherwise imperceptible cultural space for the *tusheng* as a group, the role of the *Chinatown News* in the construction of local-born Chinese identity deserves careful scrutiny.[27]

From its inception, the *Chinatown News* stood for the fullest participation of the ethnic Chinese, with the local-born as the vanguard, in all aspects of Canadian life. It lavished attention on stories of upward mobility, referring to the successful careers of many *tusheng* individuals.[28] It drew regular attention to their organizations, such as the Lions, the Elks, and the Veterans, arguing that they were the outcome of 'the attainment of ... personal status and material achievements.'[29] Editorials, like the following one in the issue of 18 June 1954, are typical:

> Trouble with us as a minority group in the larger Canadian society is that we tend to restrict ourselves too much for our own good. We think because we are Chinese we should isolate ourselves socially, occupationally and psychologically from the rest of the community. True, in the past we have suffered terribly by race prejudice, but time has changed and a new vista is dawning. The opportunity for Chinese to become an integrated part of the community is now more visible than ever before. It is up to us to take every advantage of it.
>
> A cursory examination reveals we have come a long way in the last couples of decades. Socially, we have taken advantage of all opportunities to intermingle with the society around us ... Occupationally, this generation has ventured from past practices of limited dealings with Chinese only ... Psychologically, we are undergoing a metamorphosis of losing our nationalistic feeling of being Chinese. The ill wind of World War II blew in strongly to bring about this good effect ...
>
> The foregoing does not mean we are denying there are no background differences with our Caucasian citizens, or that the existence of these differences are necessarily harmful. We are, however, advocating an attitude of looking at ourselves as individuals similar to others in this intermingled Canadian society.

From this editorial, the *Chinatown News* seems not to have stood for assimilation, meaning a total absorption into the mainstream society and the subsequent disappearance of one's ethnic heritage; instead, it exhibited an incipient belief, as early as the 1950s, in the merit of integration, implying a full identification with the country of adoption without the loss of one's native culture.[30] However, this emergent cultural position of the *tusheng* was still vaguely defined. For one thing, the retention of ethnic culture was by definition problematic in the period before cultural pluralism was accepted as the norm in Canadian society. For another, since the power to define ethnic culture was largely the preserve of the immigrants, and since the primary concern of the *tusheng* was to depart from the latter's parameters of control to embrace some form of local Canadian identity, the native-born Chinese could not be very enthusiastic about cultural retention.

Such ambivalence notwithstanding, the *Chinatown News* was quite ready for polemics within the Chinese minority. Later examples will show how it frequently defended the *tusheng* against the immigrants. At this point, two examples of local controversies will suffice to show its persistent effort to construct a distinct local-born Chinese identity.

The first one concerned the threat of urban redevelopment that beset the Chinatown neighbourhood from the late 1950s. Many local residents and Chinatown organizations feared financial loss, dislocation, and a dismantling of their community. To their dismay, the *Chinatown News* was outspoken in its support for the plan. In its many editorials on the subject, published between 1958 and 1964, it portrayed the situation as 'a choice between progress and temporary inconvenience.' The ethnic enclave, it argued, had already fulfilled its historical functions during the days of exclusion and was now mainly a 'tourist attraction.' Since the dispersal of the Chinese population from Chinatown was already under way, the magazine welcomed this latest move by the municipal government as an impetus for deghettoization.[31]

Another controversy of interest concerned the diplomatic recognition of the People's Republic of China by the Canadian government, which, after protracted negotiation, was finalized in October 1970.[32] In stark contrast to the practice of the Chinese-language press, the *Chinatown News* usually paid little attention to Old World politics and the related factional rivalries in Chinatown. This time, with typical detachment, the magazine showed its approval of Ottawa's rapprochement with Beijing, saying that it was in line with Canadian national interests. No less interesting is the way it underlined the indifference of the *tusheng* to this development. In its first editorial on the subject, which appeared in the issue of 3 December 1966, the *Chinatown News* argued that the Canadian-born Chinese 'have become too well integrated and too accustomed to the Canadian way of life to find attraction in any foreign ideology or totalitarian form of government. *Unlike the older generation* ... [they] have manifested little interest in the political fortunes of governments outside of Canada, save as an academic interest.

They are more at home with Canadian political parties' (emphasis added). The same point was driven home two years later when an editorial commented on the protest by some immigrant Chinese against Canada's move to recognize Communist China. Canadian-born Chinese were again described as 'more attuned to Canadian outlook and thinking ... In any event, recognition will have little effect [on the *tusheng*] for when it comes to clarifying our stand, we are proud that we are Canadian citizens of Chinese ancestry.'[33]

Some elements of journalistic self-promotion by the *Chinatown News* are obvious in these two examples. Nonetheless, we must pay attention to the fact that the two controversies – Chinatown redevelopment and Canada's diplomatic relationship with Mainland China – bore directly on the construction of *tusheng* identity. The *Chinatown News* seemed to be arguing that Canadian-born Chinese were not 'inscrutable Chinese,' clinging forever to the narrow perspectives of the ethnic group or holding fast to any Old World political affiliation; rather, they looked beyond the ethnic neighbourhood for their terms of reference and were Canadians at heart. By seeing the future of the Chinese minority in terms of integration into Canada, and by portraying the local-born as pioneers, the *tusheng* had projected their own discourse on Chineseness onto the public arena.

Cultural Offence and Defence

Having identified the *Chinatown News* and the key organizations of the local-born Chinese as their principal instruments of identity construction, it is now time to examine more closely the relationship between the *tusheng* and the immigrant Chinese. The fact is that *tusheng* identity did not develop in solitude; it evolved in full view of the older settlers and the new immigrants through interacting with their respective cultural assumptions and propositions. Their criticisms of one another, rejoinders, and counterattacks were landmarks in the cultural trajectory of *tusheng* identity.

I shall begin with the relationship between the local-born and the older generation of Chinese settlers. Before the 1940s, efforts at cultural maintenance within the ethnic group and the inaccessibility of social life and career choice beyond it were general conditions during the childhood and the adolescence of the *tusheng*. Both factors influenced the way these local-born Chinese, as adults in the postwar period, related to the older immigrants and to the community life and social organization the latter used to define. On the one hand, these *tusheng* were searching for autonomy, as is shown in their endeavour to delineate a sphere of their own public life. On the other hand, though they were trying to distance themselves culturally and socially from the older generation, their approach was marked by empathy. A thorough reading of the *Chinatown News* in this period, for instance, produces not a single public criticism of the older generation or anything remotely comparable to the scathing remarks by the new immigrants examined in the preceding chapter.

The reasons for this are twofold. First, despite the differences in age and outlook, the historical and emotional distance separating the older *tusheng* from the elderly settlers was relatively small. The large majority of them had grown up in Chinatown with an understanding of its cultural norms and social practices, and they were proficient in one or more of its spoken Cantonese sub-dialects. Many could further identify their own encounter with racial discrimination with the experience of their immigrant parents, which they had observed first-hand. Consequently, these native-born Chinese were more likely than, say, the postwar immigrants or the junior *tusheng* to empathize with the elderly generation.

More important, unlike the young newcomers who were locked in a conflict with the existing settlers over the same cultural and social space within the ethnic group, the Canadian-born Chinese generally looked beyond the ethnic boundary for economic and symbolic resources to nurture their sense of identity and autonomy. Seldom did they present themselves as critics of the older immigrants; instead, dressed as cultural brokers or mediators, they claimed to bring the Chinese minority ever closer to mainstream Canada. That was exactly how they handled a potentially explosive situation during the reform of the Chinese Merchants Association in the late 1950s.

The association was first founded in 1929. In the decade after the Second World War, it had remained largely a chamber of commerce for established Chinatown merchants of immigrant background.[34] In August 1957, several local-born Chinese, who had been nominal members, put forward a proposal for reform. They suggested revamping the organization to include not only merchants in the traditional lines of import-export trade, but also other businessmen and professionals. The result, it was argued, would be 'a businessmen's organization of a new kind' that encompassed the broadest spectrum of Chinese economic interests.[35] The negotiations were mostly veiled from the public, but a year later the reform was declared complete. The organization was renamed the Vancouver Chinese Association of Commerce, and it had an enlarged membership, a revised constitution, a redecorated clubhouse, and, most revealing of all, a newly elected executive committee filled by a large majority of *tusheng* from the Chinatown Lions Club.[36]

This was literally a takeover, and the apparent lack of tension attending it begs for an explanation. Perhaps, since the Chinese Merchants Association had not been active for years, the incumbents considered it unworthy of a fight. But the approach of the reformers surely contributed to the smooth transition. The *Chinatown News*, the local-born's mouthpiece, called the reorganization 'epoch-making ... [because] the appearance of this new group ... means that the vision of a more progressive, enlightened and prosperous

Chinatown has been translated into a reality, and in every businessman's heart there breathes new hope.'[37] Again, it cast the *tusheng* as the harbingers of progress and prosperity for the ethnic group. The reformers themselves also seem to have made an effort to deliver the coup de grâce peacefully. The old leadership was never criticized openly, and some previous members were given honourary positions on the new executive committee. Taking this arrangement at face value, the *Chinese Voice* praised the attempt at 'bringing pioneering merchants and young businessmen together' as the most remarkable feature of this reform.[38]

Obviously, had the local-born sought to take over a major organization of the immigrants, such as the Chinese Benevolent Association (CBA), then the episode would have ended differently. But the point here is to illustrate the temperate approach of the *tusheng* in dealing with the elderly immigrants. In fact, the latter had their share of ambivalence too. Among the old settlers there was a general feeling of resignation over the local-born's loss of Chinese cultural skills and national sentiments. They often castigated the *tusheng* organizations as too 'Westernized' (*xihua*) and continued to exclude them from any representation in the CBA.[39] On heated occasions, such as the Chinatown redevelopment controversy, they gave vent to their displeasure by heaping onto the *tusheng* scornful accusations of alleged deculturation. At one public hearing hosted by the city government in 1960, a spokesman for the Chinese opposition condemned the local-born as 'traitors' (*hanjian*) for their perceived corruption by Western culture and for their loss of interest in the well-being of their own kind.[40]

Notwithstanding the dissatisfaction with the cultural orientation of the *tusheng*, few Chinese could question the desirability of having the local-born win acceptance and respect for the ethnic group in the host country. Indeed, it is only reasonable to expect the elderly immigrants to show approval and to take pride in the competence and success of their children. A good example is provided by the scholarship awards, set up by many traditional associations from around the early 1960s, for the children of members who attended university. Despite the fear of acculturation on the part of many immigrant parents, they could not but recognize the accomplishments of their children. In this case, they actually spurred them on.[41]

In comparison, such cultural ambivalence and mutual accommodation were less evident in the *tusheng*'s relationship with the postwar immigrants. On the one hand, some local-born viewed the newcomers almost as an embarrassment, as though the latter's arrival had somehow turned back the clock of acculturation into Canadian society. On the other hand, among the new immigrants were many Chinese-educated youth who were equally intolerant. After their arrival, they took it upon themselves to revitalize Chinese culture in what they considered to be a backward community of conservative, poorly educated, elderly Chinese and their deculturated local-born descendants. With an inflated cultural pride and self-assured Chineseness, they harped on the perceived cultural deficiency and pretensions of the Canadian-born Chinese. The result was a cultural contest manifested in a series of confrontations and acrimonious disputes between the two groups.

In January 1954 a physical fight broke out between two parties of local-born and new immigrant youth in Chinatown, which, for the first time, brought considerable public attention to this internal conflict. Reportedly, this incident took place after some snowball throwing and exchanges of verbal insults. The local police intervened and arrested a number of participants. As expected, the CBA, as the leading community organization, called an emergency meeting at which it requested the native place societies to discipline their members; it then issued a public appeal to the same effect.[42]

There is no evidence of any further action taken by the various organizations, but as far as the editorial stances of the ethnic press are concerned, battle lines were quickly drawn. In their appeals for reconciliation, the two local Chinese-language newspapers – the *Chinese Times* and the *Chinese Voice* – could barely veil their sympathy for the immigrants and thus laid the blame entirely on the native-born Chinese. One of the editorials pejoratively contrasted the acculturation of the *tusheng* with the so-called 'pure ancestral country style' (*chuncui de zuguo feng*) of the immigrant youth. It chastised the local-born Chinese, insisting that they discard their pride and prejudice. 'They could *also* become the future masters of the overseas Chinese community,' as the editorial concluded, '*if* they apply their English language skill to improve the lot of the Chinese in Canada ... and learn more about their ancestral country from the immigrant Chinese' (emphasis added).[43] The denigration and marginalization of the local-born had continued unabated in the consciousness of the immigrants.

In coming to the defence of the Canadian-born Chinese, the *Chinatown News* furnished a seemingly objective and balanced assessment of the incident, as follows:

> The recent fracas in Chinatown between a group of newcomers and some [local-born] teenagers ... resulted in the arrest of seven youths charged with being in possession of offensive weapons ... Ostensibly, the incident was touched off by a snowball fight. We believe, however, that there are deeper underlying causes behind it all. At the basis of the conflict is a wide cultural gap between the two groups whose upbringing, habits and customs are totally different from the established practice of one another ...
>
> [The local-born Chinese] sometimes forget that for the newcomers from the old country, there is the tremendous problem of adjustment – both cultural and psychological – which must be met. To be successful, it will require all the sympathy and understanding that we [Canadian-born] can

show them. In a word, what the newcomers seek from us is help, not hindrance; encouragement, not ridicule; and tolerance, not prejudice.

On the other hand, the sooner the newcomers abandon their silly notions that because of their Chinese education they are culturally superior to their [local-born] brothers, the better it will be for all. After all, it will be only a matter of time before our immigrant friends too will be undergoing the same process of acculturation as [the Canadian-born] have already gone through, which means the acquiring of the cultural pattern of the land of their adoption.[44]

By attributing the event to cultural differences and mutual dislike, the *Chinatown News* held both sides responsible for causing the fight. The local-born youth should not have looked down on the newcomers because of the latter's ineptitude in a new cultural environment, it suggested; nor should the immigrants have ridiculed the *tusheng* for their poor command of Chinese cultural skills. However, this 'even-handed' appraisal was encapsulated in a larger argument about the future of the ethnic group. The ultimate issue presented here was one of cultural adjustment on the part of the new immigrants. Since acculturation was inevitable and desirable for the Chinese, the cultural arrogance of the newcomers and their self-assured Chineseness were misguided. For their own good, the *Chinatown News* argued, they should immediately embark on the process of local adaptation, and, if they did so, then the local-born Chinese would be in a better position to offer their sympathy, assistance, and support. The *Chinatown News* was steadfast in upholding the native-born's cultural agenda.

Thereafter, no further incidents involving physical assault were reported, though the chasm between the two groups endured well into the 1960s.[45] From what we know about their open altercations, the immigrant youth appeared like a group of cultural vigilantes criticizing the *tusheng* for their perceived cultural deficiency and pretensions. Bearing the brunt of these attacks were the junior Canadian-born Chinese, in part because they were the contemporaries of the young newcomers. Moreover, their progressive loss both of Chinese cultural skills and of their interest in things Chinese had rendered them more vulnerable to such disparagement than were the older native-born Chinese.

One rather amusing exchange took place in the correspondence column of the *Chinatown News* in 1956. The argument was triggered by the question: 'Could *tusheng* girls be good wives?' The background of this was the extreme imbalance in the sex ratio between the incoming youth in the early stage of renewed immigration after 1947. The male newcomers soon found that there was a dearth of suitable partners, and, by the mid-1950s, some of them reportedly went back to Hong Kong to seek spouses. In April 1956 this problem aroused even the sympathy of the Canadian government, which then made a special provision to allow Chinese to send for their fiancées.[46] Two months prior to the official announcement, a curious writer, who was intrigued by the popularity of costly 'wife hunting expeditions' to Hong Kong, posed these questions to his fellow readers: 'Why can't the Canadian [-born Chinese] girls capture these ambitious young men's hearts? Is there a shortage of girls? Or are there other reasons?'[47]

In the following issue, a frank reply was given by an immigrant youth, who seems to have decided to use the occasion not so much to reason as to vent his anger and disappointment: 'All these [Canadian-born] girls know is how to enjoy themselves and how to spend money and how to make up their faces as beautiful [sic] as white girls. They want a husband who must have a car, a house, or some other things representative of money. How can a young man afford these?' In his opinion, 'maidens in Hong Kong' were more preferable marriage partners than 'Chinese girls born in Canada,' who were ignorant of 'their Chinese parentage' and were 'prejudiced against their own kind.'[48]

The indictment was taken seriously and many *tusheng* replied in the following weeks, accusing the author of this letter of bigotry and bitterness towards the Canadian-born Chinese. The gender aspect of the controversy is especially fascinating, for explicit references to gender roles and expectations in the unfolding debate on Chinese identity are relatively rare. In this instance, we actually have a female voice in the form of a rebuttal from a local-born woman from Lethbridge, Alberta:

> Kindly allow me a couple of inches of your precious space to reply to Gerry Fong's highly amusing comments re. Canadian[-born Chinese] girls. Said he: 'All these girls know is how to enjoy themselves, how to spend money and how to make up their faces as beautiful [sic] as white girls ...' Come to think of it, Mr. Fong, if you don't find life glorious and yummy, I suggest you go and find a warm lake and do some acrobatics.
>
> And where are you going? Wherever it may be, this much is certain: even if you have money to burn, you still can't take it with you! So why be a tightwad?
>
> Your efforts sounded like the grumblings of a prejudiced mind when you insinuated that Chinese girls must use artificial makeup to be beautiful. Don't you realize that makeup is considered a necessity today, and not a vanity?
>
> Certainly we want something representative of money in a man. Security should be taken into consideration. Love and understanding can grow with the years. *How can a man afford a home and a car? Why, any young man with half an ounce of ambition can acquire these.*
>
> I have yet to meet a Canadian-born who is not proud of her heritage. And you, who harbors [sic] such thoughts, are the one who should disqualify

yourself as judge and jury ... *Having been born and educated in Canada* we naturally are a little more fussy when we come to pick our lifetime partner. Whereas many of our distant sisters [in Hong Kong] look at Canada through rose-colored glasses – using marriage as a convenient vehicle to come to Canada. And I am sure many many must have dearly regretted their quick marriage to some of you dashing, albeit feelingless, wife hunters. (Emphasis added.)[49]

Emphatically, the author of this letter believed that *tusheng* women were entitled to have their own expectations of their future spouses. Moreover, the right of the Canadian-born Chinese to be culturally different from the immigrants and not to be judged by others was fiercely defended.

Another bone of contention concerns the language preference of the native-born Chinese. Since the command of English was an economic asset and a status symbol for members of the minorities in Canadian society, immigrant resentment is understandable. They accused the *tusheng* of showing off, especially when the latter used English with other Chinese. As a young Chinese put it bluntly, 'We are learning English in order to deal with westerners. We are not supposed to use it among fellow Chinese. Otherwise, will it not mean the end of overseas Chinese culture in this place?'[50] Consider the opinions of another young essayist in an article entitled 'Zhongguoren yu zhongwen' [Chinese People and Chinese Language]. After ridiculing the local-born Chinese for the neglect of their 'native language' and their lack of cultural pride, the author urged the *tusheng* to redeem themselves by attending Chinese-language classes, reading Chinese newspapers, watching Chinese movies, and so on.[51]

In the *Chinatown News*, the younger native-born were resolute in refuting the accusation of language loss and deculturation. One of them, writing in 1964, claimed: 'Our elders fear we are losing our heritage – but what they fail to realize is that our heritage is North America[n], no matter how much we or they deplore it, no matter how much they try to deny it.'[52] Perhaps English, rather than Chinese, was their native tongue. Two years later, a Canadian-born Chinese high school teacher observed that the local-born were doing much better in the postwar period than were their forefathers. Several questions then arose: 'Why should they jeopardize themselves by bringing up the past? What is this Chinese culture? Should they have a part in "it"? Since they can get along well without speaking a word of Chinese, surely it is not at all necessary for them to learn Chinese.'[53]

Interestingly, the younger *tusheng* of that time were not as adamant in claiming the right to interpret or represent Chinese culture. One would no doubt have this impression from a visit to the UBC campus. In the 1950s, the Chinese Varsity Club for the local-born was the only ethnic Chinese student organization and was, therefore, assumed to speak to the university audience for all things Chinese.[54] This changed with the arrival of an increasing number of Chinese immigrant and foreign students towards the end of the decade. With a predominantly Hong Kong background, in 1960 this group was large enough to set up the Chinese Overseas Students Association.[55]

From all indications, relations between these two Chinese student bodies at the university were poor. Common interest in recreational activities and social events did not necessarily draw them together. Actually, the Chinese Varsity Club preferred to co-sponsor campus activities with the Japanese Nisei Varsity Club, an organization of fellow Canadian-born Japanese, who were likewise in search of a locally derived identity. As for the new immigrant students, they were equally determined to dissociate themselves from the *tusheng*, evidently because they were upset by the Varsity Club's 'mis-representation' of Chinese culture.[56] One revealing episode was the argument over 'The Question of the Rickshaw,' which broke out in February 1964.

As part of the celebration of the Chinese New Year on campus, the Varsity Club performed a lion dance and displayed a rickshaw. The latter was a rather common exhibit, presented on occasions of Chinese festivity as an exotic 'Oriental' artefact. The Chinese Overseas Students Association had voiced its objection in the past, but this time it launched a publicity campaign in the *Chinese Voice* to denounce the event as 'a national disgrace' (*youru guoti*). In an open letter it took pains to point out the origin of the rickshaw as an American invention in Meiji Japan. Once transplanted to China and various colonial cities in Southeast Asia, the vehicle had become an unmistakable symbol of the West's subjugation of Chinese people. To reenact the scene was humiliating. The letter went on to ridicule the Varsity Club's undertaking as 'laughable' because it served to reveal the native-born's superficial grasp of Chinese culture.[57]

In a rejoinder submitted to the *Chinese Voice*, the Chinese Varsity Club reiterated the popularity and success of the event.[58] Unfortunately, the explanation just provided more ammunition for its critics, who jumped on the organizer for being brazen and for distorting and shortchanging Chinese culture for the satisfaction and curiosity of the non-Chinese. Reprints of letters criticizing the club ran for more than a week in the *Chinese Voice*.[59] The Varsity Club made no further effort to defend itself, even when the association published a critique in the *Chinatown News*.[60]

It seems impossible to deny the immigrant and foreign student body a victory not only with regard to publicity, but also with regard to the struggle for the power to define Chinese culture. (One may add that their self-righteous condemnation of the *tusheng*'s identification with White stereotypes of the exotic 'Orient' is eminently in line with the critique of postcolonial scholarship.) Nonetheless, the rickshaw incident also underlined the changing emphasis of different cultural attributes in the identity construction of the local-born Chinese. It may no longer have been of interest and importance to them to claim the right to represent the culture of China, especially after the new immigrants arrived on the scene. The change was a matter of conscious choice and, perhaps, the inevitable outcome of their search for some form of local identification with Canada.

To conclude, the most salient feature in the emergent identity of the *tusheng* in Vancouver was their overall cultural orientation towards Canada. The more tangible markers included their use of the English language and the locally derived formats of voluntary organizations. The latter were important instruments in delineating a distinct cultural and social space for the local-born Chinese. Furthering their cause was an outspoken and self-conscious publication, the *Chinatown News*. On numerous occasions, this English-language magazine came to the defence of the Canadian-born against the ethnic chauvinism of some Chinese immigrants by reaffirming their cultural differences and reasserting their pride.

So, like the new immigrants after 1947, in the postwar period the local-born Chinese had become a potent force for unsettling the existing discourse on Chinese identity – a discourse that had once been dominated by the older generation of immigrants. Defining Chinese identity entirely in terms of China-related experiences and cultural skills, the immigrants could easily denigrate and marginalize the local-born Chinese. Now, however, by seeing the future of the ethnic group in relation to its acculturation and integration into Canadian society, the *tusheng* shifted the point of reference from China to the place of settlement. Thus the discourse on identity changed dramatically in favour of the *tusheng*. No wonder the local-born so confidently displayed and took pride in their Canadian orientations and local competence. No wonder the immigrants were outraged.

5
Old-Timers, Public Rituals, and the Resilience of Traditional Organizations

The older generation of Chinese immigrants had good reason to be enraged by the behaviour of the newcomers and the local-born Chinese. At the beginning of the postwar period, these old-timers still formed the largest sector of the Chinese population in Vancouver. Having survived the difficulties of the exclusion era, they expected from the newcomers and local-born nothing short of filial respect and gratitude for their perseverance. Moreover, in their eyes their Chinatown organizations – including the influential Chinese Benevolent Association (CBA), the partisan groups of the Freemasons and the Kuomintang, and the numerous district and surname associations – represented the established order. These collective endeavours had always given meaning and substance to their community by defining and defending it in the larger context of a hostile, racist Canadian society. As a realm of public activity, the organizations had been instrumental in grooming a local elite, mediating internal disputes, and nurturing a shared cultural identity.

However, the dominant position of the elderly immigrants became increasingly untenable as the postwar period wore on. Not only were they soon outnumbered, the cultural norms and social practices associated with the old-style organizations were much criticized by the new immigrants and were rejected by the *tusheng*. In a nutshell, the growing diversity and plurality within the ethnic group challenged the old-timers and upset their sense of dominance.[1]

Many studies of North American Chinatowns have seemingly confirmed the demise of the citadel of the older immigrants – the traditional organizations. For instance, Gunter Baureiss has theorized that since these ethnic organizations were primarily a defence against racist rejection, their utility and relevance would have expired with the end of overt discrimination after the Second World War.[2] Referring to the communist takeover of China in 1949, Graham Johnson sees the 'cut-off from the homeland' as no less detrimental to the vitality of district and clan associations, given their preoccupation with China and the native areas.[3] More generally, the once popular modernization theory has led some of its practitioners to describe the decline of 'old-style,' 'anachronistic' organizations as inevitable once traditional societies enter the threshold of modernity.[4]

These diagnoses have underestimated the resilience of the Chinese traditional organizations in Vancouver. In spite of, or perhaps because of, their unpopularity among the newcomers and the *tusheng*, the old-timers actually intensified their activities in some of the organizations in order to substantiate their claim of authority. At the heart of their claim was the performance of public rituals, a topic that has not received much attention from concerned scholars. These rituals, in my opinion, were constitutive and expressive of a definition of identity and community that was delivered by the elderly settlers as a rejoinder to their critics.

After providing an overview of ritual activities undertaken by the traditional associations in Vancouver and a detailed case study of their fundraising practices, this chapter goes on to examine the postwar history of the CBA. So many studies pertaining to the demise of the traditional Chinatown organizations after 1945 have merely generalized about the decline of the CBA.[5] The history of the Vancouver CBA is considerably more interesting and complex than scholars have noticed thus far.

Ritual Construction of Identity

There is no disagreement that the quarter century after 1945 was a difficult time for the older generation of Chinese settlers in control of the traditional associations. The growth of the Chinese population did not have a positive effect on the inventory of their organizations.[6] Reliable and precise membership figures are unavailable, but we already know that the traditional associations were shunned by the new immigrants and the *tusheng* Chinese. Certain associations, like the Chinese Freemasons and the Wong organizations, were able to recruit young new arrivals due to their Chinese-language schools and other recreational facilities. Less successful were those associations that experimented only briefly with the youth corps in the 1950s. Least successful of all were those that had nothing with which to appeal to the young newcomers and the local-born. With regard to this last group, its vitality must have diminished considerably by the 1960s, if not earlier, as aging steadily took its toll.

The difficulties of the traditional associations did not escape the notice of the new immigrant youth. In the late 1950s and the 1960s, condescending comments on the 'lifelessness' of these organizations appeared occasionally in the Chinese press. They were portrayed as 'just a bunch of elderly people who stick together for their own goods.' 'These folks met to commemorate their predecessors, celebrate their organization's founding anniversary, rotate among themselves leadership positions, pay homage to Taiwan, and above all, have a feast,' as the critics would point out.[7]

There is an element of truth in these criticisms. Many of the public functions of these associations took the form of repetitive, ritual observances, presumably dictated by traditions. It is questionable as to whether the participants were fully conscious of the meanings of their actions. Indeed, there is an established opinion in the scholarly literature on rituals that ritual performance is '*thoughtless* action – routinized, habitual, obsessive, or mimetic' (italics in original). Catherine Bell, however, points out in a recent revisionist critique of various theoretical positions that the dichotomy between thought and action in ritual analysis may have been overdrawn.[8] As a matter of fact, Victor Turner, probably the best recognized authority on the subject, has long argued that ritual may look 'rigid,' 'empty,' and 'threadbare,' but it is 'richly textured,' with living meanings embedded within it.[9] Another one of Turner's important observations, inspired by no less an authority than Clifford Geertz, is that since ritual 'is tacitly held to communicate the deepest values of the group regularly performing it, it has a *"paradigmatic"* function ... As a *"model for,"* ritual can anticipate, even generate change; as a *"model of,"* it may inscribe order in the minds, hearts, and wills of participants' (italics in original).[10]

This last observation, that rituals communicate ideals, can be a point of departure in our attempt to understand identity construction among the older generation of immigrant Chinese. Not as educated as the newcomers and the *tusheng*, the elderly immigrants resorted to, and probably relied upon, public rituals in the traditional organizations to articulate their ideas and sentiments about identity. Their ritual behaviour thus furnishes us with a most vivid non-written script for a sketch of their cultural universe.[11] In the eyes of the critics and the uninitiated, the old-timers' obsessive nostalgia about the Old World, their expressed desire for internal unity, and the invariable claim of accomplishment and greatness for their organizations at the time of ritual observance (see below) were rhetorical at best and hypocritical at worst. Nevertheless, these memories, claims, and visions, irretrievable and unrealistic as they seemed to be, functioned as a 'model,' in Geertz's terms, for fostering a shared culture and community.[12]

In postwar Vancouver, the principal occasions of ritual performance in the Chinese traditional associations formed a fairly standard annual ritual cycle, as is shown in Table 11. These were regular public functions that occasioned general membership participation. Some activities that are not on the list, such as the executive meetings, could be equally ritualistic, but they involved only a few people. Also omitted are irregular ritual events, such as receptions for visiting dignitaries, funerals, and national conventions. As for the items in the annual cycle, my classification is arbitrary and

Table 11

Annual ritual cycle observed by traditional Chinese organizations in Vancouver during the postwar period

Items

Administrative	Election of officials	Held annually by most organizations between November and February of the following year
Religio-cultural	Spring rite at the Qingming Festival	During March and April
	Autumn rite at the Chongyang Festival	During September and October, becoming common in the early 1960s
	Birthday celebration of (fictitious) progenitors	Observed by the Chinese Freemasons and some clan associations
Socio-cultural	Spring banquet	During the Chinese New Year
	Founding anniversary	Various dates; held annually by an increasing number of organizations during the postwar period
Political	Commemoration of the 1911 revolution	Annually on 10 October
	Commemoration of the founding of the Republic of China	Annually on 1 January

Sources: Chinese Times and Chinese Voice.

is meant only to highlight their essential features because each ritual is, by nature, 'multivocal,' its various meanings and objectives being endowed by participating individuals.[13]

A collective ritual explicitly for administrative purposes was the annual election of the executive officials. Typically, a traditional organization was run by a general committee of several dozen people. Within this committee was a smaller executive group led by a chairperson and a few standing committee members. The maximum version of an election could take weeks, as it included the nomination of candidates, the preliminary election of the general committee, another round to elect the standing committee (and other subcommittees, if any), and, finally, an installation ceremony. Such an elaborate procedure was followed by the CBA and some well established and sizable clan and district organizations.

Towards the other end of the scale were the smaller societies with fewer members and less resourceful leaders. It is interesting that many of them would compress a lengthy procedure into a minimum version that was still considered dignified and presentable to outside observers. A case in point is the Ing Suey Sun Tong. With just a few dozen members, it was customary for the Tong to get everyone to sit on the executive committee. The entire election process, from the nomination to the casting and counting of votes to the installation of the new executive, could be completed at an annual general meeting attended by less than two dozen people on a weekend evening.[14]

The second type of public ritual was expressly religious-cum-cultural. It included the so-called 'spring and autumn rites,' which were dedicated to deceased members at the Qingming and Chongyang Festivals. Qingming had long been set aside for ancestral worship in Chinese tradition. It had been dutifully observed by the migrants and their organizations in Vancouver from the earliest time. The observance of Chongyang, however, seems to be an example of 'ritual intensification,' which was added to the ritual cycle in Vancouver as late as the 1960s.[15] Two circumstances in the postwar period might have compelled the traditional associations to pay more attention to the commemoration of their deceased. Not only did an increasing number of elderly Chinese pass away, but the dead were to be buried locally in a permanent fashion, the practice of exhuming bones and sending them back to China for reburial having ceased in 1951.[16]

The birthday celebration of the fictitious progenitors in the surname organizations was another ritual with strong religious overtones. The Chinese Freemasons organization was the only other Chinatown society with a comparable public function. The Freemasons regularly paid homage to the supposed founders of their secret brotherhood back in China several centuries ago, and they took great pride in their teaching of loyalty and righteous behaviour. The Freemasons' membership initiation also had a stronger religious flavour than did those of the other organizations.[17]

Compared to the second category, the collective rituals in the third category, including the spring banquets during the Chinese New Year and the anniversary celebrations, might appear more as social occasions. The New Year banquets were by far the most popular ceremonial events. The oldest members, said to have 'fulfilled their obligations [to the association]' (*jinru yiwu*), were escorted to the banquet, honoured publicly, and treated to a special meal. The occasion was further distinguished by the presence of a significant number of women and children; even nominal members who seldom set foot in the meeting hall would show up. The founding anniversaries, on the other hand, were celebrated on a smaller scale and were attended mainly by active members, unless it was something grander, such as the silver or golden jubilee.

Last, there were the political rituals associated with support for the Nationalist government. The local Kuomintang was no doubt the most enthusiastic about the commemoration of the 1911 revolution and the founding of the Chinese Republic. Assisted by the Chinese Consulate-General, it publicized those events and urged other organizations to follow its lead. Initially, many traditional associations complied, but they were getting fewer as the postwar period wore on and interest in Chinese politics waned.

With this last notable exception, the annual ritual cycle was generally observed more regularly and more widely among the traditional organizations in the 1950s and 1960s than ever before. Why did the older generation of Chinese immigrants invest more time and energy in these ceremonial functions? What kind of messages were they trying to convey? Could they have used ritual as a vehicle to defend their pride and reiterate their claim of legitimacy and authority while being disparaged by the immigrant youth and rejected by the local-born Chinese?[18]

One way of answering these questions is to decipher the layers of symbolism and meaning woven into each ritual performance. For instance, the New Year banquet clearly signified 'the presence of the group in its full numerical strength' and impressed 'those present with a deep sense of group consciousness.' As such, it became one of the most important occasions for expounding the theme of unity through delivering the appropriate speeches, through recognizing the contributions of certain individuals to the group, and through everyone partaking of a big feast to mark the sharing of abundance. To draw the maximum benefit from these moments of unity, the leadership often took the opportunity to drum up support for charities or other fund-raising activities.[19]

The ancestral rite performed in the traditional associations had its specific functions too. Unlike private ancestral worship in a family setting, in an organization the objects of veneration were the progenitors of the group and its deceased members. A public rite was therefore more than an individual expression of filial piety; it delineated the group's boundary and buttressed its collective identity. Moreover, it enabled the participants to lay claim to a larger historical memory by commemorating and honouring the pioneering generations for their perseverance, hard work, frugality, love of native place, and commitment to the well-being of the group. Celebrated as the essence and beauty of Chinese culture, these supposedly timeless values were now appropriated by the elderly Chinese. Catherine Bell nails down this analytical point when she argues that the ritual construction of tradition acquired its potency by 'the invocation of authoritative precedent with all its connotations of moralism and nostalgia.'[20]

The annual election of officials was yet another revealing ritual performance. Campaigning and open competition were rare, given the emphasis on consensus and power sharing. The participants basically rotated offices among themselves. Nevertheless, formal election both conferred procedural legality and bestowed moral approval upon the leadership. No less important was the opportunity given periodically to members to symbolically take part in deciding the future of an organization.

Though each public ritual had its specific forms and meanings, the aggregate efficacy of public rituals in general is clearly discernible in certain paradoxes embedded within almost all of them. For instance, ritual performances and communal celebrations were designed to enhance the vitality of the associations that held them. With the focus ostensibly on the group, elderly Chinese came to renew their sentiments of pride, loyalty, and unity. They redecorated the meeting hall for the occasions, and they displayed their corporate strength by means of public announcements, news reports, and parades through Chinatown. In the process, however, although individuals were transcended they were not eclipsed, and unity was emphasized without sacrificing hierarchy. By taking part in congregational activities, regular members refreshed their sense of belonging, rubbed shoulders with one another, and renewed contact with their leaders. Some were honoured by the organizations for their service or because their personal accomplishments reflected favourably on the group. Others who helped out with the event demonstrated some responsibility in the esteemed public arena. Leaders, in particular, gained visibility by speech making and financial contributions. To quote Turner, these participants all became 'heroes in [their] own dramas,' as their personal images were enlarged and their self-worth inflated.[21] In this sense, public rituals wove individuals and the corporate body of the organization into a single, almost seamless, tapestry.

Furthermore, each traditional association mounted its own rituals, so the potential for competition and rivalry among them was real. Nonetheless, by subscribing to a common corpus of ritual practices, these organizations transcended their separate identities and generated an aura of consensus – an imagined community – among the elderly Chinese. Not only did the old-timers observe the same ritual events and follow common procedures in the ceremonies, but, above all, they were in unison with one another in upholding the ideal of internal unity and harmony, the lasting value of traditional Chinese culture, and their own roles as active participants in this community. Furthering this 'ritual integration' were the cross-participation of the older immigrants in one another's public ceremonies and the overlapping membership among organizations. On those occasions, the associations exchanged gifts, and their delegations sang one another's praises. They offered some of the finest moments of calculated Chinese solidarity.[22]

The old-timers' engagement in public rituals was, therefore, purposeful. Ritual performance breathed life into the traditional organizations and enabled the older generation to articulate its visions of community and its own sense of cultural and social worth. The following section extends my ritual analysis to a relatively obscure, and yet highly important, aspect of organizational operation.

Financial Management as Ritual

At a glance, due to a dearth of pertinent information, the finances of Chinatown associations are not amenable to academic scrutiny.[23] However, I have found materials that have never been tapped, and, altogether, they provide extremely valuable insights into the process of financial mobilization.

Incoming members of Chinatown organizations were usually required to pay an enrolment fee and then to contribute a small amount to the coffers every year. Collection of this annual fee must have been frustrating, as some associations admitted that many members owed them years of back payments.[24] Another regular item on the financial statement in the early period was the so-called 'exit fee' (*chu kou fei*) of two dollars to be honoured by every member who returned to China, supposedly for good, after years of sojourning abroad. Its collection was suspended during the Sino-Japanese War, resumed briefly in the late 1940s, and finally abandoned in the early 1950s because, after that, few Chinese would go back to Mainland China. Even when it was being collected, however, the exit fee was not really a source of income. It was, instead, earmarked for the cost of exhuming the bones of deceased members and shipping them to China for reburial. Practically, this money all ended up in the Chinese Consolidated Benevolent Association in Victoria, which coordinated this effort across Canada.[25]

Over the years, the traditional organizations devised other means to supplement their income. The Hoy Ping District Association ran an in-house lottery that netted more than $3,000 at the end of the Second World War. The Lee Clan Association made the lottery into an annual event for its fee-paying members.[26] It was also common to raise funds for special projects such as the various Chinatown language schools. These campaigns were typically organized in such a way as to distinguish the benefactors and to articulate the differences in the contribution amounts (see Figure 5). Other than promoting the event, this practice of 'competitive generosity' was a well established way of grooming and recognizing leaders.[27]

Sometimes, financial contributions were made as part of public events. Traditional organizations routinely collected fees for New Year's or anniversary celebrations. These and other ceremonial occasions were most appropriate times for the expression of public spirit and group loyalty by means of a donation. Carefully managed, a costly public ritual could cover its expenses.[28]

This same logic of turning an item of expenditure into a source of income can be seen in the way some associations acquired their own quarters. Most Chinatown organizations had started in the early years by renting their clubhouses, but a few had managed to mobilize enough support from their

---

In order to encourage donation to the School, the Board of Directors has decided to use the following scheme to recognize the contributions of our benefactors:

1. For those contributing $5 or above, their names will be inscribed on a mirror hanging in the hall.
2. For those contributing $25 or above, their personal pictures of two inches large will be hung in the hall.
3. For those contributing $50 or above, their personal picture of three inches large will be hung in the hall.
4. For those contributing $100 or above, their personal pictures of four inches large will be hung in the hall.
5. For those contributing $200 or above, their personal pictures of six inches large will be hung in the hall.
6. For those contributing $500 or above, their personal pictures of eight inches large will be hung in the hall.
7. For those contributing $1,000 or above, their personal pictures of twelve inches large will be hung in the hall. The classrooms will also be named after these benefactors individually.
8. For the one contributing $3,000 to $5,000, a personal picture of twenty inches large will be hung in the hall. The school playground will also be named after this benefactor.

Foon Sien Wong
Chairman, Board of Directors
Mon Keong School
9 October 1944

Figure 5   Recognition of financial contributions to the Mon Keong School, 1944

Note: Apparently, the board was expecting only one benefactor who would contribute a sum of $3,000 or more, since only one school playground would be built. The competitive potential of the scheme is obvious.
Source: Extract from 'Wenqiang xuexiao xiaodonghui dongshizhang huang wenfu baogao shu' [Report by Foon Sien Wong, Chairman, Board of Directors, Mon Keong School], 1944. In Foon Sien Wong Papers, Special Collections, UBC, box 3.

members to purchase properties. This not only saved the payment of a monthly rental, but it often provided a source of additional income as any extra floor space could be rented out. The Wong Kung Har Tong, a leading Chinatown organization representing the biggest surname group, was a case in point. Using membership contributions, it bought a large building on East Pender Street in 1922. The second and third levels were used for the meeting hall and the Mon Keong School, respectively, and the ground floor was rented out. By 1950, this piece of property was said to be worth $100,000.[29]

The Wong association was not alone in acquiring institutional properties in this early period, but what seems remarkable in the postwar years is the large number of traditional associations purchasing real estate in Chinatown for the first time (see Table 12). Perhaps economic recovery and rising property values made this a sound investment. At the same time, the interruption of remittances to the homeland as a result of warfare and political upheavals since 1937 should have left Vancouver Chinese with more

Table 12

Vancouver's traditional Chinese associations with real estate investment during the postwar period

Year(s)	Association
1945	Ming Sing Reading Room*
1946	Chee Duck Tong*
1949-52	Oylin Society HQs*
1950	Yee Fung Toy Tong HQs*
1951	Fong Loon Tong HQs*
1951	Hoy Ping District Association HQs*
1951-52	Nam Ping Bitsuey*
1952-53	Wong Wun San Society HQs*
1953	Lee Clan Association HQs
1956	Nam Yeung Tong HQs*
1956	Chung Shan Lung Jen Association*
1957	Shon Yee Benevolent Association HQs
1957-59	Hoy Sun Ning Yung Benevolent Association
1958-59	Cheng Wing Yeong Tong HQs
1959-60	Sue Yuen Tong
1960	Mah Society
1960	Kong Chow District Association HQs
1961	Fong Loon Tong HQs
1962-66	Gee How Oak Tin Association*
1963	Lee Clan Association HQs

* First-time property owners
HQs = national headquarters
Sources: Chinese Times, Chinese Voice, and various organizational publications.

disposable capital. Steady progress in reuniting families after 1947 might have also reduced remittances, though, arguably, it cost more to support a family in Vancouver than in China.[30] Whatever led to the upsurge in corporate property ownership, which lasted well into the early 1960s, the ingenious method of financial mobilization known locally as the *baizi hui* deserves a careful analysis.

The origin of *baizi hui* is not known, but its literal meaning, 'a club of a hundred sons,' quite aptly captures the idea that it was an undertaking involving the many rather than the few. The reference to *baizi*, perhaps taken from '*baizi qiansun*' (lit. a hundred sons and a thousand grandchildren), suggests that the project had implications for posterity. As for *hui*, despite a common denominator, the *baizi hui* was very different from the popular money pool. In that traditional enterprise, a dozen individuals would rotate their access to a sum of money in order to meet their need for some family occasion, investment capital, or emergency funds.[31] In the case of *baizi hui*, the association would take the lead in setting up a real estate company and then invite the entire membership to contribute in the form of shares. The money raised would be used to buy a property to house the association and to generate rental income. Part of the proceeds so derived could be credited to shareholders as dividends and as repayment of the principal. An ideal scenario was for an organization to buy back all the shares and for the members to be duly compensated for their investment.

The *baizi hui* in the Hoy Ping District Association was one such successful example. In late 1951, the association raised $40,000 through a *baizi hui*. In the following year, the money was invested in a two-story building on Main

Figure 6   Official opening of Chee Duck Tong's new clubhouse, 1947

Figure 7 Principal of Mon Keong School plays host to visitors, 1950. Notice the signs in the upper left showing the 'Chinese Culture Room' (in English and Chinese on the top) and, beneath them, the 'Wong Kung Har Tong Real Estate Company Classroom' (in Chinese).

Street. Apparently the property generated such good income that the payment of dividends and principal began in 1955. By 1970 the association had acquired sole ownership after buying back a total of 800 shares from its members.[32]

Though failures were not unheard of, the *baizi hui* seems to have been an appealing and sound financial scheme.[33] Not only did many traditional associations become property owners by this means, but the project often provided stable revenue for membership welfare and public charities. It was also a way of enhancing institutional staying power and prestige, rendering the organizations more attractive for leaders and members alike. Moreover, another beauty of the *baizi hui* was that it did not ask members for donations. Seto Gock, a Chinese leader, once explained the advantages of joining a *baizi hui* as follows: it was a safe investment with a relatively high degree of liquidity; its 5 percent guaranteed annual interest was comparable to the yield of government bonds; above all, the *baizi hui* was a good *private* investment that contributed to a *public* cause.[34]

The idea of melding public and private suggests that *baizi hui* was not simply a financial set-up but also a ceremonial activity for the traditional organizations. Similar to other public rituals, *baizi hui* emphasized group identity. The associations usually limited participation to their respective members and claimed the right to buy back any shares fallen into the hands of 'outsiders.' These provisions were, of course, meant to safeguard corporate ownership, which was the ultimate purpose of the venture.[35]

Our Headquarters has decided to buy a building in the northeast corner of Hastings and Carrall Streets at the price of $90,000. The following regulations will be applied regarding our ownership and investment:

1.   A real estate department is set up in the Fong Loon Tong Headquarters.
2.   The legal ownership is in the name of the Fong Loon Tong.
3.   All shares are of uniform value, i.e., $20 each.
4.   The basic capital consists of the money we got from the city government when our previous building was expropriated and our savings in the bank.
5.   All See and Seto clansmen, sisters (including those who have already 'married out'), and our close relatives who are residing in Canada should subscribe at least one share ($20) as a responsibility. A maximum ownership of 100 shares ($2,000) is prescribed to prevent control by any single member.
6.   There is an annual interest of five percent for the amount of investment. By drawing lots, the dividends and the principal will be paid to each investor in order. The amount of interest will be calculated from the date of the actual payment of the capital.
7.   The ownership of the shares is transferrable to the spouses, siblings and close relatives upon a written notification to our department.
8.   People who want to cash their shares before maturity can do so by giving the department a one-month notice. Those who withdraw during the first half of the year will forfeit all the interest of the year, and those who withdraw during the second half will be paid half of their annual interest for that year.

Figure 8   Regulations of the *baizi hui* in Fong Loon Tong Headquarters, 1961

Note: The explicit invitation of female contribution is noteworthy because the large majority of the participants in *baizi hui* during this period were elderly immigrant men. In this case, this might be a strategy to maximize participation because this clan organization had too small a membership.
Source: An extract from 'Jianada fenglun zongtang shiyebu qishi' [Public Notice by the Real Estate Department of the Fong Loon Tong Headquarters], *Chinese Voice*, 5 May 1961.

In contrast to fund-raising methods that emphasized distinction in the amounts of contribution, another characteristic of *baizi hui* was its egalitarian spirit. With few exceptions, the unit value of shares was kept very low – usually between five and twenty dollars – to make them affordable. A flat interest rate was the norm, regardless of the difference in the amount of subscription. The date of maturity was decided by drawing lots, and each investor was to collect the principal and dividends in turn. To prevent

Table 13

**Classification of shareholders in the *baizi hui* of the
Wong Wun San Society Headquarters, 1953**

Capital $	Investors No.	Investors %	Investment %
1,000	5	0.97	12.59
500	15	2.91	18.88
400	1	0.19	1.00
300	10	1.94	7.55
250	4	0.77	2.51
200	23	4.47	11.58
150	3	0.58	1.13
110	1	0.19	0.27
100	77	14.98	19.39
80	4	0.77	0.80
50	107	20.81	13.47
40	3	0.58	0.30
30	26	5.05	1.96
20	103	20.03	5.18
10	132	25.68	3.32
	(514)	(99.92)	(99.93)

Source: Compiled from *Huang yunshang zong gongsuo gouzhi louye baogaoshu*
[A Report on the Purchase of Land Properties by the Wong Wun San Society
Headquarters], 1957, 5-12.

excessive ownership and control by any single member, the Fong Loon Tong
went as far as limiting the number of shares bought by each investor (see
Figure 8). Of all the public rituals practised by the traditional organizations,
the *baizi hui* probably gave the most substance to the popular saying that
'the association belongs to all of the members.'

Some of the records I found provide exceptional documentation of *baizi
hui* in two organizations. In 1953, the Wong Wun San Society Headquarters
organized a *baizi hui* to buy a building on East Pender Street. A report, printed
in 1957, gives the details of this financial mobilization.[36] Issuing some 5,500
shares at a value of $10 each, a sum of $55,000 was raised. Among the
institutional shareholders were the Wong Wun San Societies in Calgary,
Edmonton, Toronto, and Montreal, and the headquarters in Vancouver,
which altogether contributed 1,000 shares. There were seventy-eight individual shareholders from various Canadian Chinatowns, but the bulk of
the capital was raised from local members. Table 13 classifies the 514 shareholders from Vancouver according to the amount of their investment. It
should be pointed out that the report itself made no such distinction, and
the names of shareholders were probably arranged based on the sequence
of subscription.

The egalitarian spirit of *baizi hui* is borne out by the evidence in this table. Over 70 percent of the participants contributed $50 or less. In fact, one out of four subscribed only the minimum amount of one share. The bigger investors – those who bought more than $100 worth of shares – made up only 12 percent of all investors. This application of the *baizi hui* formula apparently yielded good results, with the building generating a monthly rental income of $570, not to mention new quarters for the society and the Hon Hsing Athletic Club.

Due to its elitist impulse, the *baizi hui* organized by the Lee Clan Association around the same time was very different from the others.[37] Even its origin was unconventional. In late 1952, the association was presented with an opportunity to acquire the ownership of a hotel on Main Street. Considering this a profitable undertaking, the association promptly raised a loan of $75,000 from seventy-five local members. In the following months, a *baizi hui* was set up with contributions from some 180 individual members and the loan was repaid. In stark contrast to the above example of the Wong organization, the minimum amount of shareholding in this case was $50, but only three people came under this category. In fact, some twenty-five individuals bought at least $1,000 worth of shares. Peculiar among the contemporary *baizi hui*, this pattern of distribution resembled more closely the fund-raising rituals that encouraged competition and articulated leadership distinction. The fact that the names of creditors and shareholders in the original documents were arranged according to the amount of money they rendered also supports this conjecture.[38]

Such a penchant for the ritual of 'competitive generosity' came to the fore again when the Lee Clan Association decided to build a new clubhouse at its Second National Convention in 1963. This time, the *baizi hui* formula was simply shelved and a fund-raising committee was formed to solicit donations from members across Canada. My sources give no explanation for this preference, but the effort proved to be misguided. The uncertainty over the future of Chinatown caused by the city government's urban renewal programs must have dampened the appeal of the project. Compounding the problem was the expectation for donations, which went against the deeply ingrained practice of *baizi hui*. It is a tribute to the Lee association's organizational strength that $70,000 was raised, though it still fell short of the original target. In 1970, the project was finally aborted after being put off several times. Clearly, performing the right ritual was critical.

In retrospect, the successful completion of many *baizi hui* and the faithful performance of other public rituals should put the traditional organizations in a different light. The older generation of immigrants did not just indulge in ceremonial formalities, as their critics insisted. In a period of drastic social and cultural change, ritual performances enabled the old-timers to reenact their community visions and to reaffirm a sense of cultural vitality vis-à-vis their detractors. The following case study of the CBA amplifies some of these points.

Ritual of Unity and Representation at the CBA

At the beginning of the postwar period, it is arguable that the Vancouver CBA was the Chinese organization that best captured the meaning of community. Since its founding at the turn of the century, it had signified the early immigrants' persistent quest for an organization that could encompass partisan interests and provide a sense of unity. By 1925, the CBA had put into place a system of electing its executive committee that guaranteed representation to both the major district associations and to members at large. The system placed the CBA at the apex of the Chinese organizational hierarchy and supported its claim to speak for all Chinese in Vancouver. The claim seems to have been generally well taken, despite ongoing factional strife and leadership rivalries among the ethnic Chinese.

This structure of representation underwent no fundamental change throughout the postwar years. Minor alterations were made in the 1950s to enlarge the executive committee.[39] More important was the rearrangement in 1948 to elect three co-chairmen instead of one. The conflict between the Kuomintang and the Freemasons was accentuated by the civil war in China. The new modus operandi would allow both parties to be represented, with a 'neutralist' providing the balance.[40] In effect, a niche was created for Foon Sien Wong, under whose competent and skillful leadership the CBA was to rise to the peak of its power in the following years.

Before we say more about Foon Sien's leadership, it is important to pinpoint the fundamental reason for the preeminence of the CBA throughout the 1950s. Contrary to Baureiss's assertion that the decline of racism and the improved racial relations in postwar Canada would spell the downfall of the traditional organizations, these developments actually benefited the CBA. Various government authorities suddenly became eager to inform or even consult the Chinese on issues such as the exercise of the latter's newly acquired franchise. Likewise, non-government organizations committed to better ethnic relations and public charities were enthusiastic about involving ethnic Chinese in their work. Invariably, they all approached the Chinese minority through the CBA. This increasing demand for brokerage from outside enhanced the CBA's role as the spokesperson for the Chinese.

Into this new climate of cooperation stepped Foon Sien, whose public career as a Chinatown leader really deserves a fuller examination than this book allows. Having been born in China in 1899 and having emigrated to Canada at age nine, Foon Sien fits my definition of the first generation of *tusheng* Chinese. What distinguished him from his peers was his ability to work with not just the immigrant Chinese in general, but also with the different factions in Chinatown. Combined with his English education, his social skills made him a recognized 'public relations' person well before the Second World War. When he became one of the co-chairmen of the CBA in 1948, he brought to that position numerous outside connections, including his Canadian Liberal Party membership and wide acquaintance with mainstream journalists and leaders of other minority groups.[41]

In the eyes of Foon Sien's many admirers and critics, he is likely to be best remembered for championing fair immigration legislation. Throughout the 1950s, Foon Sien lobbied annually in Ottawa for the relaxation of immigration measures. Various petitions and other legal documents were carefully prepared by Foon Sien and his advisors.[42] The CBA also sought to drum up public support among the Vancouver Chinese. For instance, members of the executive committee would solicit donations on the streets of Chinatown, in addition to tapping their own business and organizational networks. In 1953, some 300 individuals and 150 business firms, all from Vancouver, gave more than $4,000. Only four of the donors contributed as much as fifty dollars; the majority gave the minimum amount of several dollars. The records of the campaign in 1957 suggest a similar pattern, except that total contributions increased to $10,000 and the number of donors to almost 600, with some coming from other western Canadian Chinatowns. In line with the CBA's general fund-raising strategy, stress was put on solidarity rather than competitive generosity.[43]

Integral to the ritual celebration of unity and representation was the management of publicity. Foon Sien himself was most visible in speaking to the mainstream media. The Chinese newspapers, on the other hand, always supplied his trips with full coverage and editorial support. They also printed leaflets showing his entire itinerary. Various Chinatown organizations would hold farewell banquets in his honour before his departure, and upon his return to Vancouver the CBA always convened a general meeting for the representatives from the traditional organizations to hear his report.[44]

All of these functions aimed to convey a unanimous opinion to both participants and observers. They were successful, for Foon Sien was widely accepted as the spokesperson for the Chinese on the subject of immigration both inside and outside the community. The campaigns worked as a powerful machine to manufacture consensus and a sense of unity. They further gave Foon Sien and the CBA unprecedented prestige and influence. It was in the course of these carefully staged public campaigns that the Vancouver CBA appropriated the title of the National Headquarters of all Canadian CBAs. This status appealed to the Vancouver Chinese, though the claim was sometimes contested by other CBAs.[45]

Admittedly, even in their heyday in the 1950s, the CBA and its leadership occasionally came under attack. Some people accused Foon Sien of manipulating the CBA for his personal aggrandizement, and others resented the way the mainstream media addressed him as the 'mayor of Chinatown.'[46] However, criticisms from within the ethnic group were largely muted, reflecting the potency of consensus-making in the CBA's mobilization rituals at that time.

In retrospect, the ultimate downturn in the CBA's fortune began with a seemingly unrelated event: the coming to power of the Progressive Conservatives in Ottawa in June 1957. Foon Sien's useful connection with the Liberal Party might not have been a liability but it certainly did not help him in his negotiation with the new government over the subject of Chinese immigration. Within two years Foon Sien insisted on retiring from the CBA executive committee.[47] The CBA thus entered the 1960s without its most resourceful leader and the single issue that had preoccupied and empowered it for many years. Its prestige was further damaged when it was implicated by the police crackdown on illegal Chinese immigration in the following years.[48]

Against this background, Chinese criticism of the CBA surfaced dramatically in late 1961 during a big argument over its reform.[49] Triggering the debate was an open letter in the *Chinese Times* on 30 October 1961. Penned by someone identified as 'Old-timer' (*Lao huaqiao*), it was addressed to the CBA concerning the coming executive committee election. The author began by acknowledging the strong leadership of the CBA among the Chinese in Canada. Nevertheless, he was troubled by the 'imperfection' (*bu wanshan*) in the election. In his opinion, the problem was caused by a 'lack of transparency' (*bu touming*), and he suspected that the CBA had fallen into the hands of a clique. He then suggested a series of democratic measures – such as the provision of full biographical data on the nominees – to rectify the situation.

This letter was the first of its kind publicly to address problems within the CBA during the postwar period. Its appearance in the *Chinese Times* suggests that it was endorsed by the Chinese Freemasons and was possibly directed at the Kuomintang. In any case, the letter prompted emergency meetings of the CBA. Even more drastic reform suggestions appeared in the following days. Writing in the *Chinese Voice*, Mah Fat Sing, a reform-minded leader at the CBA, admitted that the present election system was defective because it was based principally on the representation of the district associations. He believed that the scope of representation should be broadened to include 'all kinds of organizations,' but he did not elaborate.[50] Echoing a similar complaint but going much further in his proposal was K. Tong Au, a young lawyer associated with the Hai Fung Club. Au argued against using organizations as electoral colleges because of the obvious differences in the size of their memberships and the multiple memberships held by certain individuals. The best option, he insisted, was to implement 'universal suffrage' by giving every adult Chinese in Vancouver a vote.[51]

So, the discussion had grown from a complaint about the abuse of the election system to a general critique of the system even before a general meeting of the CBA was convened. From the various accounts, the atmosphere at that meeting was tense. Reform opinions were heard from the delegates of the Chinese Freemasons, the Wong Kung Har Tong, and the Hai Fung Club. Apparently they spoke for the post-1947 generation of new immigrants, who now desired to be included in the CBA. However, their opinions did not prevail. At the insistence of the Kuomintang delegates, the meeting was adjourned and it was decided to pass the issue of reform onto the executive committee for the following year. The reform advocates reportedly protested against any procrastination but to little avail.[52]

Several months later, when the new CBA executive committee invited the traditional associations to forward their proposals for change, the discussion in the Chinese press suddenly became intense again. Interestingly, all the writers kept their anonymity by using pen names during this second phase of the debate. The search for a new election system continued to be the greatest concern. The old format based on the representation of district associations and an at-large election was generally considered too limited to reflect the growing diversity among the ethnic Chinese. Of the different proposals, Tong Au's idea of a Chinese 'universal suffrage' was much criticized as impractical. For the older generation of immigrants, that proposal, in eliminating all distinctions by granting the new immigrants as well as the *tusheng* equal admission into this leading organization, perhaps went too far.[53] Other proposals suggested extending representation to the clan organizations and various professional groups, such as lawyers, physicians, dentists, and clergy, because of their unique social status and their contributions to the ethnic group.[54]

The debate also indicated that many Vancouver Chinese believed that there was an urgent need for the CBA to find new directions and specific new tasks – otherwise how it could possibly justify its claim as the national headquarters.[55] Clearly, the quest for an inclusive and vital community organization was still alive. Here was a historic opportunity for the CBA to bring itself in line with the growing diversity and changing expectations in the Chinese minority and, once again, to breathe life and efficacy into its consensus-making and community-inspiring functions.

The outcome was very unexpected, to say the least. As far as the debate in the press was concerned, the turning point came in June 1962 with the publication of a relatively lengthy, orthodox-sounding article in the *Chinese Voice*. The author, 'Ning Yang' (signifying that the author was a native of Taishan), talked at length about the CBA's historical mission 'not as another charitable organization' among the Vancouver Chinese but as their 'channel of communication' with the home country and the local Canadian authority. As for the existing system of election, it may have been 'loosen[ed] up,' the author conceded, but it had been practised by CBAs across North America, 'from New York to San Francisco, and from Victoria to Halifax.' 'Ning Yang' concluded at the end that the so-called 'question of election' was a conspiracy in disguise, 'simply a pretext used by those savages who hold heterodox views to infiltrate the organization.'[56] For whatever reason, and perhaps people had become alienated, frustrated, or intimidated by this familiar 'Red Scare' story, the debate halted abruptly.

By the end of 1962, after the heated argument had subsided for several months, the CBA finally publicized its proposal for reform. The blueprint outlined an executive committee of sixty-one members, twenty of whom were to be elected at-large and the rest of whom were to be nominated by the district and surname associations. Incredibly, even this conservative proposal was defeated at a representative meeting of the traditional organizations, turning the entire episode into a fiasco.[57]

This debate was a landmark in the history of the CBA. The existing Kuomintang-Freemason division seems to have been the major determinant of the outcome, but it is interesting to see in the process the expressed desire of the postwar new immigrants to get involved in the CBA and the determination of some elderly, conservative Chinese not to lose control of this organization. The latter appeared to be successful in the politics of exclusion. Ironically, among the victims this time was the CBA itself, for, in the aftermath, excitement and expectation concerning the organization evaporated. Three years later, in the same fashion, 'Ning Yang' nipped in the bud a brief attempt by another young Chinese lawyer of new immigrant background, Harry Fan, to stir up discussion on the reform issue.[58] From then on there were frequent insinuations that the CBA had been captured by the local Kuomintang in order to keep the Chinese in Canada subservient to the Nationalist government in Taiwan. The CBA's pro-Kuomintang stance became conspicuous, and its executive committee was dominated by the Kuomintang supporters led by Lam Fong. Lam occupied both chief executive positions in the CBA and the local Kuomintang from the early 1960s until 1979.[59] Inevitably, this was to marginalize the CBA in the eyes of not only the new immigrant generation, but also of other elderly Chinese who were not toeing the Kuomintang line. The CBA had nullified its own claim to embodying the Vancouver Chinese.

In view of the debacle of the CBA reform in the early 1960s, it is tempting to generalize about the decline of the CBA and, by extension, the traditional organizations in Chinatown during the postwar period. After all, the arrival of the new immigrants and the rise of the local-born Chinese did undermine the dominance of the older generation. It would be a mistake, however, to assume that the elderly immigrants and their cherished organizations had become a spent force. As a matter of fact, the CBA had just reached the zenith of its influence during the 1950s. Meanwhile, other traditional associations were able to harness the emotional and financial support of their members through a rich repertoire of ritual performance. Rituals were very effective in constituting a sense of cultural identity and community among the elderly Chinese. The successful operation of the *baizi hui*, in particular, provided a critical foundation for long-term institutional development. This accomplishment alone guaranteed that the older generation would leave an important legacy in Chinatown's social, cultural, and institutional practices well beyond the postwar years.

6
Negotiating Identities between Two Worlds, 1945-70

Corresponding to the changing demographic composition of Vancouver's Chinese population during the postwar period, a range of different opinions as to the definitions of Chineseness and visions of community had emerged. The respective positions of the new immigrants, the local-born Chinese, and the old-timers have already been examined. Much attention has been given to the way their different propositions and agendas evolved, not separately but interactively, in dialogue and contestation with one another. It is important, however, not to reduce this emergent identity discourse and intramural battle to a matter of demographic plurality.

The quarter century after the Second World War was a time when many Chinese throughout the diaspora experienced momentous changes in their relationships with China and their country of residence. Concerning North America, the story of the ethnic Chinese is often generalized as a lineal process of local adaptation. The era of the sojourner had essentially been brought to an end in 1949 with the triumph of communism in China and the ensuing Cold War confrontation between Mao's regime and the Western world. Replacing this sojourner paradigm are the themes of settlement, acculturation, and assimilation in the new context of receding racism and greater acceptance in the host society. This rather simplistic and linear historical narrative is hardly adequate for capturing the complexities of identity construction and contestation among the Chinese overseas.

We can better contextualize the process of identity formation and negotiation among Vancouver's Chinese after 1945 by dissecting their ongoing relationships with China and Canada. These relationships were multi-layered as well as dynamic, and this chapter seeks to identify the specific components and to discern their respective trajectories from 1945 to 1970. To support the larger arguments of this book, the following account pays particular attention to the differential positions and strategies of the three groups – the old-timers, the local-born Chinese, and the newcomers – with reference to their shifting sense of cultural identity.

Native Place Sentiments

The emotional and cultural attachment to one's place of origin had been an important strand in the history of Chinese domestic and foreign migration since late imperial times. The works of Ho Ping-ti and Dou Jiliang provide the classic explanations for the primacy of these regional specific affiliations and sentiments in Chinese society. Among the important factors were the Confucian notion of filial piety, the institutional emphasis of the imperial bureaucracy, and the great diversity in the natural environment and local culture across the empire.[1] More recent studies by Western scholars have illuminated the centrality of regional identities in structuring geographical mobility, informing social and economic adaptation, and organizing political and cultural life in a myriad of situations of migration inside China down to the modern period.[2]

The continuity is striking as we look at the Chinese migrant communities overseas. Whether it was in Southeast Asia or North America, native place identities – usually articulated at the county level but, in some cases, extending down to the local villages – provided these migrants with connections to friendships, jobs, and means of protection. As in China, regional identities had a powerful institutional expression in the form of native place associations. These associations contributed to local adjustment, resolved internal conflicts, and also represented collective interests to other Chinese groups and the local authorities while keeping migrants abreast of developments at home. Their entrenched position and widespread influence rendered them indispensable channels for any popular mobilization, including the patriotic movements of republican revolution and, later, anti-Japanese national salvation. Such were the dynamics of native place identities as they meshed with, but were not obliterated by, rising national consciousness.[3]

When the Second World War ended in August 1945, the native place sentiments of the Vancouver Chinese were again on display. The future of China remained troubled as a result of the unresolved conflict between the Kuomintang government and the Chinese communists. Notwithstanding, some Chinese seized the opportunity to return to South China, prompting the traditional organizations to resume the collection of exit fees. Canadian immigration authorities registered 635 ethnic Chinese leaving for China in the year 1945-46, and the number increased to 2,112 in the following year. By August 1947, the *Chinese Times* estimated that an average of 160 Chinese – mostly in their sixties – took the home-bound journey from Vancouver each month.[4]

For those Chinese who stayed, their native place associations quickly involved them in activities aiming at the recovery of the home areas. There were campaigns, one after another, to raise funds for charity, local defence, flood relief, improvement of local transportation, restoration of market towns, and so on, all reminiscent of similar undertakings by the same organizations before and during the Second World War. For this first generation of immigrants, their native place sentiments and sense of responsibility towards their home locality were all part and parcel of being Chinese.[5]

These efforts were not deterred even as China slipped into a full-scale civil war between the Kuomintang and the Chinese Communist Party. However, a turning point did come with the final communist victory in 1949. Chinatown had been following events in China with great anxiety and with a general apprehension about the prospects of communist rule, both of which were confirmed after Mao's takeover. The onset of the land reform in Guangdong in 1950 further aroused widespread anger and despair as news arrived that families at home had been dispossessed of their land and penalized as class enemies.[6] To make it worse, in late 1951, cases of alleged communist 'blackmail' were reported in Vancouver English-language dailies and Chinatown newspapers. Apparently, some Chinese had received letters from home requesting large remittances. Rumours spread that the RCMP had begun an investigation of suspected communist activities in Chinatown. Under the circumstances, the much publicized work of the traditional organizations for the native areas came to a halt, though clandestine assistance to individual families in South China must have continued.[7]

In retrospect, the traumatic events of 1949-51 were to usher in a new phase of development, in which the immigrant Chinese found an outlet for their native place concerns in the British colony of Hong Kong, not too far from their home areas. The substitution was imperfect as long as some family members, land holdings, and ancestral graves remained in the native villages, but it made perfect sense under the circumstances. Hong Kong, of course, would have little problem in capturing the attention of the Chinese in diaspora. Being the major port of embarkation for emigrants from South China and a regional commercial hub since the mid-nineteenth century, Hong Kong was pivotal to the extensive transnational webs of personal, organizational, business, and social networks spun by the Chinese overseas. As the southern gateway to China, Hong Kong functioned additionally as an interface between the Chinese migrants and their native areas and China. A case in point was the Tung Wah Hospital, the leading Chinese charitable organization in the colony. Since its founding in 1869, it had coordinated the shipment of bones of deceased migrants back to the home villages for reburial. The organization and its leadership commanded such respect that it was often designated to administer relief work in China on behalf of Chinese communities abroad.[8]

The outbreak of the civil war and the communist victory disrupted the existing triangular relationships between Hong Kong, South China, and the Chinese overseas. The tiny British colony of less than 400 square miles provided sanctuary for hundreds of thousands of refugees fleeing the Mainland. There assembled a critical mass of fellow natives, among whom were the families and relatives of many Chinese migrants. At the same time, the home districts became inaccessible, in part because of the revolutionary upheavals inside China, but also due to the United States-initiated international sanctions against the communist regime during the Korean War. Thus Cold War politics and the domestic turbulence in China conspired to make Hong Kong a surrogate native place of the Chinese overseas.

It did not take long for the situation in Hong Kong to draw the attention of the Vancouver Chinese. Almost immediately after the founding of the People's Republic of China in October 1949, the CBA petitioned Canadian immigration authorities and some members of Parliament to expedite the processing of immigration applications at the Hong Kong office. The CBA repeated the request at least three more times in 1950, but all these turned out to be only initial reactions, signalling more persistent Hong Kong-bound engagements among the immigrants in the following years.[9]

Hong Kong was greatly in need of assistance after the Pacific War. The massive influx of refugees from Mainland China had swollen its population from 650,000 at the time of the Japanese surrender to more than two million in 1951. Ten years later, the number had increased to 3.1 million. The demographic explosion exhausted all available resources, forcing the colonial government to take action to settle this displaced population. Playing a significant role in this effort were many local voluntary organizations, including the native place associations in Hong Kong. These groups appealed to their overseas counterparts for support.[10]

One particularly memorable incident was the Shek Kip Mei fire on Christmas Day, 1953, which destroyed the largest squatter settlement in the colony. That event jolted the Hong Kong government into launching a rudimentary housing program for the homeless and aroused considerable sympathy among the Vancouver Chinese. The Hoy Sun Ning Yung Benevolent Association took the lead in a drive to raise funds to aid fire victims, believing that fellow Taishan natives made up the majority of those affected. A sum of HK$20,000 was remitted immediately to its sister organization in Hong Kong, and a general appeal for relief was sent to other Chinatown associations.[11]

There were numerous other examples of Vancouver's Chinese organizations dispensing charity in Hong Kong during the 1950s and 1960s. A movement to collect clothes took place in the winter of 1959, when the first wave of refugees arrived in the colony following the outbreak of famine in the Chinese countryside. With the Great Leap Forward causing more havoc and putting more people to flight in the next several years, the operation was repeated until at least 1962.[12] Besides these responses to immediate needs, long-term commitments were not unheard of. For instance, the Chung Shan Lung Jen Association seems to have made regular contributions to its sister organization's charities in Hong Kong every winter.[13] Likewise, the Hoy Ping District Association was so involved in its Hong Kong counterpart's effort to provide low-cost education that it was represented on a school board there.[14]

The Hong Kong-bound charities of the traditional organizations were primarily expressions of native place sentiments among the older generation of immigrants. These undertakings came to an end towards the late 1960s, as members of that generation gradually passed away. Moreover, Hong Kong society had become more settled by then and was actually on its way towards great prosperity. This declining activity contrasts most interestingly with the steadily growing cultural influence of Hong Kong on the post-1947 generation of immigrants in Vancouver. Before we examine this fascinating trans-Pacific cultural flow, let us first consider the vicissitudes of Old World politics as they influenced the ongoing construction of Chinese identity in the postwar years.

Old World Politics

For the first generation of migrants from South China, the national salvation movement of the 1930s and early 1940s had left behind a powerful legacy. From a position of relative powerlessness in Canada, these individuals had shown what they could do from afar when their native country was in crisis. Right after the war, their concern for political change in China was much alive, as was demonstrated in a rapid succession of electoral campaigns, during the winter of 1947-48, to send overseas delegates to several political bodies in the Nationalist government of China. Vancouver's Chinatown was the scene of keen competition among the traditional associations on behalf of their respective nominees.[15] Gaining representation in the government of China was considered important, but local prestige and influence were equally at stake.

The Kuomintang was undoubtedly the most enthusiastic participant in Chinese politics in Vancouver. To its supporters, patriotism to China meant allegiance to the Kuomintang regime. Party orthodoxy long insisted that overseas support had contributed significantly to the republican revolution led by Sun Yat-sen. After the Kuomintang's military debacle and subsequent withdrawal to Taiwan, such steadfast loyalty was now even more critical to its political legitimacy.[16]

In Vancouver, the Kuomintang appeared well positioned to pursue its agenda through its base in the Canadian national headquarters and the overlapping western Canadian regional head branch. There, in Chinatown, the party faithful organized activities to drum up public support. In 1958, they took over the publication of the party newspaper, the *New Republic*, from Victoria.[17] The Kuomintang supporters seemed to have dominated the leadership in a number of traditional organizations, including the Lee Clan Association, the Lung Kong Kung So, the Lam Sai Ho Tong, the Hoy Sun Ning Yung Benevolent Association, and the Hoy Ping District Association. These supposedly non-partisan groups were useful in creating an aura of massive support for the Nationalist regime. A case in point was the founding of the Anti-Communist National Salvation Association in 1953, reportedly with the participation of some forty Chinatown organizations.[18] By 1962, the list of pro-Kuomintang organizations was to include the CBA.

Another advantage for the local Kuomintang was the presence, until 1970, of the diplomatic representatives of the Nationalist government in Vancouver. Enjoying the privileges afforded the foreign diplomatic corps, the staff of the Chinese Consulate-General was actively involved in Chinatown affairs. Led by the consul-general, Chinese officials routinely attended public functions to cement ties with various organizations and their leaders. They showered praises on those who were considered staunch supporters of Taiwan and vehemently condemned alleged communist sympathizers infiltrating Chinatown. A widely covered episode occurred in the summer of 1962, when several Ottawa-sponsored Mainland Chinese refugee families arrived in Vancouver. At a welcoming party hosted by the CBA, Wang Meng-hsien, the Chinese consul-general, urged them to speak out against the Beijing regime.[19]

Despite these efforts by the Kuomintang, from the mid-1950s on, partisan Chinese politics no longer resonated widely among the immigrant Chinese. The intense hostility of some elderly immigrants towards the communists did generate initial support for the Nationalist regime; however, apathy set in as Taiwan's anti-communist rhetoric and its promise to retake Mainland China began to sound increasingly hollow with the passage of each postwar year. Though the Consulate-General could claim leadership and, at times, substantial influence, its relationship with the immigrant Chinese was a complicated one. The fact that the Cantonese-speaking immigrants perceived the Mandarin-speaking consular staff to be guilty of bureaucratism and cultural elitism presented an underlying problem. Even party loyalists were not immune from disillusionment. They resented the priority given to the Chinese in various Southeast Asian countries and in the United States, where Taiwan perceived and pursued greater economic and diplomatic interests.[20]

While the older generation often simply became resigned to the course of political change in China, many Canadian-born Chinese strove to unlink Old World politics from the question of cultural identity. They might have some thoughts on the Communist-Nationalist rivalry, especially when they were approached by non-Chinese for a 'Chinese' opinion, but they did not feel that Chinese politics was relevant to their lives. The *tusheng* organizations were typically indifferent to Old World politics. Equally revealing was the unequivocal refusal of many immigrant youth societies to get entangled in debates on China. The constitution of the Hai Fung Club, for example, stated categorically that this subject was too controversial.[21] Promotion of cultural events and social activities apparently sufficed to anchor its members' sense of Chineseness, whereas Chinese politics as such allegedly had nothing to do with being Chinese.

Such abstention from Chinese politics notwithstanding, echoes of Old World politics could still be heard intermittently in Chinatown. On the one hand, the long-standing rivalry between the Kuomintang and the Chinese Freemasons lingered on. The Freemasons had no effective channel to influence political events in China, but they continued to take stands. On various occasions, such as national conventions, they would issue lengthy declarations condemning the dictatorial regimes on both sides of the Taiwan Strait.[22]

On the other hand, there was a small group of young new immigrants who were decidedly sympathetic to Mainland China. Represented by the Chinese Youth Association, they were few in number but very vocal, especially after launching the *Da Zhong Bao* in 1961 as their mouthpiece. This bimonthly (and later weekly) newspaper always carried laudatory reports on Mainland China, referring to its economic advancement, technological and scientific breakthroughs, competitiveness in the world of sports, and victories on the diplomatic front.[23] These 'accomplishments,' purportedly a new foundation for Chinese pride, were typically juxtaposed with the 'unenviable' records of the Nationalist government, which was disparaged as a corrupt and weak-kneed regime, devoid of dignity and competence. In *Da Zhong Bao*'s favourite phrase, the Kuomintang and its overseas underlings were all 'scum of the [Chinese] nation' (*minzu bailei*).[24]

Given its enthusiasm for associating national and cultural pride with allegiance to the People's Republic of China, the *Da Zhong Bao* never hesitated to defame its local adversaries. Nineteen seventy seems to have been an especially eventful year. In January, *Da Zhong Bao* was the first to report on the secret sale of the Chinese consul-general's official residence in the exclusive neighbourhood of Shaughnessy. According to its sources, the incumbent from Taiwan had already absconded to Seattle with the proceeds, in anticipation of Ottawa's pending switch of diplomatic recognition to Beijing. *Da Zhong Bao* went on to accuse the local Kuomintang of covering up the scandal and criticized the other Chinese newspapers for their complicity.[25]

Later in the year, *Da Zhong Bao* got into a bitter argument with the *Chinese Times*. Accusing the Chinese Freemasons of disregarding the manifold accomplishments of Mainland China, *Da Zhong Bao* launched an editorial barrage that lasted for five months. It castigated the Freemasons for their 'phoney neutrality' (*jia zhongli*), for being 'pseudo-patriotic' (*jia aiguo*), and for being 'anti-communist, anti-China, anti-people' (*fangong, fanhua, fan renmin*). Deprived of 'ethnic and national pride' (*minzu zunyan*), the Freemasons were allegedly another group of 'scum.'[26] In response, the *Chinese Times* asserted its right to express non-communist, non-Kuomintang opinions and characterized the *Da Zhong Bao* as a victim of Maoist radicalism.[27]

So Old World politics had by no means been exorcised from the ongoing debate over Chinese identity in Vancouver, although it may have mattered less, and to a smaller number of people, than it had previously. In contrast, retaining its considerable influence on the discourse of Chineseness, and causing great divisiveness among the different generations, was the question of Chinese culture.

Chinese Cultural Retention

As expected of any first generation immigrant population, the Chinese minority in Vancouver entered the postwar period with a solid record in cultural retention. The numerous organizations in Chinatown, as ethnic institutions par excellence, had been instrumental in maintaining a distinct cultural and social space for the immigrant Chinese. They enshrined certain traditional cultural values, such as clanship loyalty, native place sentiments, filial piety, mutual assistance, and public harmony, through their routine activities and ritual performances. They also rendered primary support to the Chinese-language schools, where the teaching of the native language along with the history, geography, and ethics of China would presumably keep the younger generation Chinese. With the same spirit of defiance vis-à-vis the tide of acculturation, and also with the hope of promoting Chinese studies in Canadian higher education, several surname and native place associations made donations to the founding of an Asian Library at the University of British Columbia in the early 1950s.[28]

The Chinese press obviously played an important role in this. All three Chinese-language newspapers in Vancouver -- the *Chinese Times*, the *Chinese Voice*, and the *New Republic* -- could claim some credit for sustaining the interest of a Chinese readership, furnishing a Chinese perspective in their reportage, and providing space for Chinese literary publication.

In many ways, the arrival of the post-1947 new immigrants, many of them much younger and better educated than the old-timers, was to add vitality to Chinese cultural expression and community life. As indicated in an earlier chapter, some newcomers were quite conscious of themselves as cultural keepers and promoters. Consider, for example, the following passage from the writings of David Lee, the author of the first book-length account of the Chinese in Canada. He was teaching at the Chinese Public School in Victoria and was occasionally on the editorial staff of the *New Republic* when he wrote:

The profound civilization of China has been our country's foundation for the last five thousand years ... Those of us who are overseas must understand that we are Chinese above all else, even though our norms and social customs might be at variance with those of our ancestral country. Being Chinese, our thoughts and consciousness must be based on the civilization of China ...

At present [in the mid-1960s], there are not a few self-degrading local-born Chinese youth in our community. Influenced by western culture, they completely disregard the greatness of our country's civilization and claim to be Canadians. As a matter of fact, westerners still keep us ethnic Chinese at a distance and seldom consider us Canadians. How embarrassing it is [for them]!

We must realize that it is not at all shameful to be Chinese. Rather, it is honourable. Our people have been residing in foreign countries for generations. However, we have not been assimilated because of our superior heritage and highly developed civilization. So, Chinese people should not feel inferior at all. On the contrary, we should take great pride in our own people, respect and learn the civilization of our ancestral country, and care for our nation at all times.[29]

Evidently, postwar immigrants such as Lee continued to anchor their sense of being Chinese in the historical civilization of China, perhaps not unlike the older Chinese. It was said that by holding on to this culture of their homeland, ethnic Chinese could overcome the problem of foreign residence and maintain cultural authenticity. Thinly veiled in Lee's assertive chauvinism was, ironically, a tortuous response to the cultural dominance of the Canadian host. For Lee, the problem was not the essentialized culture of China, nor was it the presumed cultural loyalty of the immigrant Chinese: it was the local-born, who should be ashamed of their cultural corruption and deficiency!

As I have argued earlier, for their part, the newcomers were not thrilled with the old-timers. Many immigrant youth found the existing 'Chinatown culture' pathetic, in need of surgical redefinition and reform. They decried the conservative elements of Confucian thought, the prevalent parochial identities and sentiments, and, especially, the taken-for-granted patriarchal authority among the old-timers. Their self-assured cultural sophistication prompted them to adopt the language of modernity. Their recreational clubs and literary societies promoted an interesting combination of traditional and modern Chinese artistic skills and tastes as well as Chinese martial arts and Western sports.[30]

This postwar development took place at an interesting time, when clearly competitive models of Chinese culture began to present themselves to ethnic

Chinese in Canada and elsewhere. There were always a variety of models, depending on the migrant's class background, pre-departure location, and time. But whether these models were drawn from one's ancestral village, a nearby county town in the Pearl River Delta, or the vibrant Guangzhou-Hong Kong cultural and economic nexus, they appeared to be sufficiently integrated, just as these places were themselves spatially integrated in South China. That was no longer the case after 1949, with competitive models beaming from separately demarcated territories and even from antagonistic entities.

On the one hand, there was the emerging model of Socialist China, highly nationalistic, anti-imperialistic, and consciously radical and non-traditional. Among Chinese in Vancouver, its appeal was largely limited, until 1970, to the small group centring on the Chinese Youth Association. On the other hand, there was the rival model painstakingly put together by the Kuomintang in Taiwan for ideological purposes. Typical of a regime in crisis, the Nationalist government dwelt on its rightful cultural inheritance and its conscientious magnification of Han Chinese tradition to supplement its truncated political legitimacy.[31] The Nationalist Consulate-General, the local Kuomintang, and various sympathetic organizations served as channels of propagation in and out of Chinatown. It is difficult to determine more precisely the reception of Taiwan's model in Vancouver, but, given the growing influence of yet another model of modern Chineseness, its pervasiveness is doubtful.

This third model emerged gradually but perceptibly from post-1949 Hong Kong, that surrogate native place of the immigrant Chinese. Hong Kong's strategic location on the China coast and its background – Westernized, colonial, and yet Chinese – made it special. Until 1949, its relatively transient population and the residents' close economic, cultural, and social ties with the adjacent native areas in Guangdong were not conducive to the development of a distinctive Hong Kong culture and identity. Its severance from China consequent upon the communist revolution came as a watershed. A Hong Kong identity did not appear overnight (not until the 1970s), but a Hong Kong-based Chinese culture did begin to take shape.[32]

First, there are some suggestive materials in Canadian immigration records. Based on immigration statistics, Table 14 shows that, in 1958, Hong Kong surpassed Mainland China as the self-reported 'country' of last permanent residence among the incoming Chinese. Many of them must have left China earlier and applied for entry to Canada from Hong Kong. In the 1950s and 1960s it was Canadian government policy that some years of residence in Hong Kong were mandatory in order for potential immigrants originating from China to go through security clearance.[33] Not all applicants succeeded, but for those who did, Hong Kong could be a place of extended temporary residence.

Table 14

Number of immigrants entering Canada from China and Hong Kong, 1949-65

Year	China	Hong Kong
1949-50	841	183
1950-51	2,148	26
1951-52	2,696	39
1952-53	1,904	47
1953-54	1,881	132
1954-55	1,712	219
1955-56	1,897	646
1956	1,491	572
1957	828	778
1958	883	1,696
1959	513	1,968
1960	178	1,105
1961	110	680
1962	244	426
1963	179	1,008
1964	184	2,490
1965	197	4,155

Note: For some unknown reason, from 1966 to 1970 Hong Kong was subsumed under the category of 'China' on the list of countries of last permanent residence of the new immigrants.
Sources: Immigration Branch, Department of Mines and Resources, *Annual Reports* 1946-49; Department of Citizenship and Immigration, *Annual Reports,* 1949-56; and *Immigration Statistics,* 1956-70.

More important, with Mainland China and Taiwan each under the ideological straitjacket imposed by their respective governments, Hong Kong was to develop into a viable centre of Chinese cultural production in the postwar years. The colony quickly replaced Shanghai after 1949 as the capital of the Chinese film industry. Its locally produced Cantonese movies were particularly popular among the overseas migrants from Guangdong. Indeed, Hong Kong's linguistic affinity with many immigrant Chinese populations provided its cultural exports with a decided advantage over those of Taiwan and Mainland China. The latter were wrapped in the supposedly more prestigious and authentic, but distinctly remote and unfamiliar, language of Mandarin.[34]

Furthermore, the young newcomers may have been drawing, consciously or unconsciously, on models from Hong Kong when they sought to promote various social, cultural, and recreational events in Chinatown. Specific information is limited on this point, but the three musical societies active in performing Cantonese operas (Jin Wah Sing, Ching Won, and Ngai

Lum) all ordered their instruments and costumes from the colony. Occasionally, their members worked alongside visiting troupes from Hong Kong to expand their repertoire. In 1961, Jin Wah Sing went so far as to import talent by sponsoring the immigration of a famous maestro from Hong Kong as its instructor. This was similar to the actions of the youth clubs and literary societies, which stacked their small libraries with Chinese-language magazines and books printed in Hong Kong.[35]

The sway of Hong Kong can also be seen in the criticism it drew. The conservative elderly Chinese were uncomfortable with Hong Kong, but it was the young pro-Mainland China radicals who critiqued it most pointedly. When the change in Canadian immigration legislation in 1967 and the Cultural Revolution-inspired riots that rocked the colony that same year were about to usher in a new wave of Chinese immigration, the *Da Zhong Bao* lamented the prospect of local cultural degradation. 'The simplistic and unsophisticated culture of our overseas Chinese community' (what a contrast to their previous criticism of the same!) was diagnosed as vulnerable to the undesirable influence of the Hong Kong arrivals. Echoing the condemnation by Mainland China, the editorial considered Hong Kong society a despicable hybrid of Chinese culture and British colonial influence.[36] Interestingly, it was at around this time that Vancouver's Chinatown was dubbed 'Little Hong Kong.'[37]

Clearly, ties to the Old World were multifaceted, with each component having its own history of evolution and contestation. The support for Chinese culture, subject to various definitions and emphases, remained vital in the negotiation of Chinese identity. Enthusiasm for the politics of China appeared to have ebbed, but rival groups continued to link their partisan interests and commitments to the question of Chineseness. Another element was the lingering attachment to the native areas in South China and the temporary transfer of such sentiment to Hong Kong after 1949. Hong Kong, of course, since it had begun to produce 'Hong Kong-filtered' immigrants and an emergent competitive model of sophisticated, modernized, and contemporary Chinese culture, was more than a mere surrogate.

Concerns for these China-related issues varied noticeably among different generations within Vancouver's Chinese population. In particular, the position of the Canadian-born Chinese was defined more by their abstention than by their active participation. The *tusheng* rarely got involved in the above debates and, when they did, it was defensively – to fend for their pride and articulate their sense of being different from the immigrants. This was not the case when it came to their engagement with local Canadian issues. As will be seen in the following pages, the *tusheng* wanted to add new dimensions and possibilities to the meaning of being Chinese in Canada. Within the ethnic group, their efforts would alter the existing pattern of leadership and intramural relationships.

If the *tusheng*'s Canadian orientation was to complicate but not erase their Chinese sensibility, then, similarly, the immigrants' nostalgia and Old World ties did not inhibit an emerging identification with the host environment. Somehow the immigrants had to adjust to, and come to terms with, their residence in this foreign country. Conducive to this development in the postwar period was the gradual opening of Canadian society to the ethnic Chinese and other minority groups. Instead of being rejected by institutional racism and blatant discrimination, these groups were encouraged to nurture a sense of belonging and to seek greater acceptance in Canada. As one essayist for the *Chinese Voice* poignantly stated in his advice to fellow new immigrants in 1961, 'Tangshan' (referring to China, the ancestral country) had vanished. Though Chinese people might hold on to certain cultural values and customs, they should settle down in 'Jinshan' (Gold Mountain; that is, Canada).[38]

Two Roads to Ottawa
The issue closest to the hearts of the immigrant Chinese, now that they were to settle in Canada, was the right to bring over family members who remained in the homeland. The repeal of the Exclusion Act in 1947 was hardly sufficient, given the upheavals and hardship in China. From that point, the Vancouver CBA under Foon Sien Wong took the lead in the campaign for further redress.

I have mentioned Foon Sien's lobbying activities in Ottawa during the 1950s and the CBA's attempt to drum up Chinese support. These efforts yielded good results, even if, in some cases, only temporarily. Allowing children over the acceptable age to enter Canada on compassionate grounds, extending the right of sponsorship to landed immigrants who were not yet citizens, admitting parents over a certain age, and developing a special scheme for the immigration of Chinese brides are good examples of successes.[39] But the campaign for immigration liberalization was historically important in another way as well. Owing to the skills of one leader and the brokerage of the CBA, Chinese immigrants could now engage the Canadian government in fruitful negotiation, with the latter appearing to be not only approachable but even sympathetic. The annual dramatic replay of this crusade in the 1950s was symptomatic of the opening of Canadian society – a society of which ethnic Chinese could now hope to be a part.

In June 1957, the symbolic importance of the CBA and Foon Sien's leadership was undermined by a purely Canadian event. When the Progressive Conservative Party dislodged the Liberals from power, Foon Sien lost his partisan connections in Ottawa. As discussed earlier, Foon Sien ultimately resigned his position at the CBA in 1959, bringing to a close an era marked by his flamboyant leadership. But the general election of 1957 also ushered in an entirely new factor: the first ethnic Chinese was elected to the

Figure 9 Douglas Jung speaks after winning
re-election in 1958

Canadian Parliament. Douglas Jung, local-born son of an immigrant family
in Victoria, a Second World War veteran, and a lawyer then practising in
Vancouver, defeated the incumbent defence minister, Ralph Campney. In
the subsequent election of March 1958, as the Conservatives swept the country, Jung widened his margin over his Liberal opponent by some 10,000
votes.[40] He served as Member of Parliament for the district of Vancouver
Centre until 1962 and literally blazed another trail by which the Vancouver
Chinese could reach Ottawa.

Douglas Jung's successful bid for a seat in the Canadian Parliament should
be traced back to the enfranchisement of the Chinese in the late 1940s.
Though the *tusheng* and their Veterans organization were pivotal in securing Chinese access to the ballot box, they made little organized effort to
promote the exercise of this right. That role was first assumed by the CBA as
part of its traditional brokerage functions in ethnic politics. During the
early 1950s, on the day prior to a public election, the CBA would remind
ethnic Chinese that their previous disenfranchisement had represented
the stigma of second-class status. Its standard message was an account of
the great pains taken to remove such disability and the importance of not
taking one's vote lightly. The CBA also dispensed information on voter
registration and polling procedures. At times, it would endorse candidates
considered friendly to the ethnic group.[41]

The response of the Vancouver Chinese to these efforts was rather dismal. Vancouver City Council closed its own Chinatown ad hoc office after a discouraging 1950 attempt to register neighbourhood voters.[42] A 1956 study conducted at UBC concerning ethnic Chinese participation in provincial elections reflected similar pessimism. The proportion of eligible Chinese voters in the district of Vancouver Centre who actually exercised the franchise did climb modestly from 10 percent in 1949 to 20 percent in 1952-53, and it reached 25 percent in 1956. However, the report suggested that the gain was largely a result of increased naturalization and a rise in the number of local-born reaching voting age.[43]

The same study also mentioned something special about the provincial by-election of 1956. Douglas Jung, soon-to-be the first MP of Chinese descent, was nominated by the Progressive Conservative Party to run for a seat in the BC legislature. Jung's campaign aroused excitement in Chinatown, even though, up to that point, he had been virtually unknown to the immigrant Chinese. His party affiliation was intriguing, too. Whatever minimal interest in Canadian politics existed in Chinatown tended to be pro-Liberal because the Liberals reputedly favoured putting an end to exclusion and actively tried to recruit Chinese. Notwithstanding, Jung's candidacy seems to have received widespread Chinese support. Some traditional organizations and their leaders were formally on his campaign committee. Most dramatic of all was Foon Sien's public endorsement. In an interview with the *Vancouver Sun*, this Liberal Party liaison in Chinatown dismissed the Liberal's entrenched position and predicted a solid voting bloc for Jung among Chinese voters.[44]

Regardless of these public gestures and the defeat of Jung in his campaign debut, Jung's success in the two subsequent federal elections electrified Chinatown. Especially in the 1958 election, as the coverage in the ethnic press suggests, Chinese public support was overwhelming. It was the unanimous opinion to keep Jung in office as the 'faithful spokesman' of the ethnic Chinese.[45]

It has now been over four decades since Douglas Jung first achieved his parliamentarian status (1957-62), and still his career is celebrated as an early example of Canada's openness to its Asian minorities. It is unfortunate that no follow-up study was undertaken at that time to assess the impact of Jung on Chinese electoral behaviour, but the historical significance of his political career would be hard to miss. Particularly for the Vancouver Chinese, Jung helped to lessen the remoteness of Canadian politics by giving them a voice in Ottawa. Arguably, Jung's accomplishment enabled Chinatown to shed some of its ghetto characteristics by integrating it into the larger Canadian political landscape. In the aftermath of his election, the two mainstream political parties became more active in recruiting supporters from Chinatown, more Canadian politicians chose to attend campaign rallies there, and several ethnic Chinese candidates sought public offices in Jung's footsteps in the 1960s (though none succeeded).[46]

Douglas Jung's tenure in the Canadian Parliament must have had the immediate effect of solidifying and intensifying the sense of community, as immigrant Chinese and *tusheng* alike basked in his success. However, this was, unmistakably, another case of the local-born Chinese upstaging the immigrants by demonstrating their political and cultural skills. More than any other single incident in the postwar years, Jung's electoral victory bolstered the claim, first advanced by the Veterans and the Chinatown Lions, that the *tusheng* were leading the way for ethnic Chinese to seek full acceptance in this country. Jung's election thus represented a milestone in the decline of the traditional brokerage of the CBA, which was dominated by the immigrant Chinese.

The defeats of Jung in his bid for reelection in 1962 and 1963, respectively, were equally revealing in light of such internal division. Public opinion in the ethnic press at that time suggested some disenchantment among immigrants over Jung's alleged lethargy with regard to advancing the interests of Chinatown. Equally damaging to his credibility as a faithful spokesperson for the ethnic group was the Conservative government's perceived hard-line approach to the issue of immigration and its crackdown on illegal Chinese immigration in 1960. But, interestingly, the organization most visibly involved in rebuilding the position of the Liberal Party in the ethnic neighbourhood was not a traditional Chinatown association. It was not even the CBA. It was the recently rejuvenated *tusheng* organization of the Chinese Veterans. Its leaders, Dr. S. Won Leung and Harry Con, were the acknowledged architects behind the Liberal rebound in Chinatown during the election of Jung's opponent, J.R. Nicholson, in 1962 and again in 1963.[47] These efforts did not go unrewarded. When Nicholson visited Vancouver in April 1965 as the minister of citizenship and immigration, he arranged to have the Veterans present a brief on the subject, signifying his political patronage.[48] Thus, ironically, the defeat of Jung again demonstrated, rather than calling into question, the advantage of the local-born Chinese over the immigrants in negotiating with the Canadian power structure.

From Foon Sien Wong and the CBA's traditional brokerage to Douglas Jung, we can discern a shift in identity construction and the politics of representation among the ethnic Chinese. The beginning of Chinese electoral participation undoubtedly removed a major obstacle to the ability of this minority to claim its Canadian status, but the process also enabled the *tusheng* Chinese (whose privileged position was a function of their Canadian orientation, upward mobility, and relevant social and political skills) to challenge the leadership of the immigrants with regard to representing the group's collective interests. In the last section of this chapter, which concerns the defence of Chinatown, one can see this same process at work.

Defending Chinatown in Vancouver

For the Vancouver Chinese, adding to the momentous change of the post-war period was a protracted confrontation with the city government over the issue of urban redevelopment. In December 1955, after a period of benevolent neglect, officials in the Health Department suddenly convened a series of meetings with the traditional associations to bombard the delegates with ideas about public health standards. Chinatown was portrayed as a potential health and fire hazard, and self-renovation was declared immediately mandatory. The episode was reminiscent of similar incidents earlier in this century, when Chinatown was caricatured by the mainstream media as the 'Celestial Cesspool' and a 'Vice-town.'[49] The difference in the later period seems to lie in the more conscientious official effort to provide information about problems and some consultation about remedies.

In postwar North America, municipal officials and technocrats exhibited a rising interest in slum clearance and improved transportation. Most Chinatowns happened to be close to the downtown areas, thus, in the eyes of the authorities, occupying valuable lands. The popular association of Chinatowns with unsanitary conditions and run-down buildings provided the justification for draconian measures to eradicate these 'blighted areas' and to restore them to their proper use – all, of course, in the public interest.[50] In Vancouver, as the Chinese organizations proceeded with the renovation of buildings located mainly in the commercial part of Chinatown, little did they realize that Strathcona, the adjacent residential district to its west, would soon be engulfed by a massive redevelopment plan. In 1957, senior city officials released a document that targeted Strathcona in a twenty-year urban renewal project.[51]

As a traditional working-class neighbourhood for European immigrants, Strathcona had started to attract Chinese residents during the inter-war period due to its affordable housing and its proximity to commercial Chinatown. In the late 1940s, ethnic Chinese already made up more than a quarter of its inhabitants. Later census data suggest that the proportion increased to about one-half by the late 1950s and to some three-quarters in the 1970s. So at a time when the larger Chinese population began to disperse (leaving, according to various sources, at most one-third of Vancouver's Chinese minority in Strathcona around 1960 [see Map 4]), the district was the most concentrated Chinese neighbourhood in the city, earning it the designation of 'China Valley' in the official writing of that time.[52]

In early 1958, city council officially adopted the redevelopment plan. Though the details were at first not widely known in Chinatown, the prospect of dislocation and uncertainty caused an uproar. At a meeting called by the CBA, representatives from the traditional organizations and other concerned individuals set up the Chinatown Property Owners Association (CPOA).[53] In the following years, the leaderships of the CPOA and the CBA

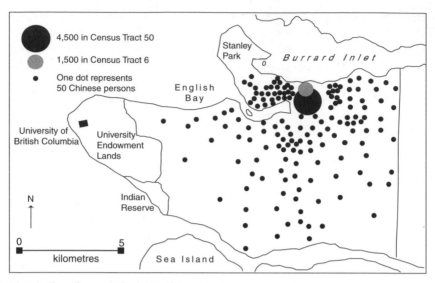

Map 4   Distribution of ethnic Chinese in Vancouver, ca. 1960

Source: George Cho and Roger Leigh, 'Patterns of Residence of the Chinese in Vancouver,' in *Peoples of the Living Land*, ed. J. Minghi, BC Geographical Series, no. 15 (Vancouver: Tantalus, 1972), 74.

were in the forefront of local opposition. On many different occasions, their delegates attended public hearings and met privately with city officials to voice their objections to the redevelopment plan. At times they raised very specific grievances, such as the freezing of land values (which rendered properties unsalable), the stoppage of public works maintenance, the refusal to grant permits for private development, and the allegedly unfair monetary compensation for expropriation. The property owners obviously had their own economic interests to protect, but quite often the underlying argument against redevelopment alluded to an imagined community of people that was defending its shared culture and identity.[54]

To begin with, the opposition pointed out that many Chinese residents in the neighbourhood were elderly settlers and recent immigrants who had little command of the English language. For them, residence in Strathcona was essential for mutual care, cultural comfort, proximity to employment, and other ethnic facilities in nearby Chinatown. Their dispersal from Strathcona would entail immense hardship. More important, it was said that the redevelopment project would not only hurt the individual residents, but it would also deprive Chinatown businesses of their customers and labour supply. Dislocation would undermine the Chinatown organizations because it would make it difficult for their members to attend social functions. Overall, it was maintained that the community still desired its own distinct and contiguous social and cultural space – a space in which the members of the larger Chinese population (not just the Chinatown-Strathcona residents) could anchor their personal and collective identities.

Appealing as these arguments might be, they failed to stop the bulldozers from coming to Strathcona. CBA and CPOA protests to the city authorities were loud and clear but piecemeal and ineffective. The opposition was galvanized into action only by specific impending crises, such as when detailed proposals for redevelopment came up for deliberation at city council or when municipal officials set out to expropriate particular properties.[55] The traditional brokerage function of Chinatown's elites was also called into question by the dissenting position of the *Chinatown News*. As the reader will recall, that local-born Chinese publication gave the redevelopment plan its blessing because it believed that it would further deghettoization. The *tusheng* belittled Chinatown as a result of their own social mobility and physical relocation – both desired and actual.

It is not clear from municipal records and other sources if the view of the local-born Chinese had emboldened local officials. But bureaucratic determination and intransigence prevailed at first, forcing the Chinese opposition to resign in despair. A surprising turning point came in the late 1960s, when Strathcona suddenly emerged as an ideological battleground for the future of Vancouver. Disturbed by the pro-development stance and heavy-handed approach of the municipal government, a group of concerned professionals spearheaded a citywide movement to support neighbourhood preservation and grass-roots involvement in the planning of future change. That movement had a far-reaching impact on local politics in Vancouver, and it ignited a new stage of opposition in Chinatown.[56]

Until this point, Chinatown had been virtually powerless in this struggle. In late 1967, riding on citywide opposition, the otherwise lethargic CBA (the CPOA had long been defunct) managed to oppose city council's proposal to run a freeway through Chinatown along Carrall Street.[57] However, further resistance to urban redevelopment soon brought a completely new organization into existence. In 1968 the first two phases of the renewal project were completed, resulting in the clearing of fifteen blocks of houses and the displacing of some 3,300 people, the large majority being ethnic Chinese. In December, when the last phase was about to start to level the remaining half of the neighbourhood, a group of local residents established the Strathcona Property Owners and Tenants Association (SPOTA) as a last-ditch effort to save their homes. SPOTA was formed with the encouragement of some non-Chinese social workers, young professionals, and university students, and this external link was to remain vital in the history of this organization.[58]

SPOTA was not a conventional ethnic organization. With over 90 percent of its several hundred members and two dozen executive committee members being Chinese, SPOTA did appeal to ethnic sentiments and did approach the traditional Chinatown associations for support. However, from its inception, SPOTA presented itself as a neighbourhood organization with legitimate interests and rights of participation in the formulation and implementation of public policy in the Strathcona area.[59] Supporting this claim was its spectacularly diverse leadership. In addition to consisting of several non-Chinese individuals, it also contained immigrant and *tusheng* Chinese of various generations. Among the Chinese leaders were a few Chinatown businesspeople and heads of traditional associations, but they were outnumbered by housewives, university students, social workers, and many others who were willing to commit their time. Facilitating such a cross-generational and cross-cultural coalition was the fact that SPOTA kept all its internal documents and records in both Chinese and English.

No less instrumental in holding together that novel leadership and broad membership base was SPOTA's intense grass-roots mobilization. Six weeks after its founding, SPOTA presented to city council a statement of its mandate, endorsed by the signatures of 200 Strathcona residents. The brief urged the municipal authority to respect the residents' desire for rehabilitation rather than to follow its own blueprint. The signatories further 'requested the Vancouver City Council and the provincial and federal governments to recognize SPOTA as an official body for negotiation on these and other matters [regarding their neighbourhood].' 'We citizens,' the brief continued, 'who are most affected by urban renewal want to be more involved in planning and have the right to full participation. This Association [SPOTA] will do all in its power to involve a cross section of local residents and to encourage positive development of this area.'[60] In the following months SPOTA conducted a general survey of 1,644 residents in Strathcona and presented its findings to Vancouver City Council in May 1969. The results showed solid opposition to redevelopment.[61]

Compared to other Chinese organizations, SPOTA had a strong system of internal communication that enabled it to keep its membership better informed and more committed. It adopted a system of block captains to circulate news. General meetings were held almost once a month during its first year in order to assure its members of an accountable leadership and, perhaps more important, to impress officials with its own credibility as a grass-roots organization.[62]

Benefiting from the growing sentiment against urban redevelopment in Vancouver and also from the new Liberal government in Ottawa, which was wary of the financial and social costs of these projects, SPOTA's struggle made history in less than a year. In October 1969 Vancouver City Council, under pressure from Ottawa, agreed to form the Strathcona Working Committee, in which SPOTA participated as an equal partner, with representatives from all three levels of government. Rehabilitation, rather than any

Figure 10   J.R. Nicholson (and his wife) pose with Harry Con (seated) at a
Chinatown function, August 1966

monstrous plan that would entail large-scale acquisition and demolition of
properties in the neighbourhood, was declared the general goal. It took
another year to reach the final agreement on the government-funded
Strathcona Rehabilitation Project, to be monitored jointly by official agents
and SPOTA.[63]

SPOTA's 1969 triumph was truly a landmark in the political empowerment of the Vancouver Chinese – a group that had experienced a history of
relative impotence. SPOTA's broad-based leadership, grass-roots mobilization, and its aggressive negotiation with the Canadian state authorities rendered obsolete the traditional brokerage conducted by the CBA. While the
support and active participation of different Chinese sectors were crucial,
the leading role of the *tusheng* was particularly noteworthy. It is no coincidence that SPOTA's spokesman was Harry Con. Con belonged to the first
generation of local-born Chinese to reach maturity after 1945. He was a
founding member of the Chinese Veterans. He also enjoyed exceptionally
good rapport with the older generation of immigrants, in part because he
had spent several years in China to acquire a Chinese education before the
Second World War and, in part, because of the active involvement of his
father and himself in the Chinese Freemasons. Notwithstanding these impressive credentials, most pivotal to his contribution to SPOTA was the Liberal Party patronage he forged tirelessly during the 1962-63 electoral

campaigns of J.R. Nicholson. His connections to Liberal politicians in Ottawa earned SPOTA much needed sympathy and leverage in the battle against the city government.[64]

Despite the privileged position of the *tusheng*, the SPOTA experience had the effect of bringing together some local-born and immigrant Chinese in a common struggle for greater Canadian openness and acceptance. Once the preservation of Chinatown acquired symbolic significance in the quest for local belonging, the *Chinatown News* turned silent on the subject of redevelopment. The upsurge in local consciousness among the Vancouver Chinese also spilled over into municipal politics during this period. There were three Chinese candidates running (albeit unsuccessfully) for municipal office in the elections of 1968 and 1970, respectively.[65] By then, the editorial messages in the Chinese-language press had switched from emphasizing past rejection and bitterness to advancing the claim for local identification and inclusion. On the eve of the December 1970 municipal election, for instance, the *Chinese Voice* encouraged its readers to lay claim to a 'future in the city.' Regardless of their different backgrounds and points of origin, ethnic Chinese were now all Vancouver residents with the civic responsibility to vote their representatives into the government.[66]

In retrospect, it can be seen that, during the postwar years, ethnic Chinese succeeded in overcoming major disabilities as a minority in Canada. The quest for immigration liberalization, the beginning of electoral participation, and the effective defence of the Chinatown neighbourhood were historical landmarks for the Vancouver Chinese, signifying their claim to be local residents and fellow Canadians. It is interesting to observe that the nurturing of such local identification took place at a time when the ties to the Old World of native place sentiments, Chinese politics, and ancestral culture lingered on, especially among the immigrants. Even the local-born Chinese, who led the immigrants in embracing the new opportunities in Canada, had to respond, or react, to the immigrants' affirmation of Old World sensibilities. It is in this sense that the two general orientations towards China and Canada intertwined to define the cultural positions of the different generations and allowed the ongoing discourse on Chinese identity in Canada to take shape. The underlying complexities of such cultural contestation defy any simple characterization of ethnic resilience; nor does any generalization about cultural reorientation from China to Canada capture the emergent diversity. The cultural universe of the Vancouver Chinese, existing between two different worlds, had its own logic and coherence.

7
Constructing Chineseness in the Multicultural Arena, 1971-80

The 1970s were a defining period in contemporary identity politics for ethnic Chinese in Canada. In terms of demography, the decade witnessed the massive influx of immigrants and the arrival on the scene of another maturing generation of local-born youth. Other things being equal, one would expect more generational differences and bitter rivalries over the question of cultural identity to unfold among this increasingly diversified population of Chinese. In Vancouver, these things did occur as the decade wore on but not without an interesting twist.

The key development was the formulation of 'Chinese Canadian' as an overarching identification among the ethnic Chinese. This new construct advanced the claim of the Chinese minority to be Canadian and at the same time embedded a Chinese cultural component as its defining and enriching characteristic. The different orientations towards the Old World and the New World, previously separating many immigrants and *tusheng* into opposite camps, were apparently reconciled. The beginnings of Chinese-Canadian identity thus effected a realignment of cultural positions among various groups of Chinese, to the extent of fostering a new consensus. However, the common ground was limited, and the salience of internal differences remained. Despite the popular subscription to a Chinese-Canadian identity, subtle variations in emphasis and open battles over the power of representation did not cease.

I begin this story with the rise of Chinese-Canadian identity. This new cultural construct acquired its currency in the 1970s as a result of the intersection of some local, national, and international developments in Vancouver's Chinatown. The Canadian government's enshrining of the cultural mosaic ideology, the changing popular perceptions and diplomatic standing of Mainland China, and an outburst of community consciousness and social activism centring on the Chinatown area provided the three overlapping historical contexts for the formulation of a Chinese-Canadian identity. The latter part of this chapter focuses on several developments within the ethnic group in order to discern how this identity was claimed and contested by its members. They include the popular movement to build a Chinese Cultural Centre, the endeavour of young *tusheng* of the 1970s to sharply define their Chinese-Canadian sensibility, and, finally, the search of the new immigrants of this period for their own legitimate position and cultural space within this expanding minority group.

Genesis of a Cultural Category

In the early days of the *Chinatown News*, the magazine sometimes used the term 'Chinese Canadian' to describe all Chinese residents in the country and sometimes to refer specifically to the local-born Chinese. The expression often emphasized the professed identification with Canada, whereas the ethnic half of the label remained largely muted.[1] Indeed, any attempt to reconcile the perceived differences between being Chinese and being Canadian before the Canadian government and society at large entertained the ideal of cultural pluralism was premature.

The origin of official multiculturalism in Canada had little to do with the ethnic Chinese. It grew out of an attempt by the federal government to contain the separatist movement of French Canada. In 1963, the Royal Commission on Bilingualism and Biculturalism was appointed to examine the issue of Canadian identity and related national policy, which, in the past, had been dominated by the assumption of Anglo-Canadian supremacy.[2]

Compared to that of other immigrant groups, the participation of the Chinese in this debate was modest. My reading of the Chinese-language newspapers in Vancouver in the 1960s finds little public interest in the commission and its work. However, the English-language *Chinatown News* responded differently. Its reportage and editorials on this issue show clearly the causal relationship between an incipient belief in Canadian pluralism and the forging of a Chinese-Canadian identity. No sooner had the public debate begun than cultural mosaic rhetoric appeared in the pages of this magazine. Its first reference to Canada as a multicultural country, in its issue of 15 June 1962, actually pre-dated the Royal Commission. Before long, there were essays lamenting the tragic loss of Chinese cultural heritage among the younger generation.[3] When the editor of the magazine, Roy Mah, met with the Royal Commission in Vancouver in June 1965, the *Chinatown News* applauded his appeal for the due recognition of the cultural and linguistic rights of the Chinese.[4]

This emphasis on cultural retention departed notably from the earlier proposition of the *tusheng* regarding conformity to Canadian norms. In the 18 February 1964 issue of the *Chinatown News*, Reverend Andrew Lam, the first local-born Chinese minister in Canada and a charter member of the Chinatown Lions, reflected on the fallacy of assimilation and the merits of integration. This piece of writing was the first exposition of a Chinese-Canadian identity and deserves to be quoted in its entirety:

The current interest in bilingualism and biculturalism has brought out to the open expressions from various ethnic groups concerning their viewpoints on the question. Such groups as the Ukrainian, Jewish and Indian segments of the population have stated unequivocally their intentions of retaining and promoting their language and cultural heritage, and for recognition of their respective language and culture as integral parts of Canadian life. All this has made me think again of the situation of the Chinese population in Canada. We have, in general, been participating as Canadian citizens, to a greater or less degree more and more in the life of Canadian society. On the other hand, there is the question raised as to how far this participation would go, and whether it would lead eventually to participation in full measure.

The answer to this question has to be considered in the light of the fact that Canada is not a melting pot of people but rather a mosaic composed of many ethnic origins [sic], who will, within the foreseeable future, continue to retain their respective racial and cultural identities. Such ethnic groups as the French-Canadians and Ukrainians do not want to become assimilated into a type that is identifiable only as Canadian – if we can imagine Canadian nationality as such – and it seems impossible that assimilation is the answer.

As far as the Chinese is concerned, unless there is a wholesale movement towards inter-racial marriage continuing for several generations, it would be difficult for them to lose their distinctive physical characteristics regardless of how assimilable they may be otherwise.

As things look now, the road ahead seems to lie in the direction of integration rather than assimilation. In other words, *let us participate wholeheartedly as Canadian citizens in the life of Canada – as fully as opportunity is given us. At the same time, let us be proud of our ethnic origin and identity.*

There is no particular merit or gain in thinking less or forgetting entirely our ethnic origin or identity. In fact, there is no need for so doing. Above all, it is not a realistic approach. Each ethnic group inherits and shares with others a way of life that contributes to the enrichment of Canadian life. It is good for the ethnic groups and Canada as well that it is possible for this enriching process to continue.

To be proud of our origin and to appreciate it fully is an attitude of mind that is not inconsistent with good citizenship or loyalty to Canada. I suggest that we should do our best to instil in our young this pride and appreciation and to teach them the language of their forbears and the culture of their father land – but with a realistic approach to the association. (Emphases added.)

In short, Reverend Lam argued that embracing a Canadian identity should not entail the loss of one's ethnic culture. In writing directly to the Royal Commission a year later, Lam further asked that an 'assurance of full acceptance' be given to the ethnic Chinese 'so that their individual contributions in their daily endeavours and the richness of their cultural heritage may add to [the] fullness and strength of Canadian life.'[5]

In October 1971, the federal government of Pierre Trudeau publicly enshrined multiculturalism as an official policy and a state ideology. The intent and content of this policy have remained controversial in contemporary Canadian studies ever since. Some scholars have drawn useful insights from this remarkable example of state intervention for the purpose of restructuring a society's cultural and symbolic order. However, little has been done to appraise official multiculturalism in the context of ongoing cultural dialogue and negotiation within a single ethnic group.[6]

As far as the Chinese are concerned, the policy of multiculturalism was pivotal in the development of the category of Chinese Canadian. The state now acknowledged cultural pluralism not just as an unmistakable reality, but also as an ideal form of Canadian life. Being Chinese should no longer be condemned as irreconcilable with being Canadian. The rise of a Chinese-Canadian identity, therefore, dovetailed with the aspiration for integration spearheaded by the *tusheng* Chinese. Moreover, by awarding legitimacy and financial support to the maintenance and expression of ethnic Chinese culture and group interests, the mosaic ideology and state policy encouraged the immigrant Chinese to celebrate their ethnicity and to identify Canada as their country. Hence, multiculturalism actually enveloped the entire Chinese minority within a sociocultural context that differed significantly from that of the past.

Nonetheless, multiculturalism seems to have particularly privileged the local-born Chinese. Hitherto in the intramural debate on identity, the immigrants had always emphasized that their credentials made them more authentically Chinese than the *tusheng*, who lacked first-hand experience in China and who had only a weak command of the Chinese language. After 1945, the local-born had managed to shift the terms of the debate by stressing local adaptation and success in Canada. Multiculturalism was to tilt the balance even further in favour of the *tusheng*. No wonder they participated so energetically in the construction of a Chinese-Canadian identity, as is seen later in my case studies.

As Canada evolved in this new direction, equally exciting developments occurred in China. In the early 1970s the new international profile of the People's Republic of China (PRC) and, particularly, the improvement in Sino-Canadian diplomatic relations had a considerable impact on ethnic Chinese in Canada. For more than twenty years after the founding of the PRC, Canada had sided with its American ally and had withheld formal recognition from Mao's regime. Canada's search for an autonomous policy on China finally bore fruit in October 1970, when Ottawa switched diplomatic recognition from Taipei to Beijing.[7] As for China, this proved to be the prelude to more significant developments in the following years, including its admission into the United Nations and its rapprochement with the United States. So, within a matter of a few years, China gained new international respect as a potential superpower, and its apparent approachability fostered an instant global interest in the country as a modern nation and a historical civilization.

This dramatic turn of events was very distressing for Taiwan and its supporters.[8] In Vancouver's Chinatown, there was a new level of public support for Mainland China. Eleven days after Canada announced its recognition of Beijing, the Hon Hsing Athletic Society paraded the first PRC flag in Chinatown. Led by the jubilant Chinese Youth Association, some Chinese organizations soon undertook preparations to welcome the first PRC ambassador en route to Ottawa.[9] Apparently, this recognition had emboldened a small number of leftists and the former silent sympathizers of the regime to come out. For some Chinese, this period may have been the first time in the last quarter century, or even in their lives, that they could think of China in such a positive and exuberant manner.

Consider the radical change in how the *Chinatown News* reported on Mainland China. Since its beginning in 1953, this magazine had been most reluctant to cover any China-related events because of a fear of tarnishing its claim to be Canadian. The uneasiness over associating with China receded perceptibly after the official recognition of the PRC. The change was first noticeable during the visit of a PRC table-tennis team in 1972. The *Chinatown News* lavished attention on this so-called 'Ping Pong diplomacy' and reported the enthusiastic attendance of more than 4,000 local Chinese fans at one of the games.[10] The following year, Roy Mah, the editor, was the only ethnic Chinese correspondent to accompany Prime Minister Trudeau to China. An interesting outcome of this trip was a series of articles written by Mah in the *Chinatown News* concerning the manifold accomplishments of Mainland China – articles not unlike those printed in the *Da Zhong Bao* over the years.[11] Commenting on this and other related changes in the *Chinatown News* in the early 1970s, two outside observers were amazed by the magazine's 'self-assured security of identity and a satisfaction with Chinese origins, now that these [attitudes] imply roots in a great and friendly nation.'[12]

In fact, the breakthrough in Sino-Canadian diplomatic relations brought forth not only new attitudes and feelings with regard to China, but it also further afforded the ethnic Chinese the opportunity to re-establish connections with the ancestral area of Guangdong. These local ties had been attenuated by several decades of war and revolution in China and had then been severed because of the state of diplomatic anomaly after 1949. Major steps towards their restoration were taken during Trudeau's visit in October 1973. The two governments agreed on a family reunion program that would allow people from Mainland China to join their close relatives in Canada. They also agreed to a consular package, leading to the opening of a PRC Consulate-General in Vancouver in November 1974.[13]

Finally, in addition to the official policy of multiculturalism mandated in Ottawa and the impact of the China factor, some local events affected the social and cultural consciousness of the Vancouver Chinese. Riding on the initial success against intrusive and disruptive urban redevelopment in 1968-69, SPOTA became the moving spirit in an enlarged and sustained movement for neighbourhood defence and enhancement. The 1970s saw this organization in the forefront of several major protests against the municipal government. As early as February 1970, SPOTA used its brand new official position in the Strathcona Rehabilitation Project to block a proposal to run freeway traffic through Chinatown.[14] Two years later, it spearheaded a most memorable protest over the firehall controversy in Chinatown.

For months, city hall refused to consider the expressed opinion of SPOTA and other Chinese organizations that locating a new fire station on the western edge of Strathcona, bordering commercial Chinatown, would cause great danger to local residents. Undaunted by bureaucratic intransigence, SPOTA resorted again to popular mobilization. A coalition of some Chinatown leaders and young activists resulted in the Committee to Fight the Firehall Site in Chinatown. In a public statement, the committee declared that the location of 'this firehall, with its administrative office, a multi-storey training centre and fire-fighting equipment for the entire downtown station ... amid a beehive of activities – schools, YWCA, churches, high density senior citizens residence and family dwellings ... – [was] totally unacceptable to the community.' Almost a thousand people responded to the call for a mass rally on 10 December 1972, making the protest the largest in Chinatown's history thus far. The most remarkable aspect came only after the demonstrators paraded through Pender Street and proceeded to the Strathcona School auditorium, where twenty-three candidates for the upcoming civic election were asked to take a stand on the issue.[15] The event was a powerful display of Chinatown's community sentiments, its resolve, and its ability to confront the authorities. The firehall plan was scrapped.

Neighbourhood self-help and improvement initiatives also flourished in the Chinatown area during those eventful years. SPOTA itself, for instance, ventured into cooperative housing in addition to maintaining its original responsibility for overseeing the rehabilitation program.[16] At the same time, it was involved in a host of other projects, including the Strathcona Community Centre, opened in 1972, and the Chinatown Historic Area Planning Committee, set up by Vancouver City Council in 1975.[17] Two other meaningful projects, unrelated to SPOTA, were the Strathcona Renovation and Design Service and the Chinese Community Reading Room, both undertaken by ethnic Chinese university students in order to address neglected areas of social service. The former was to provide timely architectural advice to local residents in the recently commenced rehabilitation scheme; the latter began as a storefront library offering Chinese-language reading materials as well as some translation and referral services. Receiving continuous public funding and popular support, this second facility was to expand into the Chinese Community Library Services Association, which still exists.[18]

In retrospect, this sudden swelling of neighbourhood activity and social consciousness in the late 1960s and early 1970s gave the construction of a Chinese-Canadian identity its immediate local context. Vancouver's Chinatown underwent a process of resignification, becoming the symbolic locus of ethnic identity and community sentiments even though it no longer physically embodied the community. Not only did the neighbourhood residents themselves participate in the struggle for Chinatown, but other Chinese who had not previously been involved in Chinatown activities now found reasons to embrace their ethnic community. For many of these participants, the successful struggle for empowerment was a concrete expression of community spirit and an assertion of local identity. Chinatown and the Chineseness it embodied were to be respected as an integral part of Canadian society.[19]

It is now necessary to turn to the various articulations of the Chinese-Canadian identity during the 1970s. This new paradigm did not obliterate the existing intramural differences in identity construction, nor did it still the ongoing debate. As Chinese-Canadian identity became a point of reference for ethnic Chinese, it displayed the potential to draw different groups together and to rekindle a spirit of community. Paradoxically, it could also be a point of contention that disclosed cultural differences and conflicting agendas. The early history of the Chinese Cultural Centre best illustrates this contentious process.

The Chinese Cultural Centre
The idea of building some sort of a cultural or community centre had been discussed among Vancouver's Chinese for quite some time. As with other immigrant groups, this type of undertaking appealed to the ethnic Chinese for some very simple reasons. Having such a facility would presumably inspire greater unity. Hence, in the mid-1950s, when the young *tusheng* and the newcomers did not get along, the *Chinese Voice* suggested the building of a community hall. Moreover, such a project would signify the group's resourcefulness and therefore be a source of pride. These suggestions appeared from time to time through the 1960s, but they were invariably general and the public was unexcited.[20]

In late 1970, the idea of building an ethnic community centre was once more resurrected. In November 1970, right after Canada's diplomatic recognition of Mainland China, some leftist Chinese youth formed a group that called itself Chinese-Canadians for a Better Community. In an interview with the *Da Zhong Bao*, the group claimed to have a broad-based membership that cut across generational boundaries, language differences, and social classes. It also made a point of criticizing the 'so-called leaders' who 'either cannot see or are indifferent to the many problems existing in the community -- the run-down conditions of Chinatown; the exploitation of cheap labour; the lack of social facilities and adequate welfare for the poor; the alienation of the young, resulting in a drift towards narcotics and crime.' The group saw the solution in a community centre that would provide social programs and instill ethnic cultural pride.[21]

Evidence indicates that this group attempted unsuccessfully to convene a meeting of interested parties in order to launch its project. This failure was not surprising, given the criticism of the Chinatown elites, and nothing more was heard from the group.[22] Nevertheless, in May 1971, Roy Mah of the *Chinatown News* made known his view, possibly to counter the group's radical proposal. According to Mah, efforts should be made to establish 'a treasure-trove of a research library and exhibits depicting the life of our community in Canada.'[23] The issue for him was not better social services and neighbourhood revitalization; it was the preservation of the historical records of the ethnic Chinese in Canada, whose contributions to this country had not been properly acknowledged.

Events took an interesting turn the following year, as the idea of a cultural centre found new champions. At a Wong's Benevolent Association Banquet in October 1972 (the occasion was the anniversary celebration of the amalgamation of the two former Wong surname organizations into a unified body), dignitaries from Ottawa, Victoria, and Vancouver City Hall all spoke positively of the government support that would be forthcoming under the new multicultural mandate should the Vancouver Chinese build a cultural centre. Kelly Ip, a regional liaison officer of the Citizenship Branch, Department of the Secretary of State, immediately followed up with a letter urging the Wong's Benevolent Association, as the biggest surname group in Chinatown, to take the lead in order to take advantage of the offer.[24] The association responded by calling a meeting on 11 February, and 150 representatives from forty-three organizations attended to discuss the issue. Apparently, enthusiasm abounded, and a building committee was elected on the spot. In the following months, this committee initiated contact with officials to confirm their support, collected public input into the design of the Chinese Cultural Centre (CCC) building, and drafted a constitution for formal incorporation. At the same time, the CCC leadership defined the objectives of the organization as the preservation and celebration of the cultural heritage of ethnic Chinese in Canada and the interpretation of that heritage to other members of the Canadian mosaic.[25]

Just how the CCC strove to realize its Chinese-Canadian aspirations and complete its multi-million-dollar building project would make an intriguing inquiry. Of particular interest to our analysis are the social dynamics and cultural negotiations behind the CCC.

Among those elected to the building committee was Roy Mah. Afterward, he wrote passionately in a *Chinatown News* editorial that the CCC would be 'a catalyst for community action.' Never before had he seen such a 'grand coalition of individuals and groups.'[26] Mah was perhaps overly optimistic, but he was right about the potential of the CCC to engender a community movement. On this point the *Da Zhong Bao*, otherwise Mah's vehement critic, concurred. A number of its articles on the subject reminded the readers that Strathcona's struggle against urban redevelopment and the recent protest against the firehall plan had generated a tremendous sense of community. To the benefit of the CCC, these earlier collective efforts had proven that, together, Chinese people could get things done, even when they were at odds with the government.[27]

What exactly was the 'grand coalition' referred to by Roy Mah? Behind the CCC were quite a number of traditional associations that together comprised the citadel of the older generation of immigrants. However, by the 1970s their constituency had expanded to include not only the few remaining elderly Chinese of the first generation, but also some post-1947 immigrants. The Wongs and the Freemasons had been relatively successful in recruiting newcomers in the 1950s and 1960s. Others were now finally beginning this stage of succession, as some former immigrant youth reached their middle age and found these organizations useful for social networking, business interests, and other purposes.[28] Many of these organizations had derived financial strength, new vitality, and a sense of importance from their successful *baizi hui* investment. Rallying behind the CCC would be part of their transition from being traditional immigrant associations to being more Canadian-oriented and progressive institutions. The CCC's mission to preserve Chinese culture and to uphold Chinese pride within the newly defined multicultural context appealed to them as they searched for local commitments and continuing relevance in a changing environment.[29]

No head count has been taken, but the impression is that the most persistent supporters of the early CCC came from the generation of post-1947 immigrants. Especially influential were those who had previously been active in the youth societies in the 1950s and 1960s. Their deep-seated cultural sentiments, interest in promoting cultural and social activities, and organizational expertise made them indispensable with regard to developing the CCC into a viable vehicle for cultural retention and celebration. The sponsorship of events such as Chinese festivals and other regular programs (e.g., the offering of classes in the Chinese language and in Chinese art) soon became integral parts of the CCC. The post-1947 immigrants had

Figure 11   The Chinese Cultural Centre celebrates its first mid-autumn festival, 1974

struggled for over two decades, not without some success, against the dominance of the older generation. Finally, in the 1970s, they emerged as part of the recognized mainstream within the Chinese minority via the CCC.[30]

Moreover, the CCC was a conduit of cultural repositioning for many Canadian-born Chinese. Some were the more senior *tusheng*, like Roy Mah, who had always been active in Chinatown affairs. Involvement in the early CCC was, for them, an extension of their ongoing interests in ethnic matters. In contrast, there were other local-born Chinese of Mah's generation whose participation in the CCC represented a turning point in their personal experiences. Stimulated by multiculturalism and the ethnic sentiments of the 1970s, they saw in the CCC a cause for them to 'return' to Chinatown and to rediscover their cultural pride. The most celebrated example of this group is Dr. S. Wah Leung, the founding dean of the Faculty of Dentistry at UBC, who served as the chairperson of the CCC's board of directors from 1975 to 1983. Wah Leung and others like him were to bring to this fledgling organization great leadership, considerable respect in mainstream society, and the skills to negotiate aggressively with Canadian government authorities.[31] Finally, there was a larger contingent of university students and young activists from the emergent third generation of *tusheng*, who were to infuse many of the CCC's popular events with their youthful creativity and enthusiasm.[32]

The local-born Chinese left their distinct imprints in the early history of the CCC. Given that their sense of rootedness in Canada was stronger than that of the immigrants, and that they were the organization's spokespeople, the *tusheng* were able to shape the CCC's overall orientation towards greater integration into Canadian society. To encourage local adaptation, the first educational services the CCC provided were English-language instruction

Figure 12   Chinatown New Year parade on East Pender Street, 1977

and citizenship classes for new Chinese immigrants. The organization also adopted a policy of open membership to Chinese and non-Chinese, and many of its activities (such as festival celebrations and cultural performances) were directed at a larger non-exclusive audience. Such confident ventures into cross-cultural sharing fit the new ethos of multiculturalism.[33] The agenda, in turn, enhanced the position of the Canadian-born within the CCC.

In addition, the CCC enabled the *tusheng* to sharpen their Chinese-Canadian sensibility. To preserve the cultural heritage derived from China was worthwhile, but, in the eyes of the local-born, it seemed remote and less meaningful than the heritage of their forebears in Canada. Some of the CCC's activities, therefore, were targeted specifically at retrieving 'Chinese-Canadian history.' They gathered historical photos and artefacts for display and ran study workshops.[34] A revealing commentary on the Chinese-Canadian perspective of the *tusheng* is a documentary entitled 'Say Yup' ('Siyi' in pinyin, referring to the famous four counties – the ancestral area of many immigrant Chinese and their families). It was made by eighteen young workers from the CCC back in South China in the summer of 1976. According to Garrick Chu, the leader of the group:

> The idea behind it [the film] was to show China through the eyes of Chinese-Canadians who were going to China for the first time ... and in particular, to show the areas where we had come from. Also the idea was to portray the reactions and feelings of ourselves, as Chinese-Canadians, to China – to the country which has had much influence over our lives as we grew up. Furthermore, it was to bring the film back to show the old overseas Chinese, who because of their age, will probably never have a chance to go to China themselves and see the village where they came from.

In his report to the CCC, Chu drove home the point that the film was not about China but, specifically, 'the origins of the Chinese coming to Canada.'[35] With this kind of disclaimer and self-positioning at the heart of the CCC, one wonders how this organization managed to bring together all the different groups and their cultural agendas.

First of all, within the CCC itself there seems to have been a growing awareness and acceptance of cultural differences among ethnic Chinese. At its first workers conference in January 1976, the subject of variations in Chinese culture aroused the most discussion. Should the CCC uphold the Chinese culture of Mainland China? Or should it draw on the latest examples of Hong Kong or Taiwan? Or should it promote the culture developed in Canada? On that occasion, it was agreed that no single model should prevail at the expense of others.[36] As one activist put it, the CCC's underlying principle was not to eliminate differences but to provide a 'positive focus' for 'our diverse Chinese-Canadian community elements.'[37] On this point, it is interesting to see how the CCC strove to incorporate elements from the two earlier proposals of Roy Mah and the radical leftist group, respectively. A museum and library facility was planned as a component of the CCC complex (though not realized until 1998). While not really a community service organization, on an ad hoc basis the CCC also offered legal assistance, translation, and help with tax returns.[38]

Second, the CCC's commitment to a wide range of cultural and social activities was not just a bid to garner Chinese support, it was an attempt to demonstrate the organization's ability to deliver ethnic culture in order to obtain major public funding under state multiculturalism. The first official recognition came in the spring of 1976, when the CCC organized a festival for Habitat – the United Nations Forum on World Housing – at the request of the municipal government. It is no coincidence that, after the event, Vancouver City Council voted unanimously to lease to the CCC, at a nominal rent, two and a half acres of land in Chinatown for its future building. The CCC never hesitated to seize this kind of opportunity to raise its profile as 'the Chinese Cultural Centre' and to develop rapport with politicians. Other examples include the hosting of the Shanghai Ballet Company in 1977 at the invitation of the Canada Council, and the co-sponsorship of the 'China Month' program with city authorities in November 1979.[39] Eventually financial support from both the federal and provincial governments came through. Clearly, the politics of multiculturalism provided great incentive for the CCC to develop an eclectic cultural agenda and a broad social base.[40]

Finally, the coalition at the CCC was sustained by the existence of a common enemy, the Kuomintang and its supporters who controlled the CBA. The leadership of the CCC had originally chosen not to do anything about the situation at the CBA. However, the CCC's growing popularity and its patronage of Chinese culture from the Mainland soon agitated the pro-Kuomintang faction in Chinatown. The latter spread rumours that the CCC was organized by communist sympathizers to promote the influence of the PRC. This smearing tactic was followed by lobbying against federal and provincial funding for the CCC. In early 1977, the CBA launched an almost identical project, the Chinese Canadian Activity Centre Society, to compete for the same government support. The CCC thus found itself catapulted into a contest for the power to represent Chinese-Canadian culture and community interests.[41]

The CCC responded to the CBA with an exposé of its own. It accused the CBA of abdicating its responsibilities in Chinatown affairs since the late 1960s. Indeed, fully preoccupied with the support for the Kuomintang regime in Taiwan, the CBA was said to have completely alienated the ethnic community. This so-called Activity Centre Society, argued Wah Leung in a public letter, represented no one, least of all the Chinese Canadian.[42] Finally, the supporters of the CCC took the CBA to the provincial Supreme Court and won an injunction requiring an open election for a new executive committee, as stipulated by the CBA's own constitution. During the final showdown in October 1978, when more than 4,000 Chinese cast their votes, the CCC group beat its opponents handsomely and gained control of the CBA.

By 1980, the first chapter of the CCC's history had come to a close. Enough funding was secured to complete the first phase of the construction project, after which the CCC relocated from its temporary office to a brand new complex on Pender Street. Between 1973 and 1980, the CCC movement held centre stage, where both immigrant and local-born Chinese had come to express their Chinese-Canadian consciousness, and where there took place both subtle negotiations as well as a dramatic battle for the power of cultural representation. Remarkable as the CCC was, there were different articulations and claims of Chinese-Canadian identities outside its confines.

Figure 13 Opening ceremony of the Chinese Cultural Centre administrative building (phase one), 1980

Figure 14   Chinese Cultural Centre and Chinese Community Library float at the PNE parade, 1977

Local-Born Chinese Youth of the 1970s

The new generation of young local-born Chinese made up a significant component of the CCC movement from its very inception. However, towards the end of the 1970s, just when fund raising was making good progress, the opposition from the old CBA had been crushed, and the initial phase of the building project was finally under way, their involvement dwindled. Statistics are lacking, but the withdrawal of the young *tusheng* was enough to puzzle some keen observers at that time, including Wah Leung, chairperson of the CCC.[43]

To account for this development, Paul Yee, a very perceptive and active member of that young generation, wrote an essay in 1981 aptly entitled 'Where Have All the Young People Gone? Vancouver's Chinese Cultural Centre and Its Native-born.' Yee suggested that his peers had dropped out of the CCC for three reasons. The first reason had to do with the growing claims of family and career, which had been of small concern to former university students and fresh graduates when they initially joined the CCC. Some of them were no doubt burned out after years of intensive volunteer work. The second reason had to do with a change in the character of the CCC and, more specifically, a decline in its idealism and vitality as a popular movement. Giving priority to fund raising from 1977 on was, to Yee, a turning point, for this was an activity in which the young activists were least interested and to which they were least likely to make a substantial contribution. The subsequent transformation of the CCC into an institution that administered various programs from within its new building seemed to come at the expense of its own dynamism and the enthusiasm of native-born youth. The third, and perhaps most important, reason for young *tusheng* leaving the CCC had to do with the fact that this new generation did not surrender its flexibility and autonomy when it joined the centre. In fact, these *tusheng* continued to explore their own channels of cultural expression (e.g., by supporting a radio program called *Pender Guy* [a colloquial Cantonese rendering of Pender Street], a writers workshop with fellow Sansei, and other publication projects). Especially after the reform of the CBA and its resumption as an active community organization, the CCC was no longer as attractive and indispensable to these local-born youth. In other words, the cultural project of young Canadian-born Chinese had a life beyond the CCC, a point that deserves elaboration.[44]

In that same essay, Yee traced his generation's search for a cultural identity to a group of about seventy undergraduate students at UBC around 1970. They were a part of the youth culture of that era, critical of traditional authorities and ready to experiment with new ideas. Additional inspiration came from the contemporary Asian American movement in the United States, where young American-born Chinese played a leading role in an ethnic movement condemning American imperialism overseas and White supremacy at home.[45] It was against this background that these young English-speaking *tusheng* at UBC, with minimal experience in Chinatown affairs, began to talk about the cultural genocide of assimilation, pride in one's ethnic background, and the need to re-identify with their ethnic community. Initially, they experimented with poetry and photography to express their fledgling cultural consciousness. Soon afterward, they showed up in Chinatown to join the public protests against the freeway and the firehall. Marching side by side with fellow Chinese in what seemed a defence of 'their' besieged neighbourhood, these local-born youth took a major step in their spiritual 'return.'[46]

Then came the CCC in 1973 and its vision of a new ethnic pride within the Canadian mosaic. The idea excited the native-born youth, and they quickly immersed themselves in Chinatown events as CCC volunteers. These activities put them in touch with other people and programs, fostering a camaraderie and a feeling of community.[47] The CCC also afforded these *tusheng* a close encounter with Chinese immigrants. Uncomfortable with these fellow workers' predilection for China-derived heritage and cultural forms, the young *tusheng* became more conscious than ever about fashioning their own Chinese-Canadian identity.

In early 1974, the young local-born Chinese published a tabloid called *Gum San Po* (lit. Gold Mountain News), in which they called for a commitment to 'make our concept of a Chinese-Canadian community a viable one.'[48] Their idea of a Chinese-Canadian identity began to take shape progressively in the second half of the 1970s. A landmark event was the Identity and

Awareness Conference organized at UBC in May 1975 by a group of young native-born activists. Drawing more than 130 participants, the conference addressed the problems of racism and assimilation as they affected the Chinese, and it discussed the current developments in Chinatown (with particular reference to SPOTA and the CCC). A common direction was evident with regard to the question of identity. Instead of nourishing a transplanted and unfamiliar culture from China, this younger generation sensed that a Chinese-Canadian consciousness must be rooted in Canada and must be derived from local experience.[49]

Out of such an awareness came a more serious probing of Chinese-Canadian history. *Pender Guy*, for instance, produced a number of historical documentaries, including a series called *The War Years* and another called *The Chinese Canadian Laundry-Worker*. In the summer of 1977, a team of its young workers travelled up the Fraser River, taking pictures of old Chinese settlements and interviewing elderly residents along the way.[50] By tracing and reaffirming the historical roots of the Chinese in Canada, these efforts empowered the *tusheng*, who now rejected outsiders' representations and aspired to narrate their own past.[51]

While the CCC continued to provide some institutional support for these local-born Chinese youth to articulate their emergent Chinese-Canadian consciousness, by 1977 the young people's centre of activity had clearly moved elsewhere. One such centre was the *Pender Guy* radio program, which grew out of the second youth conference (Between Us – Chinese) at UBC in early 1976. Having talked frankly about mutual prejudice and stereotypes at the conference, a group of local-born and immigrant youth at first agreed to take part in developing a radio program to explore the issues of identity and culture. Most immigrants, however, dropped out because of differences in language and style. The history of *Pender Guy* from 1976 to 1981 mainly reflected the concerns of the young Canadian-born Chinese.[52]

Aside from local history and domestic community issues, the radio program devoted considerable time to covering such local public issues as civic elections and the equal employment opportunity policy that affected the Chinese. Other topics explored included the subtle effects of racism, the generation gap between immigrant parents and native-born children, the prevalence of sexism, the development of Asian American music, and so on.[53] Throughout, the cultural underpinning of the program was to provide specific meanings to a Chinese-Canadian identity. As *Pender Guy* repeatedly made known:

> Our perspective is *NOT* Chinese. Nor is it Canadian. It is Chinese-Canadian. And to us on Pender Guy, a Chinese-Canadian is anyone of Chinese descent who has been in Canada long enough for Canada to affect her/him. (Emphasis in original.)

> For years, Chinese Canadians have thought of their heritage in terms of brush paintings, folkloric dances and things of that nature. But that's the culture of ancient China. As Canadians we need a culture that is relevant – such as the history, songs and literature about our people.
>
> Chinese-Canadian does not equal 'Chinese.' ... We had an identity and a culture unto ourselves.[54]

During its brief existence, *Pender Guy* assumed a leading role in challenging two cases of gross misrepresentation of ethnic Chinese by the mainstream media. The first was a 1979 National Film Board documentary called *Bamboo, Lions and Dragons*. Made with minimum consultation with the Chinese, the film was nevertheless intended to provide 'an inside look at Vancouver's Chinese community.' Confronted by serious objections from the ethnic group, including a detailed script critique submitted by two local-born Chinese, the film was held up for major revisions.[55]

The other film was a special feature entitled *Campus Giveaway*, shown on the CTV television network's *W-5* public affairs program in September 1979. Associating Chinese appearance with foreignness and accusing these 'foreign students' of depriving Canadians of their rightful place in higher education, the program aroused a nationwide protest spearheaded by the Toronto Chinese. In Vancouver, the ad hoc committee, CBA against W-5, was led by young *tusheng*. The controversy was finally settled the following April after a full apology by the CTV. An additional trophy for the native-born Chinese in Vancouver was the Annual Media Human Rights Award for radio, which was won by two special *Pender Guy* programs – one of them being its coverage of the anti-*W-5* episode.[56]

Hence, the declining interest of the local-born youth in the CCC was largely a function of their own evolving cultural consciousness. Theirs was an emergent Chinese-Canadian identity sufficiently different from, though not necessarily in opposition to, the one espoused by the CCC. In fact, adding to the diversity of the Chinese minority was yet another group arriving on the scene in the 1970s. It, too, staked out different claims as Chinese Canadians during this first decade of multiculturalism. As the new generation of immigrants, this group's Chinese-Canadian aspirations and strategies are the concern of the remainder of this chapter.

New Chinese Immigrants of the 1970s

For ethnic Chinese, Canadian immigration policy had taken a decisive turn towards a more liberal and equal arrangement in the 1960s. First, in 1962, national origins were basically eliminated as a factor in determining admission. Chinese residents in Canada were allowed to sponsor a few categories of family members. Individuals with the appropriate educational and professional background could also be qualified as independent migrants. These changes were followed by a total revamping of the immigration program in 1967, when a universal points-system was adopted to screen all applicants.[57]

The large increase in Chinese immigration into Canada from the late 1960s on, as shown in Table 15, was partly a result of these legislative changes. By themselves, however, the new immigration laws only made possible the new influx: they could not fully explain it. The roots of this population movement must be found in places like Hong Kong, Taiwan, South Africa, and various parts of Southeast Asia and Latin America, where various combinations of political uncertainties, economic problems, ethnic/racial tensions, and, in some cases, state-legislated discrimination drove Chinese settlers and their descendants to migrate to greener pastures in the Western world. In countries such as the United States, Australia, and Canada, inflow from the Chinese diaspora was augmented by direct emigration from Mainland China during an era of diplomatic normalization with Beijing.

Table 15

Number of Chinese immigrants entering Canada and British Columbia, 1961-80

Year	Canada	British Columbia
1961	861	274
1962	670	175
1963	1,187	405
1964	2,674	810
1965	4,352	1,310
1966	5,178	1,676
1967	6,409	2,413
1968	8,382	3,070
1969	8,272	2,617
1970	5,377	1,588
1971	5,817	1,500
1972	7,181	2,215
1973	16,094	4,317
1974	14,465	4,558
1975	13,166	4,150
1976	12,736	4,073
1977	8,068	2,317
1978	6,021	1,651
1979	8,731	2,673
1980	12,072	4,070

Note: Instead of ethnic origin, the figures from 1962 on indicate the numbers of immigrants whose country of last permanent residence was China, Hong Kong, or Taiwan.
Source: Immigration Statistics, 1961-80.

Table 16

Time of arrival in Canada for Chinese destined for Greater Vancouver, 1981

Period	Percentage
Before 1945	2
1946-69	23
1970-81	48
Canadian-born	27
Total number	83,845

Note: The numbers in Table 15 are drawn from *Immigration Statistics,* which record data at the point of entry to Canada. They do not cover internal migration, which obviously has a bearing on the census data rendered above.
Source: Census of Canada, 1981, 93-934, Table 4.

Table 17

Number of immigrants arriving in Canada from China, Hong Kong, and Taiwan, 1971-80

Year	China	Hong Kong	Taiwan
1971	47	5,009	761
1972	25	6,297	859
1973	60	14,662	1,372
1974	379	12,704	1,382
1975	903	11,132	1,131
1976	833	10,725	1,178
1977	798	6,371	899
1978	644	4,740	637
1979	2,058	5,966	707
1980	4,936	6,309	827

Source: Immigration Statistics, 1971-80.

The census of 1981 provides some information on the immigration background of the Chinese population in Greater Vancouver. As summarized in Table 16, of the 83,000 ethnic Chinese, close to one-half had arrived as recently as the 1970s. From *Immigration Statistics,* we notice that this wave of Chinese immigration originated from more diverse areas, compared to the previous period when almost all Chinese were admitted as sponsored immigrants from South Guangdong via Hong Kong. A Chinese newcomer in the 1970s may well have been a long-time settler in South Africa or a Chinese born in the Philippines; or he/she may have been a member of the new generation of Hong Kong immigrants, who formed the largest component of this influx (see Table 17).

Besides the many different points of embarkation, another notable characteristic of the Chinese immigrants in the 1970s was their wide socioeconomic profile. Those coming directly from the PRC were usually admitted
in order to be reunited with their families, were of working-class background,
and had few English-language skills. However, the new Canadian immigration policy mandated that a sizable number of immigrants would gain admission on the bases of educational qualifications, professional status, and
occupational skills. Augmenting the rank of this group were many former
foreign students who found employment and settled in Canada after gradu-
ation. In Vancouver, local newspapers even reported the arrival of off-shore
capital coming from the 'Hong Kong millionaires' who, it was said, clandes-
tinely bought up properties downtown and in the more exclusive areas.[58]

How did this new generation of immigrants relate to the existing Chinese
minority in Vancouver? Their organizational activities may provide some
clues. Whereas those from Mainland China tended to join the traditional
Chinatown associations, the new immigrants seem to have expanded the
inventory of ethnic organizations by developing new nexuses of their own.
The latter included some old-style regional associations, such as the two
organizations formed by the Hokkiens and the Cantonese, respectively, from
the Philippines.[59] Representing the business and professional elites from
Hong Kong were several alumni societies and the Hong Kong Merchants
Association.[60] Equally noteworthy was the proliferation of ethnic Chinese
churches, whose pastoral staff, lay leadership, and congregations typically
originated in the British colony.[61] Apparently, the sheer number and resourcefulness of these new immigrants enabled them to form alternative
clusters of voluntary associations to meet their needs.

We might expect that, for a period of time, the majority of these new
immigrants would be relatively aloof from state multiculturalism and the
cultural politics of Chinese-Canadian identity. That might be what happened, but this was hardly the case for the most high-profile and influential
organization representing this new generation: the United Chinese Community Enrichment Services Society. Known commonly as SUCCESS, this
organization was established in 1973 by a group of young professionals
who had come from Hong Kong, many as foreign students, since the late
1960s. SUCCESS's targeted clientele were the newest Chinese immigrants,
who encountered problems in adjusting to Canada because of language and
other cultural barriers. As a community service agency, the underlying phi-
losophy of SUCCESS was to serve as a 'bridge' (which is the literal meaning
of its Chinese name, *Zhong Qiao*) to make sure the newcomers would re-
ceive the necessary assistance to become full members of a multiethnic and
multicultural country.[62]

The major part of SUCCESS's operation involved running a drop-in centre
in Chinatown to provide immediate assistance with regard to translation,

referral, and counselling on a wide range of subjects, including immigration procedures, old age pensions, medical plans, unemployment benefits, family problems, and so on. It also provided English-language and citizenship classes on a regular basis. To promote self-help and to augment public funding, by 1980 SUCCESS had developed a volunteer program based on a membership of more than 2,000. Finally, SUCCESS commissioned research studies to alert mainstream social service agencies and personnel to the special needs of immigrant Chinese.[63]

Because of its stance towards integration into the larger society, SUCCESS was very conscious of how it differed from the existing networks spun by the traditional Chinatown organizations, whose concern was strictly for membership welfare and group cohesion. It also jealously guarded its image as a non-partisan, independent body by not getting entangled in Chinatown politics and disputes.[64] With its proven record of securing government funding and dispensing much-needed social services, SUCCESS soon won public recognition and respect within the ethnic community. Two years into its operation, SUCCESS was already in a position to join hands with the CCC to convene a national conference in Vancouver to discuss the Green Paper on Immigration and other issues of Canadian multiculturalism pertaining to the ethnic Chinese.[65] The end of the decade saw it expanding the service to help resettle the arriving refugees from Indochina. This and much other work earned SUCCESS the reformed CBA's first outstanding citizenship award in 1980 as part of the celebration of Canada Day.[66]

By the end of its first decade, in popular opinion SUCCESS had joined the CBA and the CCC as the so-called tripod of ethnic Chinese organizations in Vancouver. Its rapid ascendance no doubt reflected the change in the composition of the Chinese population and the growth in social service needs. The rise of SUCCESS also indicated some new dynamics in Chinese identity politics in an age of multiculturalism. Just as Canada was recognizing diversity and encouraging its expression, so the discourse of Chineseness was moving towards greater variation. The accessibility of Chinese-Canadian identity, even to the latest arrivals, was revealing, and the plurality of Chinese cultural expressions was on full display.

As a cultural construct, throughout the 1970s, Chinese identity in Vancouver continued to mean a myriad of experiences, expectations, and propositions. The popular identity of Chinese Canadian was invested with different meanings and emphases by various groups of ethnic Chinese. The early history of the CCC offers a valuable vantage point from which to observe this ongoing process of cultural negotiation. For the first time, immigrants who came in the postwar years, and the few remaining pre-exclusion arrivals, celebrated their Chinese heritage and cultural skills as a legitimate part of the Canadian mosaic. An older generation of *tusheng* saw this new identity as a tribute to what they and their forefathers had contributed to Canada.

In their eyes, the work of Chinese labourers for the Canadian Pacific Railway, the wartime records of the Chinese veterans, and their own striving for acculturation and acceptance should have entitled their ethnic group to a position in multicultural Canada. By contrast, the new generation of young local-born articulated their Chinese-Canadian sensibility not simply to claim an ethnic pride, but also to affirm their personal roots in Canada. They seem to have refused to be characterized as once foreign and exotic Chinese now turned ethnic Canadians.

Different expressions of Chinese-Canadian identity were equally discernible outside the CCC. The young *tusheng* had their own channels, such as the *Pender Guy* radio program. The new generation of primarily Hong Kong immigrants likewise made known their commitment to multicultural Canada through organizations like SUCCESS. While the perspectives of the most recent arrivals cannot be fully examined in the context of the present discussion, it is reasonable to surmise that their evolving consciousness as Chinese Canadians would be different from that of the others. Their identity construction lacked the historical dimension of early Chinese settlement in Canada cherished by the *tusheng*. Compared with those of the previous generations of immigrants, their models of Chinese culture were not based in Mainland China or in Taiwan but in Manila's Chinatown, Saigon-Cholon, Singapore, Johannesburg, or, most likely, Hong Kong.

8
Beyond a Conclusion

The foregoing is the story of an identity battle that raged within the Chinese minority in Vancouver from 1945 to 1980. First igniting and informing this debate in the quarter century after 1945 were the cultural differences and mutual prejudice that existed among three distinct generations of Chinese: pre-exclusion arrivals, the post-1947 new immigrants, and the then maturing Canadian-born Chinese. The battle entered another stage in the 1970s, when these existing groups were joined by two more cohorts: most recent arrivals and local-born youth. New protagonists aside, the debate of the 1970s departed from the previous language of cultural dichotomy – as framed by the binary opposites of Old World sensibility and New World aspiration – to embrace the emergent idioms of multiculturalism. The new construct of Chinese Canadian soon attained its paradigmatic status, not so much by eliminating the intramural differences as by realigning them within a new discursive terrain. Hence, ongoing negotiation and contestation have remained salient.

Throughout this book, the analytic focus on what I call the internal discourse of identity construction is intended to make a revisionist argument against being preoccupied with majority-minority relationships and the domination of the Chinese immigrants by the North American host. These earlier emphases have exaggerated the hegemonic nature of the Occidental imagination and have, by and large, portrayed Chineseness as an outcome of a Foucauldian genealogy of control. This study of the Vancouver Chinese, by contrast, has unveiled a different genealogy by restoring historical agency to this particular minority. These immigrants and their local-born descendants had much to say about, and experienced much internal disagreement over, the meaning of being Chinese.

It is by attending to such evolving internal diversity that we begin to see the complexity of identity construction among the ethnic Chinese. Not only is it important to address how different groups articulate Chineseness, but it is also important to look at their mutual engagement with one another over conflicting leadership claims and dissimilar cultural agendas. To characterize the social dynamics in this context as generational estrangement or succession is misleading. Nor is there much support in the preceding pages for the overdrawn and simplistic notion of cultural reorientation. When we juxtapose the different cultural positions of various groups and their ongoing efforts at negotiation between myriad Old World ties and New World situations, we must finally come to grips with the transnational potential (or is it reality?) of lives in the Chinese diaspora. 该格作

I would like to do two things in the remaining pages in order to broaden the context of discussion. First, I would like to put the salient features of this book into comparative perspective. A comparative treatment will raise new questions, stimulate future research, and move us closer to understanding the important subject of identity within the larger history of Chinese migration overseas. Second, in view of the rapidly changing conditions of the Chinese in Vancouver (and also around the world) during the last two decades of the twentieth century, I would like to bring my findings to bear on attempting to understand more recent trends.

Some Comparative Perspectives

I raise five major issues, implicitly or explicitly, that lend themselves to comparative discussion with regard to the question of ethnic Chinese identities: (1) immigration patterns and their related demographic variables; (2) the relative importance of subethnicity in Chinese identity discourse; (3) various forms of ethnic institutions as arenas and agents of identity construction; (4) the China factor and its mutations; and (5) the influence of the host country.

First of all, demography was clearly a primary determinant of the identity discourse among the Vancouver Chinese, with several generations of immigrants and local-born forming distinct cohorts to take sides in the debate. Though one should be cautious not to exaggerate the rigidity of the group boundaries and the relative homogeneity within each of the groups, the evidence in Vancouver points to marked generational cleavages. Here the importance of the anti-Chinese exclusion laws, in effect between 1923 and 1947, cannot be overstated. The virtual stoppage of immigration for almost a quarter century created two separate waves of inflow, whose members differed considerably in terms of cultural background, experience, outlook, and age. Moreover, the exclusion legislation, including the earlier head tax, frustrated family formation and delayed until the 1940s the coming of age of the first Canadian-born generation. The result was a tripartite division among the elderly old-timers, the young newcomers, and the *tusheng* in the postwar decades; what ensued was a triangular debate.

One may expect a similar development in the United States, given the comparable patterns of Chinese immigration there: unrestricted immigration starting in the mid-nineteenth century, tightening control from the

1880s, stringent implementation of exclusion in the 1920s until its repeal in the 1940s, and subsequent liberalization of immigration measures in the 1960s. However, a closer look at the American situation suggests at least two important differences between it and that in Vancouver.

First, the anti-Chinese immigration legislation in the United States, while no less racist than its Canadian counterpart, never achieved the degree of exclusion that was reached in Canada. The 'paper son' phenomenon, with the incoming person claiming the right of entry into the country based on the citizenship of the father, appears to have been far more common in the United States than in Canada during the early twentieth century.[1] Unlike the Canadian case, this continuing immigration ameliorated generational distinctions among US immigrants of Chinese descent. In addition, American-born Chinese emerged as a cohort within the Chinese community well before the Second World War, much earlier than did their Canadian counterparts, and they also enjoyed stronger legal rights as citizens. Altogether, for the American Chinese these differences may suggest a different population mix and a different time line from those associated with the Canadian Chinese.[2]

The experience of Vancouver Chinese reflects, more closely, parallel situations created by the unprecedented influx of Chinese, many of them coolie labourers, into various parts of Southeast Asia in the late nineteenth century. During this period, the term 'sinkheh,' which is Hokkien and means newcomer, became popular. A typical sinkheh, arriving in the Philippines or Malaya in the second half of the century, was economically dependent on established immigrants for employment and was culturally unaccustomed to his new surroundings. Under these circumstances, it is plausible that the word was used by the earlier settlers as a term of disparagement, referring to someone without experience and know-how. Individual Chinese often managed to shed this epithet after a period of time (especially those who had some economic success) only to turn around and hurl it at whomever came after them.[3]

The situation in postwar Vancouver did not perfectly replicate the sinkheh phenomenon in Southeast Asia. In Vancouver the old-timers looked upon the new young arrivals with similar feelings of superiority (based on experience and buttressed by patriarchal authority). Newcomers, like the sinkheh, also found themselves initially disadvantaged. But in Vancouver the division between old-timers and sinkheh transcended individual reference to become a signifier of cultural difference and generational boundary. Later, the post-1947 immigrants would themselves play established settlers vis-à-vis the newcomers of the 1970s, but in the meantime they coalesced as a generation in challenging the position of the elderly pre-exclusion arrivals.

More pertinent to my comparative discussion is a set of local terms denoting the creolized Chinese in colonial Southeast Asia. These groups include the Peranakan Chinese in the Dutch East Indies (Indonesia), the Chinese Mestizos in the Philippines, and the Baba Chinese in the Straits Settlements of British Malaya. In each case, what William Skinner calls an 'intermediate society' of creolized Chinese formed after an earlier wave of Chinese immigration had subsided and those who stayed behind had inter-married with native women and become somewhat acculturated to the lo-cal environment. According to Skinner, these three groups reached their highest point of cultural development and economic strength by about the mid-nineteenth century – the period before the next wave of Chinese im-migrants arrived. In all three cases, the new immigrants' entrepreneurial drive, their control of the labour supply from China, and the expanding trading networks undermined the position of the creolized Chinese. The newcomers further exhibited cultural practices and sensibilities freshly de-rived from China and challenged the deculturated to resinicize themselves.[4]

The ensuing cultural battle in the Dutch East Indies (dating from about the turn of the nineteenth century) between the Peranakan community on the one hand and the so-called Totok (culturally pure) Chinese on the other, has been well researched. The situations in the Philippines and Malaya were similar. Indeed, across many Chinese settlements in Southeast Asia in the early decades of the twentieth century, the arrival of more Chinese women and the impact of rising Chinese nationalism made for more stable, self-sufficient, and culturally self-conscious 'Chinese' immigrant commu-nities. Inevitably, when the Peranakans, the Mestizos, and the Babas found themselves hard pressed to defend their pride against the Totok, they all came to define more clearly than ever their own sense of cultural identity.[5]

This experience of the creolized Chinese in Southeast Asia yields interest-ing insights into a major issue in this book. To be sure, there was no inter-mediate society formed by mixed parentage between the immigrant Chinese and the local people in Vancouver (or anywhere else in North America). Nonetheless, creolization, as a process of partial acculturation and adapta-tion to the normative values and practices of the host society, proved to be no less divisive among the Vancouver Chinese. For one thing, in terms of common local orientation, the cultural position of the Canadian-born Chi-nese bears a striking resemblance to that of the Peranakan Chinese. For another, the *tusheng* nurtured a strong sense of their own difference by con-fronting the Totok-style challenge of the post-1947 immigrants. At a later point, I will attempt to show how this kind of Peranakan-Totok cultural cleavage can help us understand Vancouver's more recent development.

The next comparative question I want to address concerns the relative importance of subethnicity in the identity discourse of overseas Chinese. In Vancouver, and in North America as a whole, until recently Chinese immi-gration consisted almost entirely of Cantonese-speaking natives of South-ern Guangdong (though there were further linguistic subdivision based on local districts). Dialect-based subethnic identity was therefore mute. Because what was Cantonese could easily pass by default as Chinese, this was not unlike the situations in the Philippines and Thailand, where the Chinese populations were dominated by huge Hokkien and Teochew majorities, respectively. There were, however, many contrasting examples of Chinese settlements in Southeast Asia that had a good mix of dialect groups from Guangdong and Fujian. In the Malay Peninsula, Indochina, and, to a lesser extent, Indonesia, dialect groups – widely known as *bang* in Chinese – presided over a wide range of situations involving subethnic conflict, competition, and cooperation. The *bang*-defined interests and rivalries became the essential staple of Chinese community politics.[6]

In Vancouver, as in other places where a single dialect group is in preponderance, subethnic differentiation typically unfolded at the levels of native place origin and clanship. The large number of traditional home county and surname organizations in Vancouver's Chinatown testifies to their importance, but there is more to this than meets the eye. Whereas the Chinese immigrants in many Southeast Asian contexts had developed their native place institutions and/or *bang* mentalities in the early nineteenth century, similar endeavours by the Guangdong natives in Vancouver were undertaken almost a century later and in a different environment. By then, two powerful forces were at work to contain internal subethnic differences among Chinese overseas. On the one hand, whether it was in Southeast Asia or North America, the powerful current of modern nationalism emanating from China touched the lives of many ethnic Chinese and raised their national-level consciousness. On the other hand, rising native – and also colonial (in the case of Southeast Asia) – prejudice and discrimination bracketed existing regional identities and parochialism into a racialized and homogenized Chinese category.

In Vancouver there is good evidence that subethnicity was being submerged or suppressed in the identity discourse. Note, for instance, the early establishment of the CBA for the purpose of bridging intramural differences and its persistent efforts to forge an inclusive community. Equally revealing, if we recall the details of the postwar debate, are the antipathy of the immigrant youth towards native place parochialism and the *tusheng*'s total disregard of it. Even the generation of elderly immigrants apparently clung to their native place identities and organizations as part of their construction of a Chinese – or, perhaps, a pan-Chinese – identity.

All this is to say that the role of subethnicity seems to have been relatively subdued in the identity discourse of the Chinese in Vancouver compared to what it was in some of the better known cases in Southeast Asia. It would be naive to write off subethnicity in the history of the North American Chinese, given its function in institution building and in facilitating immigrant adaptation. Nor would it be wise to assume that its secondary role will remain unchanged. As a matter of fact, subethnicity, in terms of both spoken dialect and native place, may have emerged as a new force when an increasing number of Chinese immigrants started coming to Canada (and the United States) from different shores in the 1970s. More will be said about this in the last section, but I will now move on to the topic of ethnic institutions.

At a glance, the institutional analysis that forms a large part of this book may appear somewhat conventional and even old-fashioned; thus it is all the more important for me to highlight exactly where I depart from the existing literature. The first generation of scholarship on the overseas Chinese organizations, emerging in the 1950s and 1960s, has taught us much about institutional categories, functions, leadership, and the larger community structure (especially in the Southeast Asian context). William Skinner's painstaking anthropological research on the Chinese in Thailand, Maurice Freedman's insightful thesis on organizational proliferation in nineteenth-century Singapore, and the segmentary model of Lawrence Crissmen based on a more generalized understanding of urban Chinese social organizations at home and abroad are all classics.[7] These pioneering works and others in their wake are an important first step in gathering empirical data and rendering social scientific analysis, but they are sometimes short on human agency and often lack historical depth.

In order to illuminate the theme of identity negotiation, I have drawn on the specific and collective histories of numerous and wide-ranging organizations made up of Vancouver's immigrant and local-born Chinese. I consider these associations not simply as social manifestations of some underlying mentalities or consciousness but, rather, as a contested public arena where identity politics unfolded. In other words, these associations were active agents in identity construction. Of course, not all of them were necessarily or equally involved, but, conceptually, this approach has allowed me to discern dynamism, agency, and complexity whereas previous approaches have primarily discerned structures and categories.[8]

Three related findings concerning the Chinese organizations in Vancouver are noteworthy, both intrinsically and because they may be broadly applied to analogous situations. I began with the cultural contest in postwar Vancouver – a contest in which the new immigrants and the *tusheng* built up their organizational arsenals and advanced competitive claims about Chineseness vis-à-vis one another and against the old-timers. Since 1945, this contentious process of organizational proliferation seems to have been a common thread in overseas Chinese communities and their development towards greater social and cultural plurality amidst rapidly changing environments. It was, for the most part, a function of increased diversity in the population (either because of the appearance of a younger, often local-born, generation or renewed immigration or both) and a corresponding growth in membership needs, leadership aspirations, and new demands and possibilities for adaptation.[9]

In addition, I have presented fresh evidence of the resilience of the traditional native place and other Chinese-style associations in Vancouver's Chinatown. Previous analyses of the overseas Chinese organizational scene, especially in the North American context (and, until recently, in Singapore), typically privilege newer types of professional or social service-oriented organizations and dismiss traditional ones as by definition archaic, conservative, and irrelevant to the contemporary period. For years, the late See Chinben was almost alone in drawing attention to the continuous popularity of these old-style organizations among the Chinese in the Philippines in the 1960s and 1970s.[10]

To some extent, the traditional associations in postwar Vancouver may appear to have been languishing compared to the associations of the young newcomers and the *tusheng.* What have not been noticed are the new intensity in public ritual performances orchestrated by the elderly immigrants and the remarkable success of the equally ritualized domain of the *baizi hui.* The demonstrated efficacy of these supposedly traditional ritual practices in articulating cultural claims and enabling organizational adaptation suggests an important direction for future inquiry, as scholars are now more cognizant of the staying power and vitality of these old-style institutions in many ethnic Chinese communities.

Last but not least, the early history of the CCC tells us an intriguing story about changing identity. At one level, the CCC is a wonderful prism that helps us to see the mix of Chinese-Canadian sensibilities that was emerging in the 1970s. Being a battleground from the very beginning, the CCC was (and still is) about Chinese-Canadian identity in the making – always in motion and contestation, never fully made. At another level, the CCC story shows how contemporary Chinese have renegotiated their ties with China and Chinese culture as well as with the new pluralistic environment in Canada. With Chinese ethnic sentiments on the rise and a multicultural ethos becoming fashionable in many other settlement countries since the 1970s (notably in the United States but also, to a lesser extent, elsewhere in different parts of the world) it will be interesting to see whether similar processes were working to bring forth more Chinese organizations like the CCC, at once proudly ethnic and committed to local integration.[11]

This brings my two remaining comparative topics: the changing relationship between (1) the ethnic Chinese and China and (2) the ethnic Chinese and the host country. One reason behind the alleged demise of the traditional associations was the 'loss of China' when the Chinese Communist Party came to power in 1949. To the extent that the early twentieth century represented the high tide of *huaqiao* nationalism, the influence of China on the Chinese abroad was certainly in decline after 1945. In most Southeast

Asian countries, where nearby Communist China was perceived as a threat, native nationalists often charged ethnic Chinese with foreign political allegiance and cultural loyalty to the now suspect Chinese state. Strangely enough, though, Cold War politics in the United States and allied countries such as Canada and the Philippines prompted their resident Chinese to proclaim their support for Taiwan.

Under these circumstances, it is interesting to observe how divisive the politics of China remained among the Chinese in Vancouver and how this issue helped give rise to different debating positions on the question of identity. The Kuomintang hardliners, the Chinese Freemasons, and the leftist Chinese Youth Association each had strong opinions about the regimes on the two sides of the Taiwan Strait. Even the otherwise non-partisan Hai Fung Club and its fellow immigrant youth societies, as well as the *tusheng* Chinese, used their overt disinterest in Chinese politics to make a statement about cultural identity.

Another of my findings that has significant implications for our understanding of late twentieth-century Chinese identity concerns the nature of the ties of the Chinese overseas with the Old World. This so-called China factor could mean more than just politics; it could even transcend territorial China itself. Here, evidence from Vancouver allows me to develop an argument that historian Tu Wei-ming and others have sought to delineate in a more general way. If one wants to specify the time when China was first decentred spatially within the modern discourse of Chineseness, then, unlike Tu and the recent literature on the rise of South China, one should look at the 1950s and 1960s rather than the 1970s and 1980s.[12] It was then that Hong Kong, on the periphery of China, became a surrogate native place for many immigrants in Vancouver and enhanced its position as a production centre of modern Chinese culture for the Chinese overseas. My observations are far from conclusive, but I suspect that later findings in other locales and the burgeoning research on historical Hong Kong may radically change our understanding of Chinese identities overseas.

This new history will be spatially (and temporally) configured and will not have a purported centre in China, although China, and its influence on the Chinese abroad, need not be excluded from the larger picture. In Vancouver, as has been seen, China regained influence in the 1970s when Beijing gradually ceased to be a pariah and acquired great-power status in the international arena. The re-established diplomatic channel was one thing, but the renewed contact with the ancestral native areas, not to mention the subsequent investment opportunities with China's Open Door policy beginning in 1979, once again enlarged the potential influence of the China factor on the lives of the ethnic Chinese. Compared to the more settled Chinese populations in Southeast Asia, where new immigration has been minimal since 1945, since the 1970s the Chinese in North America seem to have responded to China's overture with relative enthusiasm. Perhaps this was due to the larger number of more recent arrivals from the Mainland.[13] But this development in Canada and the United States can be fully understood only if we consider the changing attitude and state policy of these two host countries towards their ethnic Chinese around that time.

The relationship with the host society was surely an important factor in the identity discourse of the ethnic Chinese in any settlement country. The fact is that, as an immigrant minority under alien rule, the Chinese bore the consequences of official policy and prevailing public attitude towards the group. A case in point is the creolized Chinese in Southeast Asia. There the Mestizos, the Peranakans, and the Babas were given various degrees of legal recognition, distinct from the immigrant Chinese, by the colonial authorities.[14] Likewise, the *bang* designations, so salient and deep-seated in many Southeast Asian Chinese communities, owed much to the fact that the former colonial governments not only did not dispute or disrupt the boundaries between the dialect groups, but they usually co-opted the subethnic structure and its leadership into a system of indirect rule.[15]

The host environment changed for the worse for the ethnic Chinese in Southeast Asia after the Pacific War. The removal of the colonial regimes meant, among other things, that the Chinese would have to take the full brunt of native nationalisms. In countries such as the Philippines – and also Indonesia – nationalization measures targeting the perceived economic domination of the Chinese were in full swing, and escape from the negative consequences of being Chinese was not immediately available in the form of local citizenship. In Malaya the Chinese were sufficiently numerous to find some relief by taking part in communal politics. Only in Thailand was citizenship more accessible, and acculturation proceeded relatively smoothly under the strong pressure of assimilation. Still, throughout Southeast Asia, the shadow of Communist China cast a thick cloud of suspicion over the loyalty of the ethnic Chinese.[16]

The Chinese in North America did not face this kind of hostility, since by the postwar period overt and legislative discrimination was over. Nevertheless, in Canada as in the United States, racial prejudice remained a barrier, and the pressure to accommodate to the host society's expectations and to seek acceptance by the mainstream was very strong. Hence in Vancouver in the 1950s and 1960s one sees the acculturation agenda of the *tusheng* Chinese, who, based on their Canadian cultural skills and career success, fought with the immigrants for leadership. The immigrants were often apologetic about their cultural ineptitude, yet another testimony to the prevailing pressure for conformity.

Given this situation, the rise of a multicultural ethos and ethnic consciousness in North America in the late 1960s and early 1970s was to have profound and far-reaching consequences for the ethnic Chinese. Canada's and the United States's growing acceptance of their pluralistic nature lessened the pressure to conform to Anglo-defined norms and afforded new space for ethnic expression and identity renegotiation. While multiculturalism as such did not unfold this way in any part of Southeast Asia, by the 1980s the independent states of the region had become decidedly more relaxed in their relationships with Mainland China and with their resident Chinese (the latest upheavals in Indonesia, sadly, remind us of the tenacity of anti-Chinese sentiments and how vulnerable ethnic Chinese still remain in that country).

Here it would be interesting to compare my findings with regard to the late 1960s and 1970s in Vancouver with the situation in the United States, which has been more thoroughly researched. Not only would this help to draw out the unique features of the Chinese experience in Vancouver, but it would also provide a better understanding of the Canadian context and so put to rest the notion that any significant development in this country was only a mild and belated variant of whatever happened in the United States.

As a matter of fact, contemporary Canadian multiculturalism hailed intellectually from the mosaic rhetoric and continued a historic search for a distinct Canadian identity free from American cultural hegemony. Adding to the urgency of the 1960s were the domestic outcry of Francophone Canada against Anglo-Canadian supremacy in all aspects of Canadian life and the subsequent demands for cultural rights by other ethnic groups. Official multiculturalism thus began in 1971 in response to a cacophony of petitions and requests. It was a nation-building project launched by a relatively young country, with a proactive government eagerly setting the agenda. As we have seen, this new state ideology had a decisive impact on the ongoing identity debate among the Chinese in Vancouver. By encapsulating the rising ethnic sentiments in the Chinese minority and by reaffirming a sense of belonging to Canada, a Chinese-Canadian identity quickly emerged as a common reference point for various groups contending for state recognition and public support.

The ethnic movement in the United States contrasted with the Canadian movement in some important respects. In the first place, the cry for cultural pluralism in the United States had its radical beginnings in the 1960s. Inspired by the Civil Rights Movement and anti-Vietnam War protests, young ethnic Chinese of local-born and immigrant backgrounds joined other Asian minorities and People of Colour to condemn White America for racial domination at home and imperialism abroad (mainly in Asia). They also shared with Americans of their generation a growing distrust and disdain for public institutions and authorities. The confrontational character, assertiveness, and combative style of the earliest phase of the Asian American movement left behind a powerful legacy.[17]

Perhaps such radicalism can be attributed to the more intense political environment in the contemporary United States, which also explains the interest in coalition politics among the ethnic Chinese and other Asian minorities. Such groping for an encompassing pan-Asian identity stems in part from the awareness of a common history of racial exploitation and marginalization in American society. Even more important, as Yen Le Espiritu has pointed out, was institution building among Asians in the United States. Broadly based Asian American organizations were established expressly to tap public funding and to provide a means of political empowerment, but they also became vehicles for bridging ethnicities and constructing a new identity.[18]

On this point, it is interesting to notice that in Canada the state recognized various Asian ethnicities as diverse components of the mosaic and provided funding and other benefits to each, usually through their respective ethnic organizations. Unlike in the United States, where the 'ethno-racial pentagon' (a term coined by David Hollinger to refer to the African American, Asian American, Euro-American, Indigenous, and Latino segments of the population) was deeply ingrained in bureaucratic structure and popular discourse, Canadian multiculturalism endorsed a different classificatory scheme, one that offered limited incentives for coalition between, say, the ethnic Chinese and Japanese. Consequently, an 'Asian Canadian' identity never really took shape.[19]

Another unique American phenomenon that illustrates the importance of the larger sociocultural environment concerns the development of Asian American Studies as a discipline in the United States. Since the beginning of the ethnic movement in the 1960s, there has always been a much larger contingent of college students among the Chinese and other Asian minorities in the United States than in Canada. These students helped to carry the torch of radicalism just mentioned. Their demand for courses, and for a curriculum that reflected the conditions of the Asian minorities in the host country, launched Asian American Studies as a field of teaching and research. Some of these former radical students later became university professors. Under their leadership academic programs were built and research was conducted, giving Asian Americans a critical arena for continuous soul-searching, theorizing, and community action. Related to this was, of course, a much larger reading public and literary scene in the United States, which allowed Asian American authors to carve a niche and to thrive on their creativity.[20] To the extent that similar academic institutions and non-state cultural resources were unavailable to the Chinese and other Asian groups in Canada, its government, bound to a multicultural mandate, would play a stronger role in shaping the discourse on ethnic identity.

More Recent Trends

In this last section, I draw on my findings with regard to postwar Chinese identity discourse and the above comparative discussion to shed light on the exciting and rapidly changing conditions of the Chinese in Vancouver since 1980. The more recent trends reflect local as well as global developments that are still unfolding as I write. My analysis will be necessarily brief and preliminary.

In Vancouver the last two decades of the twentieth century will probably be best remembered for the massive influx of immigrants from the Asia Pacific, most notably the Chinese. By the mid-1990s, popular estimates put the Chinese population in the Vancouver area at 300,000, or even higher, out of a total population of 1.8 million. The large majority of these latest arrivals are from Hong Kong, followed by significant minorities from Mainland China and Taiwan, with a smaller number from many other locations in the existing diaspora.

In light of the generational differences and social dynamics we have discerned since 1945, this wave of contemporary immigration is striking in terms of its enormous size and its transformative impact on the local Chinese scene. Far more than the Totok of the postwar era and of the 1970s, the Totok of the 1980s and 1990s have come in even greater numbers, bringing with them such considerable financial resources and ample social capital that they appear to have taken over.[21] Within a relatively short period of time, these newest immigrants have spun their social networks through professional and business organizations, Christian churches and other religious groups, alumni societies, social service agencies, charities, and so on. In the process they have enlarged and added complexity to the nexus of ethnic Chinese organizations.[22] Another unmistakable sign of change concerns the Chinese press, with the appearance of *Sing Tao* (1983) and *Ming Po* (1993), both of Hong Kong background, as well as the *World Journal* (1991) favoured by the immigrants from Taiwan. Their deleterious effects on the older publications were completed when the historical *Chinese Times* and, finally, the *Chinatown News* closed down in the early 1990s.

This type of situation almost guarantees a cultural clash between the newcomers and the existing settlers – a clash reminiscent of the 1945-80 era. This is not to say that the existing immigrants and local-born Chinese have not enjoyed the significant rise in the social and economic profile of the Chinese minority as a whole, or the wider range and better quality of all kinds of ethnic goods and services made available by the new immigrants. However, so numerous were the Totok of the 1980s and 1990s, and so capable did they seem of projecting their own images of a contemporary, sophisticated, and success-oriented Chinese (derivative of their upbringing in Hong Kong and/or other parts of the rapidly ascending Asia Pacific economies), that some Peranakan reactions seem inevitable. Just as the newcomers promised to take the ethnic Chinese in Canada to a new level of accomplishment and recognition, so the existing settlers complained about the former holding on to their familiar lifestyles (especially the flaunting of wealth), their affront to Canadian sensitivity, and their lack of genuine commitment to their new country. The controversy surrounding the CCC board election in 1993, recounted at the beginning of this book, was simply one of the more dramatic displays of this and other related rivalries.

Such inter-generational conflict is, of course, a consistent theme in Chinese migration history in Vancouver, discernible each time a new wave of immigrants arrives on the scene. Nevertheless, this latest influx takes on additional interest because the new arrivals have come from several major source countries, all of which have very different social, political, and economic environments. In Toronto, a preliminary study by Bernard Luk and Fatima Lee has presented some fascinating data on burgeoning Chinese subethnicities. Even though the recent Chinese immigrants from Hong Kong, Taiwan, and Mainland China may appear to be all 'Chinese' in their physical appearance, their dissimilar pre-migration experiences, their lack of a common language, and their different trajectories of entry and settlement have led to the formation of culturally distinct and largely separate communities.[23] In other words, there are not one but several Totok groups.

Similar studies on Vancouver have yet to be attempted, but it is safe to assume that the differences between the Chinese settlements here and in Toronto would be a matter of degree, depending on the relative size and strength of the various groups and the extent of their mutual interaction. For instance, whereas the Hong Kong components are indisputably dominant in both Toronto and Vancouver, since the late 1980s relatively well-off Taiwan immigrants, a good number of whom entered Canada under the business immigration program as investors or entrepreneurs, have made Vancouver their choice destination. The impressive economic power of the Taiwanese, their organizational activities (especially their highly visible public charities), and their ability to fashion a distinct cultural identity within a Canadian context have opened up a new subethnic dimension in an ongoing identity discourse that awaits further study.[24]

Interesting as the above trends are, I would argue that the most significant development since 1980 has been the rise in transnational practices and consciousness among the ethnic Chinese. Here in Vancouver, as in other global cities, among Chinese as well as non-Chinese the postmodern conditions in late capitalism, manifested in the heightened mobility and fluidity of capital, information, people, and commodities across territorial boundaries and over long distances, have altered the meaning of migration and travelling. To the extent that the Vancouver Chinese have partaken of these transnational, and often trans-Pacific, movements, they now seem to belong to a mobile and cosmopolitan population of global Chinese, despite their establishment of local residence, their adaptation to the host environment, and their claim of Canadian citizenship.[25]

In a recent article, Arif Dirlik has written poignantly about the stark contradictions between local commitments stemming from the radical movement of the late 1960s and the global orientations of transnational capitalism that are currently remaking Asian America.[26] It is not difficult to discern similar tensions in evolving Chinese-Canadian consciousness, though state-mandated multiculturalism in Canada, among other things, seems to have provided a discursive space that differs from that in the United States. I will elaborate on this point by offering some empirical observations, but first I want to clarify a conceptual problem in the language of transnationalism that has, unfortunately, confounded the issue of identity.

In brief, the danger is one of cultural essentialism and the concomitant erasure of the historical specificity and complexity of identity formation in different locales. It is one thing to refer to the global spread of the Chinese as a diaspora and believe that such diaspora conditions, especially in their present postmodern settings, will impinge on the consciousness of the ethnic Chinese as they negotiate their identities *locally and globally*. It is quite another thing to assume that people have a routine or uniform engagement in transnationalism or, even worse, that there is a universal Chineseness prevailing across the global space. Such uncritical and ahistorical reference to the Chinese diaspora, the problems of which have been pointed out by several scholars, is utterly unproductive. It goes against the critical diaspora paradigm in cultural studies that inspired the present inquiry.[27]

In Canada, critical reflections on transnationalism similar to those undertaken by Dirlik and other Asian Americanists are relatively few. Canadian academe's lack of an arena comparable to Asian American Studies means that much rethinking and probing is conducted by artists, literary critics, and other cultural workers.[28] Yet the impacts of transnationalism on the Chinese in Vancouver have been real and profound. Consider, for example, the high incidence of female-headed households and the 'astronaut' phenomenon (i.e., the husband flying back and forth between his job or business in Asia and his family in Canada). Often glamourized by the mainstream media, such diaspora living is a dramatic reversal of the 'bachelor society' of earlier times, perhaps mandated by economic necessity but nonetheless causing untold hardship within marital and parent-child relationships.

Fortunately, most aspects of transnationalism seem to have been generally uplifting and positive. Ethnic Chinese voluntary organizations have been actively pursuing extra-local ties with their counterparts around the world for business and professional networking and other worthy causes.[29] Likewise, the vibrant Chinese press in Vancouver is now part of global Chinese media that provide extensive coverage of China, Taiwan, Hong Kong, and other parts of the Chinese diaspora, in addition to energetic reportage on Canadian local and national news. Ethnic Chinese have undoubtedly been playing a leading role in the globalization and, particularly, the Asianization of this part of the Canadian Pacific coast.

Such transformation of the local scene has not been without tensions both inside and outside the ethnic group. Among the Chinese themselves, conflict and competition between the different Totok groups appears rather subtle and discrete. More often heard, as mentioned earlier, are insinuations that the latest immigrants have been all too boastful of their Hong Kong origin and ostentatious consumption.[30] Although mainstream society seems to have been generally appreciative of the cultural diversity and economic benefits generated by the recent influx from Asia, negative reactions have also surfaced. Despite evidence to the contrary, local opinion has it that the new immigrants have caused real estate prices to rise beyond the reach of other Vancouver residents. For a period of time, emotions have run very high, especially in some traditionally upper middle-class White neighbourhoods, over the alleged Chinese preference for big mansions, the so-called 'Monster Houses,' and their disruption of well-blended housing designs and landscape.[31]

Whether we want to give credit to some of these thinly disguised racist sentiments or not, they have raised some important questions about the multiculturalism at the heart of contemporary Canadian identity. Since the 1970s, state multiculturalism has coincided with a period of high immigration from non-traditional source countries. For many members of the Chinese minority (and other groups as well), Canada's pluralistic ethos has encouraged them to emphasize their roots and to display their ethnic and cultural consciousness. Has state multiculturalism been producing the desired integration? Has it promoted sheer cultural permissiveness and condoned differences at the expense of national unity and a Canadian identity? Or, as critics on the other side have asked, is multiculturalism just a benign variant of a deep-seated racism that legislates 'otherness,' defining 'ethnics' as always on the margins?[32]

In the midst of soul-searching, it is fascinating to see how the Canadian state has doubled its efforts to entrench and deploy multiculturalism. Important legislative initiatives include, for example, the 1982 Canadian Charter of Rights and Freedom, and the Canadian Multiculturalism Act, 1988. Meanwhile, official and corporate Canada have increasingly portrayed multiculturalism as a growth strategy. Forging links with the larger Chinese diaspora and plugging into its international business networks are considered to be what will constitute Canada's bridge to the twenty-first century.[33]

How will the ethnic Chinese respond to the fast-changing local and global environments? How will the ongoing discourse on Chineseness evolve from this time on? Who will be debating the meaning of being Chinese, against whom, and with what outcomes? We will only know the answers as the future unfolds. But if the past is any indicator, the Chinese immigrants and their Canadian-born descendants in Vancouver will continue to weave a fascinating story about identity construction and contestation as we cross the threshold into the next century.

Notes

Chapter 1: Introduction

1 *Sing Tao,* 26-27 April 1993.

2 In a meeting with the Chinese media on 15 February, the CCC Renewal Committee named its candidates for the upcoming board election. In response, the incumbents established the Committee to Maintain the Participation of Chinese Organizations in the CCC and issued a statement the following day appealing for public support. *Sing Tao,* 16-17 February 1993. For a charge of conspiracy, see John Ko's letter to the editor in the *Vancouver Sun,* 24 March 1993.

3 For a preliminary analysis of these two political battles, see Katharyne Mitchell, 'Reworking Democracy: Contemporary Immigration and Community Politics in Vancouver's Chinatown,' *Political Geography* 17.6 (1998): 729-50. Her observations on immigrant political culture and community conflicts in the context of the more recent influxes from Hong Kong and elsewhere are theoretically interesting and in line with my own argument. Note, however, her erroneous information on S. Wah Leung (740) and a tendency to take the views of the contestants concerning democracy and open society at face value.

4 This literature is quite sizable. Among the best known are the works of William Skinner, Maurice Freedman, C.P. FitzGerald, Lea Williams, Edgar Wickberg, Donald Willmott, and William Willmott. See a bibliographical discussion in Leo Suryadinata, 'The Ethnic Chinese in the ASEAN States,' in *The Ethnic Chinese in the ASEAN States: Bibliographical Essays,* ed. L. Suryadinata (Singapore: Institute of Southeast Asian Studies, 1989), 4-42.

5 Though the connection has seldom been made, from the 1920s until well into the postwar years sociologists associated with the Chicago School combined the same kind of Parsonian structuralist analysis with Robert Park's assimilation theory in examining the changing identity and social organization of the American Chinese. Two excellent examples are Paul C.P. Siu, *The Chinese Laundryman: A Study of Social Isolation* (New York: New York University Press, 1987); and Rose Hum Lee, *The Chinese in the United States of America* (Hong Kong: Hong Kong University Press, 1960).

6 Frederik Barth, 'Introduction,' in *Ethnic Groups and Boundaries,* ed. F. Barth (Boston: Little, Brown, 1969), 9-38. Charles Keyes and Judith Nagata, two Southeast Asianists, were among the first to apply Barth's insights to their research. See Charles Keyes, 'Towards a New Formulation of the Concept of Ethnic Group,' *Ethnicity* 3 (1976): 202-13; ibid., 'The Dialectics of Ethnic Change,' in *Ethnic Change,* ed. C. Keyes (Seattle: University of Washington Press, 1981), 3-30; and Nagata, 'What Is a Malay? Situational Selection of Ethnic Identity in a Plural Society,' *American Ethnologist* 1.2 (1974): 331-50. They, in turn, have influenced many scholars studying ethnic Chinese in Southeast Asia. The best examples are the two volumes of essays, mostly by anthropologists, edited by Linda Y.C. Lim and A. Peter Gosling, entitled *The Chinese in Southeast Asia,* Vol. 1, *Ethnicity and Economic Activity;* Vol. 2, *Identity, Culture and Politics* (Singapore: Maruzen Asia, 1983). Even the more recent surge of interest in ethnicity among China specialists bore the imprint of Keyes and Nagata. See 'Ethnicity in Qing China' (special issue) *Late Imperial China* 11.1 (1990).

7 In the case of Canada, for instance, the histories of several other immigrant groups, such as the Japanese, the Croatians, and the Hungarians, have been delineated in terms of 'waves' of arrivals and generational sequence. See, for example, Tomoko Makabe, *The Canadian Sansei* (Toronto: University of Toronto Press, 1998); Anthony W. Rasporich, *For a Better Life: A History of the Croatians in Canada* (Toronto: McClelland and Stewart, 1982), especially 192-248; and D.F. Dreisziger with M.L. Kovacs, Paul Body, and Bennett Kovrig, *Struggle and Hope: The Hungarian-Canadian Experience* (Toronto: McClelland and Stewart, 1982).

8 For generational analysis of the ethnic Chinese experience, see the seminal essay by Wang Gungwu on group orientations, 'Chinese Politics in Malaya,' first published in *China Quarterly* 43 (1970) and reprinted in his *Community and Nation: China, Southeast Asia and Australia* (St. Leonards, Australia: Allen and Unwin, 1992), 251-80. Note also a more recent and considerably expanded discussion on contemporary trends that includes the new migrant states in North America and Australia, 'Greater China and the Chinese Overseas,' *China Quarterly* 136 (1993): 926-48. Regarding the Chinese in the United States, see the San Francisco study by Victor G. Nee and Brett de Bary Nee, *Longtime Californ': A Documentary Study of an American Chinatown* (Stanford: Stanford University Press, 1972); and the case study on Sacramento by Melford S. Weiss, *Valley City: A Chinese Community in America* (Cambridge, MA: Schenkman, 1974). However, the theme of group interaction and contestation has seldom been pursued. See Bernard Wong's exceptionally interesting piece, 'Elites and Ethnic Boundary Maintenance: A Study of the Roles of Elites in Chinatown, New York City,' *Urban Anthropology* 6.1 (1977): 1-22.

9 Especially Edgar Wickberg, ed., *From China to Canada: A History of the Chinese Communities in Canada* (Toronto: McClelland and Stewart, 1982). On Vancouver, see Paul Yee, *An Illustrated History of the Chinese in Vancouver* (Vancouver: Douglas and McIntyre, 1988). Note also the recent appearance of some autobiographical works and collections of oral history, as reviewed in a short essay by Patricia E. Roy, '"Active Voices": A Third Generation of Studies of the Chinese and Japanese in British Columbia,' *BC Studies* 117 (spring 1998): 51-61. This last group of materials seems to have raised the possibility of a major foray into gender analysis, which I have not attempted here. For some preliminary efforts in this new direction, see Tamara Adilman, 'A Preliminary Sketch of Chinese Women and Work in British Columbia, 1858-1950,' in *Not Just Pin Money: Selected Essays on the History of Women's Work in British Columbia*, ed. B. Latham, R. Latham, and R. Pazdro (Victoria: Camosun College Press, 1984), 53-78, and reprinted in *British Columbia Reconsidered: Essays on Women*, ed. Gillian Creese and Veronica Strong-Boag (Vancouver: Press Gang, 1992), 309-39; Women's Book Committee, Chinese Canadian National Council, *Jin Guo: Voices of Chinese Canadian Women* (Toronto: Women's Press, 1992); and two new MA theses: Joanne M. Poon, 'Miss Queen of Cathay (1954): Chinese Women, Families and Associations in Vancouver' (MA thesis, University of British Columbia, 1995); and Belinda Huang, 'Gender, Race, and Power: The Chinese in Canada, 1920-1950' (MA thesis, McGill University, 1998). Finally, two recent novels – Denise Chong's *The Concubine's Children: Portrait of a Family Divided* (Toronto: Viking, 1994) and Yuen-fong Woon's *The Excluded Wife* (Montreal and Kingston: McGill-Queen's University Press, 1998) -- are especially noteworthy in drawing attention to the role of women in Canada's immigrant Chinese community.

10 Major representatives of this historiography include Peter Ward, *White Canada Forever: Popular Attitudes and Public Policy towards Orientals in British Columbia*, 2nd ed. (Montreal and Kingston: McGill-Queen's University Press, 1990) and Patricia Roy, *A White Man's Province: British Columbia Politicians and Chinese and Japanese Immigrants, 1858-1914* (Vancouver: UBC Press, 1989). One important question raised by this literature is whether anti-Asian racism in British Columbia was culturally or economically motivated. A variation on the same theme is the stress on the damaging effects of institutional racism, as presented in the historical account of Anthony Chan, *Gold Mountain: The Chinese in the New World* (Vancouver: New Star, 1983) and the sociological analysis of Peter S. Li, *The Chinese in Canada* (Toronto: Oxford University Press, 1988).

11 Kay Anderson, *Vancouver's Chinatown: Racial Discourse in Canada, 1875-1980* (Montreal and Kingston: McGill-Queen's University Press, 1991).

12 See my review of Anderson's book in *Histoire Sociale – Social History* 26 (May 1993): 135-36. On the same note, Ronald Takaki, 'Teaching American History through a Different Mirror,'

Perspectives 32.7 (1994): 9, has pointed out the irony of reproducing cultural hegemony in American scholarship on the Asian minorities: 'Some of us sometimes also unknowingly contribute to the continued marginalization of minorities ... In our very critique [of racial stereotypes], we reinforce stereotypes by failing to penetrate beyond the notion of the exotic and by leaving Asians still faceless and voiceless ... In our examination of the nature of white racism, we have, in effect, reproduced the very monocultural perspective we have been aiming to challenge.' In a more recent state-of-the-art survey of the Asian American field, Sucheng Chan, 'Asian American Historiography,' *Pacific Historical Review* 65.3 (1996): 370-75, has convincingly argued for the necessary balance between structural oppression and historical agency in scholarly analysis.

13 Immigrant populations commonly deployed institution building as a strategy for dealing with problems of adaptation and advancement in the course of their settlement, and the Chinese were no exception. The historical and anthropological literature on this subject is substantial. On the Chinese overseas, note the earlier influential work of William Skinner, *Leadership and Power in the Chinese Community of Thailand* (Ithaca: Cornell University Press, 1958); Maurice Freedman, 'Immigrants and Associations: Chinese in Nineteenth-Century Singapore,' *Comparative Studies in Society and History* 3.1 (1960): 25-48; and Lawrence Crissman, 'The Segmentary Structure of Urban Overseas Chinese Communities,' *Man* (n.s.) 2.2 (1967): 185-204. While interest in the topic has persisted, as in my 'Urban Chinese Social Organization: Some Unexplored Aspects in *Huiguan* Development in Singapore, 1900-1941' *Modern Asian Studies* 26.3 (1992): 469-94, it is the study of immigrant organizations within China itself that has made important strides in recent years. See William Rowe, *Hankow: Commerce and Society in a Chinese City, 1796-1889* (Stanford: Stanford University Press, 1984), 252-340; and Bryna Goodman, *Native Place, City, and Nation: Regional Networks and Identities in Shanghai, 1853-1937* (Berkeley: University of California Press, 1995). A useful overview of the overseas development of immigrant organizations with reference to the China-derived experience is Edgar Wickberg, 'Overseas Chinese Adaptive Organizations, Past and Present,' in *Reluctant Exiles? Migration from Hong Kong and the New Overseas Chinese*, ed. Ronald Skeldon (Armonk, NY: Sharpe, 1994), 69-84.

14 For an unequivocal objection, see Tan Chee Beng's comment in Suryadinata, *Ethnic Chinese as Southeast Asians*, 28. William Safran, 'Diasporas in Modern Societies: Myths of Homeland and Return,' *Diaspora* 1.1 (spring 1991): 83-99; and Robin Cohen, *Global Diasporas: An Introduction* (Seattle: University of Washington Press, 1997). A recent attempt to compare and contrast the historical experiences of Chinese and Jews is Daniel Chirot and Anthony Reid, eds., *Essential Outsiders: Chinese and Jews in the Modern Transformation of Southeast Asia and Central Europe* (Seattle: University of Washington Press, 1997).

15 Lynn Pan, *Sons of the Yellow Emperor: The Story of the Overseas Chinese* (London: Secker and Warburg, 1990); Sterling Seagrave, *Lords of the Rim: The Invisible Empire of the Overseas Chinese* (New York: Putnam, 1995). The growth of Chinese economic power in the Asia Pacific and its cultural foundation, allegedly based on Confucianism, have spawned an industry since the 1980s. The literature is voluminous, but see J.A.C. Mackie, 'Overseas Chinese Entrepreneurship,' *Asian-Pacific Economic Literature* 6.1 (1992): 41-64, for a summary of research issues and findings. Note also an incisive critique by Arif Dirlik, 'Critical Reflections on "Chinese Capitalism" as Paradigm,' in *South China: State, Culture and Social Change during the 20th Century*, ed. Leo Douw and Peter Post (Amsterdam: Royal Netherlands Academy of Arts and Sciences, 1996), 3-17.

16 Among Hall's more influential writings are: 'Cultural Identity and Diaspora,' in *Identity: Community, Culture, and Difference*, ed. Jonathan Rutherford (London: Lawrence and Wishart, 1990), 222-37; 'The Local and the Global: Globalization and Ethnicity,' in *Culture, Globalization and the World System*, ed. Anthony D. King (Binghamton: Department of Art and Art History, State University of New York at Binghamton, 1991), 19-39; 'Old and New Identities, Old and New Ethnicities,' in ibid., 41-68; and 'The Question of Cultural Identity,' in *Modernity and Its Futures*, ed. Stuart Hall, David Held, and Tong McGrew (Cambridge: Polity, 1992), 273-325. For several other well known contributors to this literature, see Paul Gilroy, *The Black Atlantic: Modernity and Double Consciousness* (Cambridge, MA: Harvard University Press, 1993); James Clifford, 'Traveling Cultures,' in *Cultural Studies*, ed. L.

Grossberg, C. Nelson, and P. Treichler (New York: Routledge, 1992), 96-116; ibid., 'Diasporas,' *Cultural Anthropology* 9.3 (1994): 302-38; and Arjun Appadurai, 'Global Ethnoscapes: Notes and Queries for a Transnational Anthropology,' in *Recapturing Anthropology: Writing in the Present*, ed. Richard G. Fox (Santa Fe: School of American Research Press, 1991), 191-210; and ibid., 'Sovereignty Without Territoriality: Notes for a Postnational Geography,' in *The Geography of Identity*, ed. Patricia Yaeger (Ann Arbor: University of Michigan Press, 1996), 40-58. With regard to ethnic Chinese, see the recent collection in Aihwa Ong and Donald Nonini, eds., *Ungrounded Empires: The Cultural Politics of Modern Chinese Transnationalism* (New York: Routledge, 1997). In addition, see a very insightful piece by Ien Ang, an Australian scholar of Peranakan Chinese background. In a reflective autobiographical essay, 'To Be or Not to Be Chinese: Diaspora, Culture and Postmodern Ethnicity,' *Southeast Asian Journal of Social Science* 21.1 (1993): 1-17, she argues for a critical diaspora paradigm that would afford ethnic Chinese 'an autonomous space to determine their own trajectories for constructing cultural identities' (11), without being fixated in a position at once inferior to an imagined Chinese motherland and marginal to the mainstream society.

17 The search for a more complex and nuanced historical analysis of the period since 1945 is clearly evident in the following four volumes published between 1988 and 1998: Jennifer Cushman and Wang Gungwu, eds., *Changing Identities of the Southeast Asian Chinese since World War II* (Hong Kong: Hong Kong University Press, 1988); Suryadinata, *Ethnic Chinese as Southeast Asians*; Elizabeth Sinn, ed., *The Last Half Century of Chinese Overseas* (Hong Kong: Hong Kong University Press, 1998); and Gregor Benton and Frank N. Pieke, eds., *The Chinese in Europe* (New York: St. Martin's, 1998).

18 See two 1996 PhD dissertations on comparable transnational themes and diaspora conditions among the Chinese in the United States in the early twentieth century: Madeline Yuan-Yin Hsu, 'Living Abroad and Faring Well: Migration and Transnationalism in Taishan County, Guangdong, 1904-1939' (PhD diss., Yale University, 1996) and Haiming Liu, 'Between China and America: The Trans-Pacific History of the Chang Family' (PhD diss., University of California, Irvine, 1996).

19 This literature, primarily historical and anthropological, is growing fast, and I mention only a few examples of book-length monographs and conference volumes. On the Manchus, see Pamela Crossley, *Orphan Warriors: Three Manchu Generations and the End of the Qing World* (Princeton: Princeton University Press, 1990); and, more recently, *The Manchus* (Cambridge, MA: Blackwell, 1997). Important studies on the Muslims in China include Dru Gladney, *Muslim Chinese: Ethnic Nationalism in the People's Republic* (Cambridge, MA: Council on East Asian Studies, Harvard University, 1991); Jonathan N. Lipman, *Familiar Strangers: A History of Muslims in Northwest China* (Seattle: University of Washington Press, 1997); and Justin Jon Rudelson, *Oasis Identities: Uyghur Nationalism Along China's Silk Road* (New York: Columbia University Press, 1997). However, scholarly interest in the 'national minorities' has been extended to many other groups, as is indicated by Stevan Harrell, ed., *Cultural Encounters on China's Ethnic Frontiers* (Seattle: University of Washington Press, 1995); and Melissa J. Brown, ed., *Negotiating Ethnicities in China and Taiwan* (Berkeley: Center for Chinese Studies, University of California, 1996). On Shanghai, see Emily Honig, *Creating Chinese Ethnicity: Subei People in Shanghai, 1850-1980* (New Haven: Yale University Press, 1992); and Goodman, *Native Place, City, and Nation*. The standard reference on Hankou is, of course, William Rowe's two volumes, *Hankow: Commerce and Society* (cited earlier) and *Hankow: Conflict and Community in a Chinese City 1796-1895* (Stanford: Stanford University Press, 1989). Two important works on the Hakkas are Nicole Constable, *Christian Souls and Chinese Spirits: A Hakka Community in Hong Kong* (Berkeley: University of California Press, 1994); and the posthumous publication of Sow-Theng Leong, *Migration and Ethnicity in Chinese History: Hakkas, Pengmin, and Their Neighbors* (Stanford: Stanford University Press, 1997). For some of the latest research on the complex ethno-cultural environment along the South China coast, see David Faure and Helen F. Siu, eds., *Down to Earth: The Territorial Bond in South China* (Stanford: Stanford University Press, 1995); and Chen Chung-min, Chuang Ying-chang, and Huang Shu-min, eds., *Ethnicity in Taiwan: Social, Historical, and Cultural Perspectives* (Taipei: Institute of Ethnology, Academia Sinica, 1994).

20 I am not the first to contemplate the potential of an off-shore perspective in remapping the intellectual terrain of Chinese studies. A recent conference volume edited by David Ownby and Mary Somers Heidhues, entitled *'Secret Societies' Reconsidered: Perspectives on the Social History of Modern South China and Southeast Asia* (Armonk, NY: Sharpe, 1993), includes essays on South China and Southeast Asia. Another project, this one examining the Hakka in China and abroad, is Nicole Constable, ed., *Guest People: Hakka Identity in China and Abroad* (Seattle: University of Washington Press, 1996). See also the suggestive essays in Tu Wei-ming, ed., *The Living Tree: The Changing Meaning of Being Chinese Today* (Stanford: Stanford University Press, 1994), particularly Tu's own piece, 'Cultural China: The Periphery as the Center' (1-34); Wang Gungwu, 'Among Non-Chinese' (127-46); and Leo Lee, 'On the Margins of the Chinese Diaspora' (221-38). Another important work that claims the privilege of diaspora self-positioning is Rey Chow, *Writing Diaspora: Tactics of Intervention in Contemporary Cultural Studies* (Bloomington: Indiana University Press, 1993). While not really related, it is fascinating to discern similar pro-diaspora elements in modern Jewish thought. Especially among American Jewry, many have discussed the diaspora as a historical vehicle for the construction of Jewishness; others have pointed out that the precarious existence of the Israeli state makes it less than an ideal 'home.' Anti-Zionist radicals have even questioned the theological and moral foundation of a Jewish regime and proposed the diaspora as the best form of Jewish life. See Arnold M. Eisen, *Galut: Modern Jewish Reflection on Homelessness and Homecoming* (Bloomington: Indiana University Press, 1986), 148-80; Jonathan Webber, 'Modern Jewish Identities: The Ethnographic Complexities,' *Journal of Jewish Studies* 43.2 (1992): 246-67; and Daniel Boyarin and Jonathan Boyarin, 'Diaspora: Generation and the Ground of Jewish Identity,' in *Identities*, ed. Kwame Anthony Appiah and Henry Louis Gates, Jr. (Chicago: University of Chicago Press, 1995), 305-37.

Chapter 2: Early Settlement

1 David Lai, *Chinatowns: Towns within Cities in Canada* (Vancouver: UBC Press, 1988), 15-51. The 1885 *Report of the Royal Commission on Chinese Immigration* also contains valuable information on this earliest phase of Chinese settlement, which was confined basically to British Columbia.
2 James Morton, *In the Sea of Sterile Mountains: The Chinese in British Columbia* (Vancouver: Douglas, 1977), 144.
3 *Census of Canada*, 1911, vol. 1, 372-73. Lai, *Chinatowns*, 59, Table 12.
4 *Report of the Royal Commission on Chinese and Japanese Immigration* (1902), 13. The 1911 estimate is from Paul Yee, *Saltwater City: An Illustrated History of the Chinese in Vancouver* (Vancouver: Douglas and McIntyre, 1988), 49. There were Chinese prostitutes as well, though we know very little about this subject. The situation in early San Francisco is depicted in Benson Tong, *Unsubmissive Women: Chinese Prostitutes in Nineteenth-Century San Francisco* (Norman: University of Oklahoma Press, 1994).
5 Paul Yee, 'Chinese Business in Vancouver, 1886-1914' (MA thesis, University of British Columbia, 1983), 51-53.
6 The case of the Southeast Asian Chinese is well known. Michael Godley, *The Mandarin-Capitalists from Nanyang: Overseas Chinese Enterprise in the Modernization of China, 1893-1911* (Cambridge: Cambridge University Press, 1981). On Vancouver, see Edgar Wickberg, ed., *From China to Canada: A History of the Chinese Communities in Canada* (Toronto: McClelland and Stewart, 1982), 78.
7 The literature on secret societies in China is substantial. A recent collective effort is David Ownby and Mary Somers Heidhues, eds., *'Secret Societies' Reconsidered: Perspectives on the Social History of Modern South China and Southeast Asia* (Armonk, NY: Sharpe, 1993).
8 Lai, *Chinatowns*, 83; Wickberg, *From China to Canada*, 78.
9 For a succinct account of these events, see Jonathan Spence, *The Search for Modern China* (New York: Norton, 1990), 216-44.
10 Patricia Roy's *A White Man's Province: British Columbia Politicians and Chinese and Japanese Immigrants, 1858-1914* (Vancouver: UBC Press, 1989) has the most comprehensive discussion on anti-Asian legislation in early British Columbia. On anti-Asian riots, see Wickberg, *From China to Canada*, 62-63; and Howard Sugimoto, 'The Vancouver Riots of 1907: A

Canadian Episode,' in *East Across the Pacific*, ed. Hilary Conroy and Scott Miyakawa (Honolulu: University of Hawaii Press, 1972), 92-126.

11 David T.H. Lee, *Jianada huaqiao shi* [A History of the Chinese in Canada] (Taipei: Canada Free Press, 1967), 227-320; Eve Armentrout Ma, *Revolutionaries, Monarchists and Chinatowns: Chinese Politics in Americas and the 1911 Revolution* (Honolulu: University of Hawaii Press, 1990). On '*huaqiao*' as an ideological and nationalistic construct of this period, see Wang Gungwu, 'A Note on the Origins of *Hua-ch'iao* [huaqiao],' in his *Community and Nation: Essays on Southeast Asia and the Chinese* (Singapore: Heinemenn, 1981), 118-27.

12 The figures are from Wickberg, *From China to Canada*, 94-95, 306, Table 10; and Yee, *Saltwater City*, 49-52 ff.

13 Wickberg, *From China to Canada*, 112-13, 315-18, Tables 19 and 20.

14 Gillian Creese, 'Organizing Against Racism in the Workplace: Chinese Workers in Vancouver before the Second World War,' *Canadian Ethnic Studies* 19.3 (1987): 35-46.

15 Wickberg, *From China to Canada*, 101-15; Harry Con, *Zhongguo hongmen zai jianada* [The Chinese Freemasons in Canada] (Vancouver: Chinese Freemasons Canadian Headquarters, 1989), 15-39.

16 Wickberg, 'Overseas Chinese Adaptive Organizations, Past and Present,' in *Reluctant Exiles? Migration from Hong Kong and the New Overseas Chinese*, ed. Ronald Skeldon (Armonk, NY: Sharpe, 1994), 69-84.

17 Wickberg, *From China to Canada*, 108-9. On the segmentary structure, the classic treatment is Lawrence Crissmen, 'The Segmentary Structure of Urban Overseas Chinese Communities,' *Man* (n.s.) 2.2 (1967): 185-204.

18 In 1923, the Canadian Parliament passed the Chinese Immigration Act, which aimed at virtual exclusion. The only exceptions under the new regulations were university students, merchants of substantial fortune engaged in import-export trade, Canadian-born Chinese returning from several years of education in China, and diplomatic personnel. See Wickberg, *From China to Canada*, 135-45.

19 In 1931, for the first time, more Chinese in British Columbia reportedly resided in the two cities of Vancouver and Victoria than in the scattered smaller settlements in the province. Wickberg, *From China to Canada*, 303-4, Tables 7 and 8.

20 Quoted in Lai, *Chinatowns*, 85, note 81.

21 Lee, *Jianada huaqiao shi*, 334-44. Wickberg, *From China to Canada*, 166-67, 174-77, 319-21, Table 21.

22 The most detailed study on Chinese education in early British Columbia is Timothy Stanley, 'Defining the Chinese Other: White Supremacy, Schooling and Social Structure in British Columbia before 1923' (PhD diss., University of British Columbia, 1991), see especially 266-318. Unfortunately, his work only covers the period up to the eve of exclusion.

23 Wickberg, *From China to Canada*, 157-68, 188-91; Yee, *Saltwater City*, 94-99.

24 Stanley has focused on this complex subject of Chinese identity construction in the public realm in turn-of-the-century British Columbia in his latest work: 'Schooling, White Supremacy and the Formation of a Chinese Merchant Public in British Columbia,' *BC Studies* 107 (autumn 1995): 3-29; and '"Chinamen, Wherever We Go": Chinese Nationalism and Guangdong Merchants in British Columbia, 1871-1911,' *Canadian Historical Review* 77.4 (1996): 475-503.

Chapter 3: Renewed Immigration

1 For an account of this campaign, see Edgar Wickberg, ed., *From China to Canada: A History of the Chinese Communities in Canada* (Toronto: McClelland and Stewart, 1982), 204-9. He has given more attention to the larger Canadian context in his article, 'Chinese Organizations and the Canadian Political Process: Two Case Studies,' in *Ethnicity, Power and Politics in Canada*, ed. Jorgen Dahlie and Tissa Fernando (Toronto: Methuen, 1981), 172-76. Note also E.J. McEvoy, '"A Symbol of Racial Discrimination": The Chinese Immigration Act and Canada's Relations with China, 1942-1947,' *Canadian Ethnic Studies* 14.3 (1982): 24-42, which suggests that the effort at redress benefited from the wartime communication between the governments of Canada and Nationalist China.

2 In Wickberg, *From China to Canada*, 207.

3   See Peter Li's earlier work, co-authored with Singh Bolaria, 'Canadian Immigration Policy and Assimilationist Theories,' in *Economy, Class and Social Reality*, ed. John Fry (Scarborough, Ontario: Butterworths, 1979), 411-22; and his own *The Chinese in Canada* (Toronto: Oxford University Press, 1988), 88-92.

4   There is a rather sketchy research report written by William Willmott in the early 1960s, in which he briefly identifies three different groups within the Chinese population in Vancouver at that time; namely, the elderly immigrants, the local-born Chinese, and those 'recently arrived immigrants of the Orient.' Entitled 'A Study of the Chinese Community in Vancouver: Preliminary Report' (n.d.), the report is buried in the Chinese Canadian Research Collections, Special Collections, UBC, along with some interview materials on Chinese leaders under restricted access.

5   Wickberg, *From China to Canada*, 148-203. See also the demographic analysis by Li in *The Chinese in Canada*, 60-70.

6   *Census of Canada*, 1951, 54-11, 55-30, 60-11, and 61-30.

7   William Willmott, 'Some Aspects of Chinese Communities in British Columbia Towns,' *BC Studies* 1 (winter 1968-69): 27-36. Graham Johnson has also remarked on the disintegration of minor Chinese settlements and the increasing concentration of the Chinese population in large metropolitan centres after the Second World War. See Wickberg, *From China to Canada*, 217-18. David Lai's recent study of the lifecycle of Canadian Chinatowns is also relevant. See his explanations for their general decline in the 1950s and 1960s in *Chinatowns: Towns within Cities in Canada* (Vancouver: UBC Press, 1988), 122-26.

8   This special concession was withdrawn in 1955, though those granted admission under this arrangement continued to arrive at the point of entry in 1956. Many scholars seem to be unaware of the effect of this policy. Peter Li, for instance, takes the decline of child immigration in the early 1950s at face value when he discusses the same statistical information in *The Chinese in Canada*, 92-93.

9   See Yuen-fong Woon's *The Excluded Wife* (Montreal and Kingston: McGill-Queen's University Press, 1998) for a fictional account of the experience of Sau Ping, who joined her husband in Vancouver for the first time in 1955.

10   *Chinese Times*, 14 November 1948, reported on one of these gatherings.

11   See Peter Li's national-level analysis in 'Immigration Laws and Family Patterns: Some Demographic Changes among Chinese Families in Canada, 1885-1971,' *Canadian Ethnic Studies* 12.1 (1980): 58-73.

12   *Chinatown News*, 3 February 1955. The circulation of ethnic newspapers in Canada is often a matter of speculation, as Jean Burnet has pointed out in *Coming Canadians: An Introduction to a History of Canada's Peoples* (Toronto: McClelland and Stewart, 1988), 200; my following estimation is no exception. The leading *Chinese Times* increased its local circulation from about 2,000 to 3,000 copies during the postwar period. It was followed closely by the *Chinese Voice*, which was founded in 1953. The *New Republic*, relocated from Victoria in 1958, was way behind. As for the language schools – namely, the Chinese Public School, Mon Keong, and Tai Kung – all underwent major renovation and expansion to accommodate a larger student body, which increased from about 400 in 1945 to 1,000 in the 1960s. *Huaqiao gongli xuexiao choumu jingfei zhengxinlu* [Chinese Public School Fund-raising Report] 1962; *Wenjiang xuexiao xiaokan* [Mon Keong School, 1925-1985] 1985; and David T.H. Lee, *Jianada huaqiao shi* [A History of the Chinese in Canada] (Taipei: Canada Free Press, 1967), 334-39.

13   See the following published church histories: *Yunbu huaren zhanglaohui qishi zhounian jinian ji mingxie* [Thanksgiving and Souvenir Publication of the Seventieth Anniversary of the Chinese Presbyterian Church in Vancouver, 1895-1965] 1965; *Yunbu huaren zhanglaohui jiushi zhounian tangqing* [Chinese Presbyterian Church of Vancouver Ninetieth Anniversary Souvenir, 1895-1985] 1985; 'A Brief History of the Parish Church of the Good Shepherd,' in *The Dedication of the Church of the Good Shepherd Souvenir*, 1985; *Zili zhonghua jidu jiaohui qishiwu zhounian gan'en jinian kan* [Seventy-fifth Anniversary Thanksgiving Report of the Christ Church of China] 1986; and *Jianada yungaohua huaren xiehe jiaohui jiushisan zhounian jinian tekan* [Ninety-third Anniversary of the Chinese United Church, Vancouver, BC, 1881-1981] 1981. My reading of archival materials of the Chinese United Church in Vancouver gives the same

impression. See *Minutes of the Official Board*, 1953-67, and *Annual Reports*, 1959-67. Because of the focus of this study, not to mention the rather undeveloped state of research on the history of Chinese Christian churches in Canada, I am able to make only scattered references to Christianity in these pages. Perhaps the cases of some exceptionally interesting individuals, such as Father Peter Chow (mentioned later in Chapter 3) and Reverend Andrew Lam (mentioned in Chapters 4 and 7) will stimulate future inquiry into the impact of Christianity on the ethnic Chinese and their evolving sense of identity. For some pioneering work on Chinese Christian churches in the United States, see the following two dissertations: Wesley S. Woo, 'Protestant Work among the Chinese in the San Francisco Bay Area, 1850-1920' (PhD diss., Graduate Theological Union, Berkeley, 1983); and Timothy Tseng, 'Ministry at Arms' Length: Asian Americans in the Racial Ideology of American Mainline Protestants, 1882-1952' (PhD diss., Union Theological Seminary, New York, 1994).

14 *Chinese Voice*, 25 April 1958. Also Jack Eng, interview by author, 12 June 1992; Beven Jangze, interview by author, 12 June 1992. Both of them started their real estate businesses targeting Chinese customers in the early 1960s.

15 Several articles in *Chinese Voice* – 10 November 1954, 5 August and 12 November 1955, and 1 March 1956 – state their views.

16 The boarding houses were a typical ethnic institution found among many immigrant societies in North America in the first phase of their migration and settlement. However, we know little about their history, especially among the Chinese. For an illuminating study of the Italian 'lodging houses' in Canada, see Robert Harney, 'Boarding and Belonging: Thoughts on Sojourning Institutions,' *Urban History Review* 2 (October 1987): 8-37.

17 *Wu xushan tong caoliu bao* [Ing Suey Sun Tong Account Books], 1936-43, 1944-51, and 1952-55.

18 City of Vancouver, Planning Department for Housing Research Committee, *Vancouver Redevelopment Study* 1957, 43-44.

19 *Wu xushan tong caoliu bao*.

20 *Vancouver Redevelopment Study*, 43-44.

21 Two typical examples are essays by 'Cen Hai' on 'Fangkou' [The Boarding Houses] and 'Ma Bing' on 'Danshen Guahan' [The Bachelors], in *Chinese Voice*, 27 June 1955 and 26 October 1957, respectively.

22 *Chinatown News*, 18 October 1953. More will be said about the Pender Y in Chapter 4.

23 *Jiayun hansheng tiyuhui disi zhounian jinian tekan* [Fourth Anniversary Souvenir Issue of the Hon Hsing Athletic Club, Vancouver, Canada] 1944; *Huang hansheng tiyuhui qi zhounian jinian ji* [Chronicle of the Wong Hon Hsing Athletic Club Seventh Anniversary] 1947; and *Jiayun hansheng tiyuhui chengli ershiwu zhounian jinian tekan* [Twenty-Fifth Anniversary Souvenir Issue of the Hon Hsing Athletic Club, Vancouver, Canada] 1965.

24 *Chinese Voice*, 12-13 September 1955.

25 Ibid., 8 April 1954 and 4-5 December 1957. The following piece of reminiscence by Feng Langfan, 'Ru zhen hua sheng shiwu nian' [Having Joined Jin Wah Sing for Fifteen Years] is very informed. It was serialized in ibid., 1-18 October 1969. I also benefited from my interviews with George K. Louie (19 November 1990, 23 and 27 February 1991) and Y.S. Lee (18 January and 23 February 1991). Both Louie and Lee are Jin Wah Sing veterans who participated in its revival in 1954, not long after their arrival in Canada. Later, they became regular Freemasons, then joined the more exclusive Dart Coon Club, and eventually proceeded to the executive level.

26 The article, entitled 'You zhen hua shen jinian shou dao ta de lichang' [Let Me Talk about Jin Wah Sing's Anniversary and Its Standpoint], was written by 'Yi Yang,' *Chinese Voice*, 5-8 June 1957.

27 *Chinese Voice*, 7 and 15 June 1961.

28 The case of the Lee Clan Association was reported in the *Chinese Voice*, 2 August and 14 November 1965. Another unfortunate example is the Shon Yee Benevolent Association, as admitted in its official history, *Jianada wengehua tiecheng chongyi zonghui chengli qishi zhounian jinian tekan* [Souvenir Publication of the Seventieth Anniversary of the Shon Yee Benevolent Association of Canada, Vancouver, 1914-1984] 1984, 24-27. William Willmott has offered some contemporary observations on the demise of the youth corps by the early

1960s in his 'Chinese Clan Associations in Vancouver,' *Man* 64 (1964): 33-37, but he has provided no explanation.

29 Two representative articles are 'Qingnian de renwu' [The Responsibilities of the Youth] by 'Tong Gang,' and 'Huaqiao shehui yingyou de renshi' [Things that Overseas Chinese Society Should Know] by 'Zhong Wai,' in *Chinese Voice*, 26 February and 4 July 1958.

30 Unfortunately, no survey data of any kind exist on the backgrounds of the new immigrants. In addition to personal interviews, I have based my discussion primarily on their writings. As I suggest in Chapter 6, it is likely that the youthful and educational backgrounds of the newcomers and the potential cultural influence of postwar Hong Kong shaped the outlooks and the styles of this generation.

31 For example, full of anger and frustration over this issue is an essay by Chen Zongchao, 'Huaqiao qingnian de chulu wenti' [The Prospect for the Overseas Chinese Youth], *Chinese Voice*, 30 October 1954. Highly critical of the myth of the 'Gold Mountain' is another by 'Jiang Qing,' 'Dao jia liangnian de huiyi' [A Reminiscence of My Two Years in Canada], ibid., 7-9 July 1954. It is not clear how many young Chinese immigrants of this period had the opportunity to attain further education in Vancouver and how many were immediately ushered into the labour force. For the older cohort, say, between eighteen and twenty-five, who were admitted on compassionate grounds up to 1955, the chance to go to school must have been rather slim.

32 For example, Wu Yihong, 'Qiaotuan shi "fengjian de baolei" ma?' [Are the Traditional Organizations a 'Feudalist Citadel?'] and 'Xin Huaqiao,' 'Shicha qiaowu' [Inspecting Overseas Chinese Affairs], in *Chinese Voice*, 20 May 1958 and 12 June 1954, respectively.

33 Essays written by young Chinese on this issue are the most numerous, indicating the intensity of this grievance. See two typical pieces in 'Ma Bing,' 'Fu yu zi' [Father and Son], and 'Ling Ding,' 'Laonian yu qingnian' [The Elderly and the Youth], in *Chinese Voice*, 10 November 1956 and 11-13 April 1959.

34 Such was the title of the essay by 'Ai Ming' in *Chinese Voice*, 12 May 1954. A similarly disparaging assessment can be found in Zhen Jianyun, 'Huaqiao shehui wenhua de wojian' [My View of the Culture of Overseas Chinese Society], ibid., 14-21 January 1956.

35 For a statement on its editorial stance, see 10-11 February 1954.

36 *Chinese Voice*, 30-31 May 1956, reprinted in Peter Chow, *Jing quan ji* [The Fountain] (Vancouver: Chinese Catholic Publishing Bureau 1956; 2nd edition 1958), 132-34. *Shengfangji tong jinqing jinian* [Saint Francis Xavier Parish Golden Jubilee 1933-1983] 1983, contains a piece of Father Chow's reminiscences. Father Peter Chow, interview by author, 9 June 1992.

37 *Chinatown News*, 3 July 1956.

38 *Chinese Times*, 18 February 1955.

39 *Chinese Voice*, 1-2 August 1954. Yee, *Saltwater City: An Illustrated History of the Chinese in Vancouver* (Vancouver: Douglas and McIntyre, 1988), 109-10, 126-27.

40 *Chinese Voice*, 3 and 14 February 1958. *Enping zong huiguan nanping bieshu lianhe kenqinhui tekan* [Yin Ping District Association Headquarters Nam Ping Bitsuey Joint Convention Special Publication] 1981, 105. On the Mah Society see *Chinese Voice*, 31 October and 16 November 1964, and 15 April 1966.

41 *Chinese Voice*, 8 February 1954.

42 Information on membership is sparse. Also, the extent of overlapping membership between the autonomous societies and the auxiliaries, and among the independent societies themselves, is not clear, though a few cases of dual membership are known.

43 *Chinese Voice*, 17 and 19 October 1959. My interviews with two Hai Fung Club members were very helpful to my understanding of its visions and activities. Yim Tse, interview by author, 6 November 1990 and 28 February 1991. K. Tong Au, interview by author, 24 April 1991.

44 *Haifeng hui jinian kan* [Hai Fung Club: A Souvenir Publication] 1968, 3.

45 The meaning of the name 'Hai Fung' is stated in *Haifeng hui jinian kan*, 2. For an insider's perspective on the reorientation in late 1959, see the commemorative essay written by K. Tong Au, the chairperson during the fifth anniversary, in *Chinese Voice*, 30 November 1961.

46 A synopsis of the lecture is available in *Haifeng hui jinian kan*, 12.

47 *Jiayun hansheng tiyuhui chengli ershiwu zhounian jinian tekan.* See the section 'A report on recent activities.' Another indication of the close connection between two societies is the fact that, in 1961, the Hai Fung Club started to rent a floor in the Wong Kung Har Tong Headquarters Building on Pender Street as its clubhouse.

48 *Chinese Voice*, 4 March 1964 and 12 March 1965.

49 Apart from these social and cultural activities, another very revealing event was the Hai Fung Club's involvement in an intense debate on the reform of the CBA in the early 1960s. The club advocated a restructuring of the CBA's system of representation to reflect the growing diversity within the ethnic group. This episode will be discussed in Chapter 5.

50 'Zongqin shetuan yu huaqiao' [Clan Organizations and the Overseas Chinese], *Chinese Voice*, 14 December 1960.

51 For some scathing criticisms of the viability of youth auxiliaries as an option for youth organizations, see two articles furnished by 'Lao Er' and 'Lao San' (probably by the same author) in *Chinese Voice*, 13 and 22 April 1960.

52 See, for example, the Chinese Literary Society founded in early 1955. Its early activities were reported in the literary supplement of *Chinese Voice*, 11 February; 2 March; 1-5 April; 5 and 18 May; 16, 19, and 26 July; 28 December 1955; and 7-11 June 1956.

53 *Chinese Voice*, 17 March 1955, 28 January and 7 June 1956.

54 For instance, see the promotion of traditional and modern Chinese music in Wang Jiequn, 'Benbu ge yinyue tuanti jianjie' [A Brief Account of the Musical Societies in our (China)town], *Chinese Voice*, 12-14 August 1963. On the theme of rejecting cultural maintenance in favour of cultural reform and advancement, see 'You Long,' 'Haiwai qingnian ying zhuzhong zuguo wenhua' [Overseas Chinese Youth should Pay more Attention to the Culture of the Ancestral Country], ibid., 5-6 May 1959.

55 See the examples of the Chinese Literary Society and the Yun Qing Hui in *Chinese Voice*, 11 February 1955 and 4-5 March 1965, respectively.

56 Little is known about the early history of the Chinese Youth Association. The best internal source is the *Da Zhong Bao*, which started publishing in February 1961. Unfortunately, the only extant holding, at the Asian Library, UBC, begins with December 1965. The political inclinations of the association will be discussed in detail in Chapter 6.

57 Yee, *Saltwater City*, 110, 129-30, offers some vivid reminiscences by Jimmy Lum. My understanding of the Chinese Youth Association also benefits from an interview with another member, Victor Lee, 19 March 1991.

58 *Chinese Voice*, 26 January 1963.

59 *New Republic*, 29-31 January 1963. The article also appeared in *Chinese Times*, 1-2 February 1963.

60 *Chinese Times*, 8-9 February 1963.

61 *Chinese Voice*, 25 February 1963.

Chapter 4: Local-Born Chinese

1 David Lee, *Jianada huaqiao shi* [A History of the Chinese in Canada] (Taipei: Canada Free Press, 1967), 388-89.

2 On the marginalization of the local-born in other immigrant minorities in North America, see Takaki's account of the native-born Chinese Americans and Korean Americans on the eve of the Pacific War in his *Strangers from a Different Shore: A History of Asian Americans* (New York: Penguin, 1989), 257-69, 286-93.

3 Similar information seems to be more available in the case of the American-born Chinese. See Him Mark Lai's discussion of the rise of the American-born Chinese as a social force in the early twentieth century in *Cong huaqiao dao huaren: ershi shiji meiguo huaren shehui fazhanshi* [From Overseas Chinese to Ethnic Chinese: A History of Chinese Society in the United States in the Twentieth Century] (Hong Kong: Joint Publishing, 1992), 130-73; and the more recent work of Judy Yung, *Unbound Feet: A Social History of Chinese Women in San Francisco* (Berkeley: University of California Press, 1995), 106-77, 198-209.

4 *Census of Canada* 1951, 61-30.

5 Ibid., 1981, 4-13, 4-14. 'Greater Vancouver' includes the City of Vancouver and a dozen neighbouring municipalities.

6   David Lai, *Chinatowns: Towns within Cities in Canada* (Vancouver: UBC Press, 1988), 231-51.
7   From the long quotation at the beginning of this chapter, we see Lee shares this position. On Wickberg's view, see *From China to Canada: A History of the Chinese Communities in Canada* (Toronto: McClelland and Stewart, 1982), 94-98. I am aware of the activities of the Chinese Canadian Club, involving some local-born Chinese in Victoria and Vancouver, as early as the second decade of the twentieth century and continuing into the mid-1920s. Its functions were sporadic at best, indicating the lack of a critical mass.
8   Paul Yee makes the same point when he writes: 'The War focused attention on one special segment of the community: the new Canadian-borns.' See particularly the excerpts of interviews with several Chinese veterans in his *Saltwater City: An Illustrated History of the Chinese in Vancouver* (Vancouver: Douglas and McIntyre, 1988), 99-105 passim.
9   'Memorandum and Petition Submitted to the Honourable, The Premier of British Columbia, John Hart, Esq., and the Honourable Ministers of the Executive Council of the Government of the Province of British Columbia, on February 16, 1945, by a Delegation representing the Chinese Canadian Association,' National Archives of Canada, Roy Graham Dunlop Papers, MG 30 D 349, vol. 1, II 53-54, BC-1944-61. See also Carol Lee, 'The Road to Enfranchisement: Chinese and Japanese in British Columbia,' *BC Studies* 30 (summer 1976): 56-57. The relationship of this organization with the former Chinese Canadian Club (Note 7 above) is not clear.
10 See Lee, "The Road to Enfranchisement." Also useful is a brief article by Foon Sien Wong, "Past Achievements, Future Aspirations," in *Chinatown News*, 3 January 1956.
11 I have the impression from my interviews with members of the Chinese Veterans that the group was not able to identify other tangible goals. Moreover, at that time many members of the organization were preoccupied with the struggle to start a career and other personal problems of adjustment. Harry Con, interviews by author, 9 November 1990, 18 January 1991, and 12 June 1992. Gim Foon, interviews by author, 21 February 1991 and 15 March 1991.
12 *Chinese Voice*, 10-11 May 1961.
13 Also on the roster were Dr. Fred Chu, a Chinese pioneer in the medical profession; Tim and Tong Louie from the H.Y. Louie family, which operated one of the largest wholesale grocery businesses in Western Canada; and the Victoria-born brothers Charlie Kent and Ben Kent Chan, a very enterprising pair of Chinese businessmen. The group was joined by the first Chinese pharmacist in the city, another bank manager, a Chinese architect, a couple of lawyers, and some local-born businessmen, raising the membership of this elitist organization to about fifty by 1970. *Vancouver Chinatown Lions Club Thirtieth Anniversary 1954-1984* 1984, 11-17.
14 *Chinatown News*, 18 July 1958; *Vancouver Chinatown Lions Club*, introductory page, 14-17, 49.
15 *Vancouver Chinatown Lions Club*, 28-37; *Chinatown News*, 18 July 1958 and 18 December 1960.
16 My use of the 'cultural performance' analogy is inspired by Victor Turner, 'Social Drama and Ritual Metaphor,' in *Ritual, Play, and Performance: Readings in the Social Sciences/Theatre*, ed. Richard Schechner and Mady Schuman (New York: Seabury, 1976), 97-120; and *From Ritual to Theater: The Human Seriousness of Play* (New York: Performing Arts Journal Publications, 1982).
17 *Chinatown News*, 3 September 1953 and 3 December 1965. The connection was also mentioned to me during an interview with Fred Chu, 21 November 1990.
18 *Chinatown News*, 18 June, 3 July, 3 August, and 3 November 1965. See also *Chinese Voice*, 27 January and 17 June 1966. Bevan Jangze, interview by author, 12 June 1992.
19 This observation is based mainly on the reading of materials in the archives of the Chinese United Church: *Minutes of the Official Board* 1953-67, and *Annual Reports* 1959-67.
20 *POW: Ubyssey Special Edition*, vol. 75, no. 14 (27 October 1992), 1. Wickberg, *From China to Canada*, 95.
21 The official figure was reported in *Chinese Voice*, 22 and 24 February 1958. On the club's membership, see *Chinatown News*, 18 October 1955 and 18 November 1966. On its activities, see *Chinatown News*, 18 February and 18 March 1954; 3 March 1955; 18 January, 18

May, and 3 July 1961. See also *Chinese Voice*, 23 March 1954. Rod Wong, interview by author, 11 January 1991. Shirley Wong, interview by author, 23 January 1991. Both of them attended UBC in the early 1950s and were members of the Varsity Club.

22 The archives of the Chinese United Church contain some evidence of its youth ministry. Note the *Annual Reports* 1959-67, particularly the sections on youth activities and Christian education. For church sponsorship of scout teams, see *Chinatown News*, 18 October 1956 and 3 July 1961.

23 *Chinatown News*, 3 September and 18 October 1953; 3 and 18 February, 18 April 1954; 18 November 1957.

24 The magazine was originally called *Chinatown*. It is not clear why it was renamed *Chinatown News* at the beginning of its fourth year in September 1956. I will refer to it as *Chinatown News* throughout this study.

25 The *Chinese News Weekly* is mentioned in Yee, *Saltwater City*, 83. I have not seen a single copy of this publication. Only a few issues of the *New Citizen* are available in the Chinese Canadian Research Collections, Special Collections, UBC, box 21. This biweekly was relocated to Toronto in 1951 and came to an end soon thereafter.

26 Roy Mah was born in Edmonton. His father took the whole family back to the home village in South China when he was four, and Roy did not return to Canada until he was twelve. The young Roy Mah had shown interest in journalism while attending school in Victoria; he also claims to have started the *New Citizen* in 1949. For a few years after returning from the war, he worked for the International Woodworkers of America, organizing Chinese labourers in Vancouver. Evelyn Huang, *Chinese Canadians: Voices from a Community* (Vancouver: Douglas and McIntyre, 1992), 70-79, provides some biographical information from an interview. For its stance, see the editorials in the first few issues of the *Chinatown News*, – 3 September, 3 October, and 18 October 1953.

27 Regarding the importance of print-language on the imagination of cultural fields and boundaries, see Benedict Anderson, *Imagined Communities: Reflections on the Origins and Spread of Nationalism*, rev. ed.(London: Verso, 1991), 44-45.

28 For example, the hiring of the first Chinese employee at city hall was made into a cover story. Other news stories about Chinese entering the medical and legal professions were all reported diligently. See *Chinatown News*, 18 November 1953; 16 June 1954; 18 August and 3 October 1961.

29 *Chinatown News*, 3 August 1971.

30 The distinction between the two concepts is noteworthy, for it was seldom clearly made in Canadian society at large during that time. For another example of the advocacy of cultural pluralism in the early postwar period by an Asian minority in Vancouver, see Chihiro Otsuka, 'Remaking an Institution and Community: The Vancouver Japanese Language School after the War' (MA thesis, University of British Columbia, 1995).

31 *Chinatown News*, 3 May 1958; 18 April and 3 December 1959; 3 October 1960; 18 August 1961; 18 April 1962; 3 and 18 April, and 18 May 1964. The reactions to urban redevelopment from other sectors of the Chinese minority and the dramatic turn of events in the late 1960s are examined in detail in Chapter 6.

32 Paul Evans and Michael Frolic, eds., *Reluctant Adversaries: Canada and the People's Republic of China, 1949-1971* (Toronto: University of Toronto Press, 1991).

33 *Chinatown News*, 18 August 1968.

34 See its submission to the Chinese consular officials in 1936, including a membership registry, in the National Archives of Canada, Chinese Consular Records, MG 10 C2, vol. 4, file 5. Its activities in the postwar period were occasionally reported. *Chinese Times*, 7 and 12 August 1948, 25 August 1952; *Chinese Voice*, 22 February, 14 May, 24 June, 22 July 1954; 13 August 1955.

35 *Chinese Voice*, 3 August and 14 September 1957.

36 Ibid., 7, 11, 19, and 25 February, 1 and 10 March, 14-16 April, 7 and 30 June 1958. The Chinese version of the new constitution also appeared in ibid., 12-18 March 1958.

37 *Chinatown News*, 3 July 1958.

38 *Chinese Voice*, 22 March 1958. It would be too much of a digression to dwell on the history of this organization in the 1960s. For several years after the reform and before it lost its

momentum, the Chinese Association of Commerce was another centre of public activity for the senior native-born Chinese. It interceded frequently with the local authorities on behalf of Chinese business interests and organized public charities. It was best remembered for many of its social activities, including the public celebration of the Chinese New Year, starting in 1959, and the competition for the title of 'Miss Vancouver Chinatown' in the following year.

39 *Chinese Voice*, 22 March and 4 July 1958.
40 Ibid., 2-3 November 1960.
41 The case of the Lim Sai Ho Tong is documented in *Lim xihe zongtong qiumu gongsuo hebing jinxi jinian tekan* [Special Issue of the Lim Sai Ho Tong Headquarters – Kow Mock Kung So Amalgamation Golden Anniversary] 1980, Chronology section, 14. Song Ping, a Mainland Chinese scholar, has recently examined the provision of scholarships and bursaries by the Chinese clansmen organizations in the Philippines and has discerned a similar tension between cultural retention and local adaptation. 'Feilubin huaren zongqinhui de jiangzhu xuejin zhidu' [The System of Scholarship and Bursary in the Chinese Clansmen Associations in the Philippines], *Overseas Chinese Historical Studies* (Beijing) 27 (1994): 16-21.
42 *Chinese Voice*, 25 January 1954.
43 The quote is from *Chinese Voice*, 26 January 1954. See a letter by 'Cao Xingren' in the issue of 6 February 1954.
44 *Chinatown News*, 3 February 1954.
45 See, for example, various articles in *Chinese Voice*, 30 April-1 May 1954, and 1 September 1956; *Chinatown News*, 3 April 1968.
46 *Chinese Voice*, 3 November 1956; 25-29 May and 10 June 1957.
47 *Chinatown News*, 3 February 1956.
48 Ibid., 18 February 1956.
49 Ibid., 18 March 1956.
50 *Chinese Voice*, 17 November 1956.
51 Ibid., 20 October 1956.
52 *Chinatown News*, 18 March 1964.
53 Ibid., 18 March 1966.
54 Ibid., 18 February and 18 March 1954; 3 March 1955; 18 January, 18 May, and 3 July 1961. *Chinese Voice*, 23 March 1954.
55 *Huaxin ji: zhongguo liu jia tongxuehui niankan chuangkanhao* [Chinese Overseas Students Association Yearbook, the First Issue] 1962. According to a report in the *Chinese Voice*, the first Chinese student of new immigrant background graduated from UBC in 1957. *Chinese Voice*, 21 May 1957.
56 Yim Tse, interview by author, 28 February 1991. Tse arrived as a foreign student at UBC in 1959 and was actively involved in this campus organization. *Chinatown News*, 18 January and 18 May 1961. *Huaxin ji* [Chinese Overseas Students Association Yearbook] 1965, 10.
57 *Chinese Voice*, 15 and 18 February 1964.
58 Ibid., 22 February 1964.
59 Ibid., 25 February-3 March 1964.
60 *Chinatown News*, 3 March 1964.

Chapter 5: Old-Timers, Public Rituals

1 See Paul Wong, et al., 'From Despotism to Pluralism: The Evolution of Voluntary Organizations in Chinese American Communities,' *Ethnic Groups* 8 (1990): 15-33, which generalizes about the developments of ethnic Chinese organizations in the United States after the Second World War.
2 Baureiss, 'Ethnic Resilience and Discrimination: Two Chinese Communities in Canada,' *Journal of Ethnic Studies* 10.1 (1982): 69-87. For a similar argument about the Chinese in the United States, see Him Mark Lai, 'Historical Development of the Chinese Consolidated Benevolent Association/*Huiguan* System,' in *Chinese America: History and Perspectives 1987* (San Francisco: Chinese Historical Society of America, 1987), 42.
3 In Edgar Wickberg, ed., *From China to Canada: A History of the Chinese Communities in Canada* (Toronto: McClelland and Stewart, 1982), 231.

4 For example, Chia-ling Kuo, *Social and Political Change in New York's Chinatown: The Role of Voluntary Associations* (New York: Praeger, 1977). A most explicit application of modernization theory is Thomas Tsu-wee Tan, 'Singapore Modernization: A Study of Traditional Chinese Voluntary Associations in Social Change' (PhD diss., University of Virginia, 1983).

5 With reference to Vancouver, see the following: Hayne Yip Wai, 'The Chinese and the Voluntary Association in British Columbia: A Political Machine Interpretation' (MA thesis, Queen's University, 1970); and Brij Lal, 'The Chinese Benevolent Association of Vancouver, 1889-1960: An Analytical History,' unpublished paper, 1975.

6 Between 1945 and 1970, the turnover was negligible. Four existing associations, including the Chee Duck Tong, Yee Fung Toy Tong, Yue San Association, and Chew Luen Society, became national headquarters like many other organizations in Vancouver. See their files in the Chinese Canadian Research Collections, Special Collections, UBC, boxes 2 and 3. Two clan organizations, the Nam Yeung Tong and Gee How Oak Tin Association, were founded, as reported in the *Chinese Voice*, 26 November 1955 and 20 March 1962. The dissolution of the Lu Ming Bitsuey was mentioned in ibid., 20 September 1965 and 2 February 1966. Some others might have become defunct without being noticed. My estimate of some forty traditional organizations in this period agrees with that of Graham Johnson in Wickberg, *From China to Canada*, 329-31.

7 Wu Yihong, 'Qiaotuan shi "fengjian de baolei" ma?' [Are the Traditional Organizations a 'Feudalist Citadel?']; and 'Zhang Wang,' 'Weihe youren yaozuo "qiaoling"?' [Why Do Some People Want to Be 'Leaders' (in the organizations)?], in *Chinese Voice*, 20 May 1958 and 1 February 1969, respectively.

8 Catherine Bell, *Ritual Theory, Ritual Practice* (New York: Oxford University Press, 1992), 19-21.

9 Turner's numerous works include both case studies of ritual in African societies and theoretical discussions on ritual and other related concepts. I have relied principally on his collection of articles in *From Ritual to Theatre: The Human Seriousness of Play* (New York: Performing Arts Journal Publications, 1982); and an essay entitled 'Social Dramas and Ritual Metaphor,' in *Ritual, Play, and Performance: Readings in the Social Sciences/Theatre*, ed. Richard Schechner and Mady Schuman (New York: Seabury, 1976), 97-120. Among Chinese specialists, Turner's ideas have inspired some fascinating studies on political theatres and rituals, such as Joseph Esherick and Jeffrey Wasserstrom, 'Acting Out Democracy: Political Theatre in Modern China,' *Journal of Asian Studies* 49.4 (1990): 835-65; and Jeffrey Wasserstrom, *Student Protests in Twentieth-Century China: The View from Shanghai* (Stanford: Stanford University Press, 1991).

10 Turner, *From Ritual to Theatre*, 82. Clifford Geertz's original formulation is in his essay 'Religion as a Cultural System,' in *The Interpretation of Cultures* (New York: Basic, 1973), 123.

11 Steven Sangren calls this 'the ritual construction of social space' in his *History and Magical Power in a Chinese Community* (Stanford: Stanford University Press, 1987).

12 In his study of Lukang in Taiwan, Donald DeGlopper discerns the efficacy of 'ritual pretensions' for the reinvention of a gemeinschaft by the local residents, who wanted to reclaim a glorious past for their town. See Donald DeGlopper, 'Religion and Ritual in Lukang,' in *Religion and Ritual in Chinese Society*, ed. Arthur Wolf (Stanford: Stanford University Press, 1974), 66-69.

13 On 'multivocality,' see Turner, 'Social Dramas and Ritual Metaphors,' 104. To do full justice to the 'multivocality' of every ritual would require painstaking ethnographic research that is well beyond the scope of this book. My following discussion is based on extensive reading of news reports in the *Chinese Times* and the *Chinese Voice*, accounts in the publications of the organizations, interviews with people who have attended these functions, and my personal participation and observation in the field between 1988 and 1993. Documentation will be provided wherever appropriate.

14 *Wu xushan tong yi'an bao* [Ing Suey Sun Tong Minutes of Meetings] 1927-37, 1938-53, and 1976-92. The minutes of meetings between 1953 and 1976 have not been located.

15 See Sangren's use of this concept in *History and Magical Power*, chap. 5.

16 The practice was officially terminated at a meeting of the CBA in November 1951. It was decided that 860 sets of human bones that had been awaiting shipment since 1939 would

remain in Canada because of the political situation in Mainland China. See *Chinese Times,* 26 November 1951. For a commentary on the more enthusiastic observance of Qingming by the traditional organizations, see an editorial in *Chinese Voice,* 5 April 1966. A reader for UBC Press has pointed out that in Hong Kong the establishment of the Permanent Chinese Cemetery at Aberdeen in the 1930s has been regarded by scholars as perhaps the first public community gesture towards a local identity. See, for example, Bernard Luk, 'Xianggang lishi yu xianggang wenhua' [Hong Kong History and Hong Kong Culture], in *Culture and Society in Hong Kong,* ed. Elizabeth Sinn (Hong Kong: Centre of Asian Studies, University of Hong Kong, 1995), 68. Whether the new arrangement regarding burial practice effected any similar change among the Vancouver Chinese warrants further research.

17   Harry Con, *Zhongguo hongmen zai jianada* [The Chinese Freemasons in Canada] (Vancouver: Chinese Freemasons Canadian Headquarters, 1989), 101-9. C.K. Yang once suggested that, due to their members' lack of natural kinship ties, secret societies in traditional China had to rely on religion or mythology to inspire unity. See C.K. Yang, *Religion in Chinese Society: A Study of Contemporary Social Functions of Religion and Some of Their Historical Factors* (Berkeley: University of California Press, 1961), 58-64.

18   The analogy might sound far-fetched, but this was not unlike the case of the British monarchy which, according to David Cannadine, staged magnificent royal pageantry to shore up the image of a declining empire during the same period of time. See his 'The Context, Performance, and Meaning of Ritual: The British Monarchy and the "Invention of Tradition," c. 1820-1977,' in *The Invention of Tradition,* ed. Eric Hobsbawm and Terence Ranger (Cambridge: Cambridge University Press, 1983), 101-64.

19   C.K. Yang's comments on comparable communal events in traditional China are useful to my understanding of this particular form of ritual gatherings. See Yang, *Religion in Chinese Society,* chaps. 2-4, with quotations taken from page 43.

20   Bell, *Ritual Theory, Ritual Practice,* 122. See also Eric Hobsbawm, 'Introduction: Inventing Traditions,' in Hobsbawm and Ranger, *The Invention of Tradition,* 1-14.

21   In *From Ritual to Theatre,* 75, Victor Turner calls this function of ritual performance its 'reflexivity.' Bryna Goodman discerns the same orchestration of egalitarian community spirit and hierarchical elitist impulse in the public functions of the Chinese immigrant organizations in nineteenth-century Shanghai. See her *Native Place, City, and Nation: Regional Networks and Identities in Shanghai, 1853-1937* (Berkeley: University of California Press, 1995), chap. 3.

22   Among Chinese specialists, there has been a debate over whether standardized ritual practices (orthopraxy), as against shared beliefs (orthodoxy), contributed most to cultural integration. The primacy of performance is most strongly argued by James Watson in the following works: 'Standardizing the Gods: The Promotion of T'ien Hou (Empress of Heaven) along the South China Coast, 960-1960,' in *Popular Culture in Late Imperial China,* ed. David Johnson, Andrew J. Nathan, and Evelyn S. Rawski (Berkeley: University of California Press, 1985), 292-324; 'The Structure of Chinese Funerary Rites: Elementary Sequence, and the Primacy of Performance,' in *Death Ritual in Late Imperial and Modern China,* ed. James Watson and Evelyn Rawski (Berkeley: University of California Press, 1988), 3-19; and 'Rites or Beliefs? The Construction of a Unified Culture in Late Imperial China,' in *China's Quest for National Identity,* ed. Lowell Dittmer and Samuel S. Kim (Ithaca: Cornell University Press, 1993), 80-103. Based on my own experience in Vancouver, however, I would join Rawski and other historians in cautioning against such dichotomy. See Evelyn Rawski, 'A Historian's Approach to Chinese Death Ritual,' in Watson and Rawski, *Death Ritual in Late Imperial and Modern China,* 20-34.

23   Some organizations include past financial records in their publications, but the information is not always complete. See the statement of account balances of the Hoy Ping District Association from 1925 to 1946 in *Zhuyun quanjia kaiping zong huiguan tekan* [Special Issue of the Hoy Ping District Association Canadian Headquarters in Vancouver] 1947, 49-55. In many cases, bookkeeping seems to have been done rather erratically, as in the case of the Ing Suey Sun Tong, where the exact details of its budgets cannot be ascertained from its account books, *Wu xushan tong caoliu bao* [Ing Suey Sun Tong Account Books] 1936-43, 1944-51, and 1952-55.

24 For example, see *Jianada huang jiangxia zongtang di liujie quanjia kenqin dahui shimoji* [An Account of the Sixth National Convention of the Wong Kung Har Tong Canadian Headquarters] 1955, 37. Apparently, membership was not dependent on the payment of the 'annual fee.'

25 See the transaction on exit fee between the Hoy Ping District Association and the Chinese Consolidated Benevolent Association in *Zhuyun quanjia kaiping zong huiguan tekan*, 49-50. David T.H. Lee, *Jianada huaqiao shi* [A History of the Chinese in Canada] (Taipei: Canada Free Press, 1967), 221-24.

26 *Zhuyun quanjia kaiping zong huiguan tekan*, 50. It is not clear when the Lee Clan Association started its annual lottery for fee-paying members. My latest reference for this event is from *Chinese Voice*, 20 September 1957.

27 The term 'competitive generosity' is from Sangren, *History and Magical Power*, 78. For an example, see *Huaqiao gongli xuexiao choumu jingfei zhengxin lu* [Chinese Public School Fund-Raising Report] 1962, 3-8.

28 The Hoy Sun Ning Yung Benevolent Association collected an anniversary fee at the celebration of its sixtieth year. See *Chinese Times*, 8 October 1957.

29 *Jianada huang jiangxia zongtong di wujie quanjia kenqin dahui shimoji* [An Account of the Fifth National Convention of the Wong Kung Har Tong Canadian Headquarters] 1950, 46-47.

30 David Lai, *The Forbidden City within Victoria: Myth, Symbol and Streetscape of Canada's Earliest Chinatown* (Victoria: Orca, 1991), 20-22.

31 Rotating credit associations are a well studied subject among anthropologists. Among Chinese overseas, see Maurice Freedman, 'The Handling of Money: A Note on the Background to the Economic Sophistication of Overseas Chinese,' *Man* 59 (1959): 64-65; and David Wu, 'To Kill Three Birds with One Stone: The Rotating Credit Associations of the Papua New Guinea Chinese,' *American Ethnologist* 1.3 (1974): 565-84.

32 *Chinese Voice*, 6 December 1951 and 18 August 1952. An article in *Chinese Times*, 8 June 1973, also provides some of the details.

33 The unfortunate experience of the Hoy Sun Ning Yung Benevolent Association was exceptional. The building it bought with a *baizi hui* in 1959 was badly damaged by fire more than once. As a result, it rented a floor from the CBA as a clubhouse and failed to offer any compensation to its members until the mid-1970s. *Taishan ningyang huiguan liushi zhounian jinian tekan* [Hoy Sun Ning Yung Benevolent Association Sixtieth Anniversary Souvenir Publication] 1958; *Quanjia taishan yiqiao dierjie kenqin dahui tekan* [Special Issue of the Second Convention of the Taishan Overseas Chinese in Canada] 1975, 46; and *Yunbu taishan huiguan bashi zhounian jinian tekan* [Vancouver Hoy Sun Benevolent Association Eightieth Anniversary Souvenir Publication] 1977, 15-19.

34 *Chinese Voice*, 8 May 1961.

35 These conditions were stipulated in *Huang yunshang zong gongsuo shiye gongsi zhangcheng* [Constitution of the Real Estate Company of the Wong Wun San Society Headquarters] 1953. Another example can be found in *Jianada huang jiangxia tong shiye gongsi zhangcheng* [Constitution of the Real Estate Company of the Wong Kung Har Tong of Canada] 1944, 1950.

36 The discussion in the following two paragraphs is based on this report, *Huang yunshang zong gongsuo gouzhi louye baogaoshu* [Report on the Purchase of Land Properties by the Wong Wun San Society Headquarters] 1957. There is some supplementary information in *Huang yunshang zong gongsuo xinzhi luocheng kaimu ji di'er jie kenqin dahui shimoji* [An Account of the Official Opening of the New Premises of the Wong Wun San Society Headquarters and the Second National Convention] 1954.

37 Historical documentation is available in *Quanjia lishi disan jie kenqin dahui jinian tekan* [Souvenir Publication of the Third National Convention of the Lee Clan Association of Canada] 1985, 52-60; and *Quanjia lishi disi jie kenqin dahui jinian tekan* [Souvenir Publication of the Fourth National Convention of the Lee Clan Association of Canada] 1988, 74-80.

38 *Quanjia lishi disan jie kenqin dahui jinian tekan*, 54-57.

39 *Chinese Times*, 18 December 1952; *Chinese Voice*, 2 May 1962.

40 Wickberg, *From China to Canada*, 223.
41 There is no single biographical study on Foon Sien to date. His wide-ranging activities and interests can be seen from his personal papers, deposited in the Special Collections, UBC Library. See the memorial volume in *Huang wenfu xiansheng aisi lu* [*Memorial Volume of Mr. Foon Sien Wong*] 1971.
42 Synopses of the documents were usually printed in the Chinatown newspapers at the time of their submission to the Canadian government. I have been able to locate three original documents. 'A Brief Concerning Immigration Laws Submitted to the Cabinet by the Chinese Benevolent Association, March 24, 1950,' National Archives of Canada, RG 76, vol. 122, file 23635; 'A Brief Concerning Immigration Laws (and Citizenship Act) for Presentation to the Honourable Ellen L. Fairclough, Minister of Citizenship and Immigration by the Chinese Benevolent Association, 24 June 1959,' National Archives of Canada, H. W. Herridge Papers, MG 32 C13, vol. 40, file 5; and 'A Brief Concerning Immigration Laws (and Citizenship Act) for Presentation to the Honourable J. W. Pickersgill, Minister of Citizenship and Immigration, Ottawa, Ontario, Canada by the Chinese Benevolent Association, March 1957,' in Chinese Canadian Research Collections, Special Collections, UBC, box 12, file 2. Andrew Joe, interview by author, 9 December 1992. Joe was involved in the drafting of the documents.
43 *Quanjia zhonghua zong huiguan zhengxinlu* [Financial Report of the Chinese Benevolent Association of Canada] 1952-53, 65-71; *Quanjia zhonghua zong huiguan zhengxinlu* 1956-59, 99-106. For records of other CBA fund-raising activities, see, for example, *Jianada yungehua zhonghua huiguan juxing zhongxiu luocheng kaimu dianli tekan* [Special Publication on the Opening Ceremony of the Chinese Benevolent Association in Vancouver, Canada, at the Completion of its Renovation] 1952.
44 To reconstruct this sequence of events in 1955, see *Chinese Voice*, 13 April, 2 and 5-9 May, and 24 June 1955. A leaflet showing Foon Sien's itinerary during his trip to Ottawa in 1955 is available in Foon Sien Wong Papers, Special Collections, UBC, box 3.
45 Lee, *Jianada huaqiao shi*, 196-97. The Vancouver CBA refused to take part in a 'Pan-Canada Conference of CBAs' convened by the Toronto-based Chinese Community Centre of Ontario in 1952. *Chinese Times*, 3 May 1952.
46 Lal, 'The Chinese Benevolent Association,' 42-47; Wickberg, *From China to Canada*, 200.
47 *Chinese Voice*, 21 December 1959.
48 *Vancouver Sun*, 15 July 1961. Alan Phillips, 'The Criminal Society that Dominates the Chinese in Canada,' *Maclean's Magazine* 75.7 (April 7, 1962): 11, 40-48. Foon Sien's personal assessment of such dramatic developments is given in the *Chinese Voice*, 6 December 1962. As a result of the imposed age limit regarding children's immigration after 1947, prospective applicants sometimes might falsify their own age or even claim the identity of an eligible person. Hence this Canadian version of the problem of 'paper son.'
49 My reconstruction of this episode is based on the articles in the Chinese-language press. Interestingly, while all the relevant articles that appeared in the *Chinese Times* were critical of the established practices, it was in the *Chinese Voice* that wide-ranging viewpoints were exchanged. That the Kuomintang's *New Republic* carried not a single item on the debate is intriguing.
50 *Chinese Voice*, 9 November 1961.
51 His article was printed in 15 and 17 November 1961 in the *Chinese Voice* and the *Chinese Times*, respectively.
52 *Chinese Voice*, 20-21 and 23 November 1961; and *Chinese Times*, 24 November 1961.
53 See one of the critics, 'Chun Lei,' in *Chinese Voice*, 4 April 1962.
54 See the articles by Yee Keung Ping, 'Han Bai,' and 'Si Jia' in *Chinese Voice*, 12 March, 2 and 5 May 1962, respectively.
55 *Chinese Voice*, 12 March, 4, 6 April 1962, 11 May, and 4 June 1962. *Chinese Times*, 28 April 1962.
56 *Chinese Voice*, 2-4 June 1962.
57 Ibid., 24, 26 November, 10 December 1962.
58 Ibid., 17, 26-29 November 1965.

59 For criticism of the CBA, see *Da Zhong Bao*, 10 December 1965 and 21 January 1966. A good source of information on the CBA in the 1960s is *Quanjia zhonghua zong huiguan gaikuang* [Inside the Chinese Benevolent Association: A Report of Some Activities of the Highest Governing Body of the Chinese in Canada] 1969.

Chapter 6: Negotiating Identities

1 Ho Ping-ti, *Zhongguo huiguan shilun* [A Historical Survey of Landsmannschaften in China] (Taipei: Xuesheng, 1966), 1-9. Dou Jiliang, *Tongxiang zuzhi zhi yanjiu* [Studies on Native Place Organizations] (Chongqing: Zhengzhong, 1943), 1-9. Edward Shils has pointed out the universality of this often nostalgic and highly particularistic 'sense of place and past' for peoples who have left their original habitat. See his 'Roots – A Sense of Place and Past: The Cultural Gains and Losses of Migration,' in *Human Migration: Patterns and Policies*, ed. W.H. McNeill and R.S. Adams (Bloomington: Indiana University Press, 1978), 404-26.

2 Note the work of William Skinner, James Cole, William Rowe, and, more recently, Emily Honig, and Bryna Goodman in the bibliography.

3 See Goodman's study of Shanghai, *The Native Place, the City, and the Nation: Regional Networks and Identities in Shanghai, 1853-1937* (Berkeley: University of California Press, 1995); and 'The Locality as Microcosm of the Nation? Native Place Networks and Early Urban Nationalism in China,' *Modern China* 21.4 (1995): 387-419. See also my discussion of Chinese regional organizations in Singapore in the midst of rising Chinese nationalism, 'Urban Chinese Social Organization: Some Unexplored Aspects in *Huiguan* Development in Singapore, 1900-1941,' *Modern Asian Studies* 26.3 (1992): 469-94.

4 Reports on the collection of exit fees began to appear in early 1946 in the *Chinese Times*. *Annual Report* 1946-47, Immigration Branch, Department of Mines and Resources. *Chinese Times*, 6 August 1947.

5 The Chinese media were literally inundated with reports of these activities. See the English index of the *Chinese Times* in the Chinese Canadian Research Collections, Special Collections, UBC, box 5, files 11-13. See also Edgar Wickberg, ed., *From China to Canada: A History of the Chinese Communities in Canada* (Toronto: McClelland and Stewart, 1982), 230-31. One organization, the Hoy Ping District Association Headquarters, issued a special publication in 1947 to apprise its members of the devastation of the home region and to encourage contributing to its rehabilitation. See *Zhuyun quanjia kaiping zong huiguan tekan* [Special Issue of the Hoy Ping District Association Canadian Headquarters in Vancouver] 1947. See also its file in the Chinese Canadian Research Collections, box 3, particularly the transcript of an interview with Lee Quai Yut, 21 June 1961. Lee had been the secretary of the organization for more than three decades.

6 Stephen Fitzgerald, *China and the Overseas Chinese: A Study of Peking's Changing Policy, 1949-1970* (Cambridge: Cambridge University Press, 1972), chap. 4; and Glen Peterson, 'Socialist China and the Huaqiao: The Transition to Socialism in the Overseas Chinese Areas of Rural Guangdong, 1949-1956,' *Modern China* 14.3 (1988): 309-35.

7 See the November-December 1951 issues of the *Chinese Times*.

8 Elizabeth Sinn, *Power and Charity: The Early History of the Tung Wah Hospital, Hong Kong* (Hong Kong: Oxford University Press, 1990), 72-73, 77, and 103-13. See also Sinn's preliminary findings on emigration from Hong Kong before 1941, in *Emigration from Hong Kong: Tendencies and Impact*, ed. Ronald Skeldon (Hong Kong: Chinese University Press, 1995), 11-50.

9 *Chinese Times*, 15 October 1949, 10 January 1950, 7 June 1950, and 3 November 1950.

10 The story of postwar Hong Kong is often told, but it is by no means well researched. A useful contemporary account is Edvard Hambro, *The Problem of Chinese Refugees in Hong Kong: Report Submitted to the United Nations High Commissioner for Refugees* (Leyden, Holland: Sijthoff, 1955). A number of essays in Ian Jarvie and Joseph Agassi, eds., *Hong Kong: A Society in Transition* (New York: Praeger, 1968), offer insights as of the mid-1960s. On the role of the regional associations, see Elizabeth Sinn, 'Challenges and Responses: The Development of Hong Kong's Regional Associations, 1945-1990,' paper presented at the Twelfth Conference of the International Association of Historians of Asia, 24-28 June 1991,

University of Hong Kong; and 'Xin Xi Guxiang: A Study of Regional Associations as a Bonding Mechanism in the Chinese Diaspora. The Hong Kong Experience,' *Modern Asian Studies* 31.2 (1997): 375-97.

11 Huang Jisheng, 'Jianada yungaohua taishan ningyang huiguan shilue' [A Short History of the Hoy Sun Ning Yung Benevolent Association in Vancouver], in this organization's file, Chinese Canadian Research Collections, Special Collections, UBC, box 3. See also the numerous reports in the January and February 1954 issues of the *Chinese Times*.

12 See the February 1959 and early 1962 issues of the *Chinese Voice*.

13 *Chinese Voice*, 5 October 1963, 30 October 1965, and 5 November 1969.

14 *Chinese Times*, 1 March 1952; *Chinese Voice*, 1 March 1954, 22 March 1962, 17 December 1963, and 4 September 1964.

15 These bodies included the National People's Congress, the Legislative Assembly, and the Supervisory Assembly. For the details of overseas Chinese representation, see Overseas Chinese Affairs Commission, comp., *Qiaowu ershiwu nian* [Overseas Chinese Affairs, 1932-1957] (Taiwan: Overseas Chinese Affairs Commission, 1958), 56-58, 160-67. On campaigning in Chinatown, see the November 1947 issues of the *Chinese Times*.

16 Wing Chung Ng, 'Taiwan's Overseas Chinese Policy from 1949 to the Early 1980s,' in Larry Shyu et al., *East Asia Inquiry: Selected Articles from the Annual Conferences of the Canadian Asian Studies Association 1988-1990* (Montreal: CASA, 1991), especially 275-77.

17 David Lee, *Jianada huaqiao shi* [A History of the Chinese in Canada] (Taipei: Canada Free Press, 1967), 319-20, 350-51.

18 *Chinese Times*, 9, 16, and 27 March 1953.

19 The *Chinese Voice*, on 23-24 August 1962, carried a full transcript of Wang's speech. The Nationalist Consulate-General played an important role in spreading anti-communist propaganda. See one of its many 'Red Scare' stories in the English daily, the *Province*, 27 August 1959.

20 Chinese in Canada never figured significantly in the 'overseas Chinese policy' of the Kuomintang, which presumed the real battle was being fought elsewhere – in some Southeast Asian countries where the Chinese populations were more numerous and affluent, and in the United States where the support of the local Chinese could yield diplomatic benefits. The Kuomintang leadership in Vancouver occasionally complained about inadequate support from Taiwan, as occurred at the thirteenth party convention. The October 1955 issues of the *Chinese Voice* provide extensive coverage of the event and the party resolutions. For a more general criticism of the Kuomintang party-state, see an essay entitled 'Zhengqu huaqiao zhidao' [The Way to Win over the Overseas Chinese], ibid., 6-9 July 1964.

21 *Haifeng hui jinian kan* [Hai Fung Club: A Souvenir Publication] 1968, 3-4.

22 That happened during the Third All-America Chinese Freemasons Convention held in Vancouver in 1950 and another national conference in 1967. The documents are collected in Harry Con, *Zhongguo hongmen zai jianada* [The Chinese Freemasons in Canada] (Vancouver: Chinese Freemasons Canadian Headquarters, 1989), 50-53, 81-82.

23 For instance, the report on China's successful testing of its first hydrogen bomb in *Da Zhong Bao*, 17 June 1967.

24 In 'Bushi minzu bailei shi shenme?' [What Are They, If Not the Scum of the [Chinese] Nation?], the author condemned Taiwan for endorsing the suppression of the Hong Kong riots in 1967 by the British colonial authorities. See *Da Zhong Bao*, 15 September 1967.

25 *Da Zhong Bao*, 31 January, 7 February, and 14 February 1970.

26 Various issues of *Da Zhong Bao*, from May to October 1970.

27 Various issues of the *Chinese Times*, May-October 1970, especially 3 June and 23 October.

28 Among the benefactors were the Hoy Ping District Association, Shon Yee Benevolent Association, Wong Kong Har Tong, Wong Wun San Society, and Yue San Association. See *Chinese Times*, 2 April 1952, 7 and 27 November 1952, 8 January 1953, 23 February 1953, and 9 March 1953.

29 Lee, *Jianada huaqiao shi*, 470-71.

30 Chapter 3 has already provided a detailed discussion of the perspectives of the new immigrant youth on the question of identity, culture, and community.

31 Allen Chun, 'From Nationalism to Nationalizing: Cultural Imagination and State Formation in Postwar Taiwan,' *Australian Journal of Chinese Affairs* 31 (1994): 49-69.

32 On the historical link between Hong Kong and Guangdong, see Ming K. Chan, 'All in the Family: The Hong Kong-Guangdong Link in Historical Perspective,' in *The Hong Kong-Guangdong Link: Partnership in Flux*, ed. Reginald Yin-Wang Kwok and Alvin Y. So (Armonk, NY: Sharpe, 1995), 31-63. Hong Kong's quest for an identity is the subject of Choi Po-king, 'A Search for Cultural Identity: The Students' Movement of the Early Seventies,' in *Differences and Identities: Education Argument in Late Twentieth-Century Hong Kong*, ed. Anthony Sweeting (Hong Kong: Faculty of Education, University of Hong Kong, 1990), 81-107; and 'From Dependence to Self-Sufficiency: Rise of the Indigenous Culture of Hong Kong,' *Asian Culture* 14 (1990): 161-77.

33 Freda Hawkins, *Canada and Immigration: Public Policy and Public Concern* (Montreal and Kingston: McGill-Queen's University Press, 1972), 332-33.

34 Choi, 'From Dependence to Self-Sufficiency.' The section on movies in the literary supplements of the *Chinese Voice* gives a good indication of the popularity of Hong Kong-made Cantonese movies among the immigrant Chinese in Vancouver during this period.

35 On Jin Wah Sing, see *Chinese Voice*, 8 and 22 February 1961. The arrival of a shipment of publications from Hong Kong was often greeted with much enthusiasm, as is seen in ibid., 17 September 1955, and 9 December 1958.

36 *Da Zhong Bao*, 26 April 1968.

37 A Chinese handbook for prospective immigrants to Canada, published in Hong Kong in 1968, refers to Vancouver as 'Little Hong Kong.' See Lin Sen, *Yimin jianada bidu* [Must-Reading for Emigration to Canada] (Hong Kong: Lin Sen, 1968), 57-58. The first local reference I have found to this phrase is in the *Chinese Voice*, 20 March 1968.

38 *Chinese Voice*, 4 October 1961.

39 See Foon Sien's personal appraisal in *Chinatown News*, 3 May 1956. Some secondary accounts of these official concessions are inaccurate, as in Lee, *Jianada huaqiao shi*, 365-66; and Kay Anderson, *Vancouver's Chinatown: Racial Discourse in Canada, 1875-1980* (Montreal and Kingston: McGill-Queen's University Press, 1991), 179-86.

40 *Chinese Voice*, 17 June 1957, 1 April 1958.

41 Encouragement of voter registration and the use of the ballots by the CBA appeared in the *Chinese Times*, 19 April 1948, 18 August, 9 December 1952; and 8 August, 8 December 1953. A leaflet distributed by the CBA to endorse candidates in the general election of 1953 is available in Foon Sien Wong Papers, Special Collections, UBC, box 3. After 1953, a chapter of the Toronto-based Chinese Canadian Citizens Association existed in Vancouver, and it took on similar functions. Its executive committee seems to have overlapped considerably with the CBA, but its history is not at all clear.

42 *Chinese Times*, 23 February 1950. The turnout was said to be slightly above 10 percent of eligible voters.

43 Robin Sharp, 'A Study in the Voting Behaviour of the Chinese in Vancouver Centre,' undergraduate essay in Political Science, University of British Columbia, 1956, 23-42.

44 *Vancouver Sun*, 29 December 1955; *Chinese Voice*, 5 and 7 January 1956.

45 See the March 1958 issues of the *Chinese Times* and the *Chinese Voice*.

46 After securing his seat in the 1958 election, Jung attempted to build his own network of supporters in Chinatown in order to remedy his unfavorable party affiliation. See Jack Eng, interview by author, 12 June 1992. Eng was Jung's right-hand man at that time. See *Chinese Voice*, 17 May 1958, for an announcement of the Conservative membership drive. Jung's correspondence with another Chinatown-based supporter, Thomas Moore Whaum, also sheds light on this issue. See Thomas Moore Whaun Papers, Special Collections, UBC, box 1, file 4. See below on the Liberal Party's effort to recapture Chinese support. In one of those election years, 1962, a local daily named Chinatown 'a speaker's paradise' for campaigning politicians. See *Vancouver Sun*, 15 June 1962. A notable Chinese candidate in the early 1960s was Gladys Chong, who ran (albeit unsuccessfully) in the municipal election in 1962 and the federal election in 1963. See *Province*, 23 November 1962; *Chinese Voice*, 27 February 1963.

47 See the coverage of the two federal elections in Chinatown in the May-June 1962 and March-April 1963 issues of the *Chinese Times* and the *Chinese Voice*. See also, *Vancouver Sun*, 16 July 1962.

48 A synopsis of the submitted document and an account of the event can be found in *Chinatown News*, 3 April and 18 November 1965.

49 December 1955, February and April 1956 issues of the *Chinese Voice*. As for the city officials' definition of Chinatown as a public nuisance in the earlier period, see Anderson, *Vancouver's Chinatown*, chap. 3.

50 The literature on urban redevelopment in North America during this period is voluminous. For two examples that focus on Canada, see Setty Pendakur, *Cities, Citizens and Freeways* (Vancouver: Pendakur, 1972); and David Ley, 'Liberal Ideology and the Postindustrial City,' *Annals of the Association of American Geographers* 70.2 (1980): 238-58. As far as Canadian Chinatowns are concerned, see David Lai, *Chinatowns: Towns within Cities in Canada* (Vancouver: UBC Press, 1988), 146-54.

51 City of Vancouver, Planning Department for the Housing Research Committee, *Vancouver Redevelopment Study* 1957. Also relevant is Leonard Marsh, *Rebuilding a Neighbourhood: Report on a Demonstration Slum-Clearance and Urban Rehabilitation Project in a Key Central Area in Vancouver*, Research Publications, no. 1. (Vancouver: University of British Columbia, 1950), which set the tone of redevelopment thinking for almost two decades in Vancouver, with particular reference to Strathcona.

52 'History of Strathcona,' a manuscript by Hayne Y. Wai, n.d., in City of Vancouver Archives, SPOTA files, add. mss. 734, vol. 16, file 2. Systematic analysis of Chinese residential patterns in Vancouver is not available, with the exception of a preliminary study by George Cho and Roger Leigh, 'Patterns of Residence of the Chinese in Vancouver,' in *Peoples of the Living Land*, ed. J. Minghi, BC Geographical Series, no. 15 (Vancouver: Tantalus, 1972), 67-84.

53 *Chinese Voice*, 17, 19, 28, and 30 April 1958.

54 Other than newspaper reports, the best sources on this phase of Chinese resistance are the public documents presented to the various authorities by the CPOA. The first one was submitted to Vancouver City Council in June 1958. The second one was presented first to the same authority in October 1960 and then to the BC Royal Commission on Expropriation Laws and Procedures in July 1961. The CPOA's last written presentation to the city was made in October 1962. Chinese translation of the first two briefs appeared in the *Chinese Voice*, 24-27 May 1958, and 5-8 August 1961. An original copy of the second document is also available in the Chinese Canadian Research Collections, box 2, CPOA file, Special Collections, UBC. An annotated version of the last item was enclosed as appendix IV-C in the City of Vancouver, Technical Planning Board, *Redevelopment Project No. 2* (July 1963).

55 The first stage of the redevelopment project officially started in 1961. Soon thereafter, the city bureaucrats began deliberation on the second phase. In October 1962 the CBA and the CPOA led a delegation of nineteen Chinese organizations in an unsuccessful attempt to block the plan. See City of Vancouver, Technical Planning Board, *Redevelopment Project No. 2*.

56 Background information on changing popular opinions in Vancouver regarding urban planning is available in Pendakur, *Cities, Citizens and Freeways*, chap. 4. Ley's 'Liberal Ideology and the Postindustrial City' offers important insights into the larger political context, with special reference to a rising professional elite in Vancouver. Note also an informed analytical account by a group of local scholars, some of whom were participants in these events, in Graeme Wynn and Timothy Oke, eds., *Vancouver and Its Region* (Vancouver: UBC Press, 1992), 200-66.

57 See the June 1967-January 1968 issues of the *Chinese Voice*. Anderson, *Vancouver's Chinatown*, 200-6.

58 *Chinese Voice*, 17, 27-30 December 1968.

59 See, for example, the first two public documents it presented to the city government: 'A Brief to the Vancouver City Council by the SPOTA, January 27, 1969' in the Vancouver City Archives, SPOTA files, add. mss. 734, vol. 6, file 9; and 'A Brief to the Vancouver City Council by the SPOTA, May 16, 1969' in ibid., vol. 1, file 2.

60 'A Brief to the Vancouver City Council by the SPOTA, January 27, 1969.' The document was subsequently signed by almost 600 people.

61 The findings of the survey were reported in *Shidakongna qu yezhu zhuke xiehui sannian gongzuo baogao* [SPOTA Triennial Report] November 1971, available in the Chinese Canadian Research Collections, Special Collections, UBC, box 3, SPOTA file.

62 Shirley Y. Chan, 'An Overview of the Strathcona Experience with Urban Renewal by a Participant' (March 1971), offers a candid assessment of its strategies by a SPOTA activist. In Vancouver City Archives, SPOTA files, add. mss. 734, vol. 13, file 2. Two social analysts who were employed from outside in December 1972 to evaluate SPOTA's organizational structure were equally amazed by the intensity of its membership mobilization. See 'Chislett-Robinson Report 1968-1971,' in ibid., vol. 8, file 5. See also the report to SPOTA by John Chislett, 'Conclusions of the Self-Evaluation Study,' in ibid., vol. 11, file 3.

63 Minutes of meeting, Strathcona Working Committee, 1 October 1969, in Vancouver City Archives, SPOTA files, add. mss. 734, vol. 7, file 8. See also Larry Bell and Richard Moore, *The Strathcona Rehabilitation Project: Documentation and Analysis* (Vancouver: Social Policy and Research, United Way of Greater Vancouver, 1975), 10-13.

64 Chan, "An Overview of the Strathcona Experience." Harry Con, interview by author, 9 November 1990 and 12 June 1992. In many ways – such as his ties to both the immigrant sector and the local-born Chinese and his connections to the Liberal Party – Con seems to have been Foon Sien's prefect replacement.

65 *Chinese Voice*, 6 December 1968; 28 November 1970.

66 Ibid., 9 December 1970.

Chapter 7: Constructing Chineseness

1 *Chinatown News*, 3 February, 3 April, and 18 June 1954; 3 June 1955; and 18 March 1956. Perhaps the earliest example of such a usage was the Chinese Canadian Club founded in Victoria-Vancouver during the second decade of this century. See Note 7 in Chapter 4. See also Paul Yee, *Saltwater City: An Illustrated History of the Chinese in Vancouver* (Vancouver: Douglas and McIntyre, 1988), 110, for a 1949 reference to the "Chinese-Canadian youth" in a short-lived *tusheng* publication, the *New Citizen*.

2 Allan Smith has offered a penetrating discussion of the mosaic metaphor in Canadian intellectual life in his 'Metaphor and Nationality in North America,' *Canadian Historical Review* 51 (1970): 247-75. Despite its intellectual tenacity, the idea of Canada as a mosaic had very limited impact on public policy and attitudes before the 1970s. See, for example, the assessment of Peter Ward, 'Class and Race in the Social Structure of British Columbia, 1870-1939,' *BC Studies* 45 (spring 1980): 17-35; Evelyn Kallen, 'Multiculturalism: Ideology, Policy and Reality,' *Journal of Canadian Studies* 17.1 (1982): 51-63; and, more recently, Caterina Pizanias, 'Centering on Changing Communities: Multiculturalism as Meaning and Message,' *Canadian Ethnic Studies* 24.3 (1992): 87-98. Note also the classic study by John Porter, *The Vertical Mosaic* (Toronto: University of Toronto Press, 1965). Casting the public debate in a broad historical context is Robert Harney, '"So Great a Heritage as Ours": Immigration and the Survival of the Canadian Polity,' *Daedalus* 117.4 (1988): 51-97.

3 An article by William Wong, *Chinatown News*, 18 March 1964.

4 *Chinatown News*, 3 June 1965. The commission had written a report on this meeting. See 'Report: Private Meeting with [a] Chinese Canadian Group, Vancouver,' National Archives of Canada, RG 33, series 80, Royal Commission on Bilingualism and Biculturalism, vol. 120, file 634E.

5 Letter from Andrew Lam to Paul Lacoste, co-secretary, Royal Commission on Bilingualism and Biculturalism, 21 June 1965, in National Archives of Canada, RG 33, series 80, vol. 121, file 679E.

6 Raymond Breton, 'The Production and Allocation of Symbolic Resources: An Analysis of the Linguistic and Ethnocultural Fields in Canada,' *Canadian Review of Sociology and Anthropology* 21.2 (1984): 123-44; and Daiva Stasiulis, 'The Political Structuring of Ethnic Community Action: A Reformulation,' *Canadian Ethnic Studies* 12.3 (1980): 19-44. Studies of official multiculturalism are too numerous to be cited. See the work of Jean Burnet, Karl Peter, and Kogila Moodley in the bibliography for a sense of the debate. Single community

studies have mostly been limited to European groups, especially Ukrainians. For example, Wsevolod Isajiw, 'Multiculturalism and the Integration of the Canadian Community,' *Canadian Ethnic Studies* 15.2 (1983): 107 17; and Bohdan Bociurkiw, 'The Federal Policy of Multiculturalism and the Ukrainian-Canadian Community,' in *Ukrainian Canadians, Multiculturalism, and Separatism: An Assessment*, ed. Manoly R. Lupul (Alberta: Canadian Institute of Ukrainian Studies, University of Alberta Press, 1978), 98-128.

7 Our understanding of Sino-Canadian diplomatic relations leading up to recognition in 1970 and thereafter will remain incomplete until research materials on the China side become more accessible. On Canadian perspectives, see Paul Evans and Daphne Taras, 'Canadian Public Opinion on Relations with China: An Analysis of Existing Survey Research,' Working Paper No. 33 (Toronto: Joint Centre on Modern East Asia, March 1985); and 'Looking (Far) East: Parliament and Canada-China Relations, 1949-1982,' in *Parliament and Canadian Foreign Policy*, ed. David Taras (Toronto: Canadian Institute of International Affairs, 1988), 66-100. See also Maureen Appel Molot, 'Canada's Relations with China since 1968,' in *A Foremost Nation: Canadian Foreign Policy and A Changing World*, ed. Norman Hillmer and Garth Stevenson (Toronto: McClelland and Stewart, 1976), 230-67; and Michael Frolic, 'Canada and the People's Republic of China: Twenty Years of a Bilateral Relationship, 1970-1990,' in *Canada and the Growing Presence of Asia*, ed. Frank Langdon, Occasional Paper No. 9 (Vancouver: University of British Columbia, Institute of Asian Research, 1990), 41-62. The latest work by Canadian scholars is in Paul Evans and Michael Frolic, eds., *Reluctant Adversaries: Canada and the People's Republic of China, 1949-1971* (Toronto: University of Toronto Press, 1991).

8 See the initial reaction of Lam Fong, the chief Kuomintang spokesperson in Vancouver, as reported in the *Chinatown News*, 18 October 1970. Later, in September 1971, Lam again charged PRC supporters with harassing Chinatown residents. See *Province*, 11 September 1971 and *Vancouver Sun*, 13 September 1971, as quoted in *Da Zhong Bao*, 18 September 1971, and *Chinatown News*, 18 September 1971. As pointed out by Janet Lum, the centre of the Kuomintang's anti-recognition activity was Toronto. See her 'Recognition and the Toronto Chinese Community,' in Evans and Frolic, *Reluctant Adversaries*, 217-40.

9 The Chinese Youth Association and the *Da Zhong Bao*, needless to say, were the most jubilant, taking the diplomatic breakthrough as a vindication of their pro-PRC stance over the years. Some twenty Chinatown associations, including the Wong associations, Cheng Wing Yeong Tong, the Yue San Association, the Yin Ping District Association, and the influential Chinese Freemasons (represented by its Athletic Society) took part in welcoming the PRC ambassador. See *Da Zhong Bao*, 31 October 1970, 9 January 1971.

10 *Chinatown News*, 18 April 1972; *Da Zhong Bao*, 8 and 15 April 1972.

11 Ibid., 3 and 18 November, 3 and 18 December 1973, 18 January 1974, and 3 February 1974.

12 Charles Sedgwick and William Willmott, 'External Influences and Emerging Identity: The Evolution of Community Structure among Chinese Canadians,' *Canadian Forum* (September 1974): 12.

13 Frolic, 'Canada and the People's Republic of China,' 36.

14 Letter from SPOTA to Vancouver City Council, 10 February 1970, appended in Shirley Chan, "An Overview of the Strathcona Experience with Urban Renewal by a Participant," March 1971, City of Vancouver Archives, SPOTA Files, add. mss. 734, vol. 13, file 2. Three years later, SPOTA joined force with other Chinese organizations in forcing the municipal government to abandon the plan of widening a Chinatown street into a freeway connector. See *Chinatown News*, 18 June 1973; *Da Zhong Bao*, 16 June 1973.

15 *Chinatown News*, 18 April, 18 October, 3 and 18 December 1972. See also *SPOTA Annual Report December 1971-December 1972*, in City of Vancouver Archives, SPOTA Files, add. mss. 734, vol. 1, file 3.

16 On SPOTA's input into the operation of the rehabilitation program, see City of Vancouver Archives, SPOTA Files, add. mss. 734, vols. 22 and 23. Records of cooperative housing, including lease arrangements and the reports to the federal funding agent (the Central Mortgage and Housing Corporation) are stored in vol. 4, files 12 and 13, and vols. 25 and 28.

17 SPOTA's newsletters (including a tabloid called the *Mirror*, published between June 1977 and July 1978) have the details on these activities. On the Chinatown Historic Area Planning Committee, see *Chinatown Planning Newsletter*, published by the City Planning Department, November 1976, and the materials in Vancouver City Archives, SPOTA Files, add. mss. 734, vol. 13.

18 *Chinatown News*, 18 June and 3 July 1972, 18 September 1979. *Chinese Community Library Services Association Twentieth Anniversary Commemorative Special Publication 1972-1992* 1992, 9-12.

19 See, for instance, a highly reflective essay by Hayne Wai, "Strathcona – Chinatown ... Twenty Years Ago," in *Chinese Community Library Services Association Twentieth Anniversary Commemorative Special Publication 1972-1992*, 13-15.

20 *Chinese Voice*, 13 June 1955. For some later proposals, see ibid., 30 April 1958, 15 January 1964, and 21 November 1966. See also *Chinatown News*, 18 October 1958.

21 *Da Zhong Bao* (English edition), December 1970. The English edition was a brief attempt by the Chinese Youth Association to reach the local-born Chinese. However, only four issues were published in the fall of 1970. Members of this group seem to have been well aware of, and influenced by, current developments in American Chinatowns, especially San Francisco and New York, where alienated Chinese youth sought radical changes by openly challenging the traditional elites. See Stanford Lyman, 'Red Guard on Grant Avenue: The Rise of Youthful Rebellion in Chinatown,' in *The Asian in North America*, ed. S. Lyman (Santa Barbara: ABC-Clio, 1977), 177-99; and the chapter, 'Alienation, Rebellion, and the New Consciousness,' in his *Chinese Americans* (New York: Random, 1974).

22 *New Bridge* 1.1 (February 1971). This was probably the group's own publication. Only seven issues (from February to September 1971) are available, and these may be all that were published.

23 *Chinatown News*, 18 May 1971.

24 Both the 'unsolicited' official support given at the banquet and Ip's letter were quoted in the *Chinatown News*, 3 October 1972. Since then, the former has become part of the founding myth of the Chinese Cultural Centre. See John Wong, 'A Brief History of the Chinese Cultural Centre' (in both Chinese and English), in *Zhonghua wenhua zhongxin chengli shi zhounian jinian tekan* [Chinese Cultural Centre Tenth Anniversary Souvenir Publication, 1973-1983] 1983, 11-17.

25 Wong, 'A Brief History of the CCC.' 'The Constitution of the Chinese Cultural Centre,' in S. Wah Leung Papers.

26 *Chinatown News*, 3 March 1973.

27 *Da Zhong Bao*, 23 and 30 December 1972; 13 January, 17 February, 24 March, and 8 September 1973. It is noteworthy that this period, full of excitement and organizing activities in Vancouver's Chinatown, coincided with the famous Diaoyutai Movement (concerning a territorial dispute between China/Taiwan and Japan), which ignited a generation of Chinese student activism in Hong Kong and the United States. While the rallying cry 'Protecting Diaoyutai' was heard on campuses across the United States wherever there was a sizable concentration of foreign students from Taiwan and Hong Kong, the movement did not seem to have much impact on the Vancouver scene because of the still relatively small number of Chinese foreign students at UBC. On the impact of the Diaoyutai Movement on the Chinese in the United States, see Shih-shan Henry Tsai, *The Chinese Experience in America* (Bloomington: Indiana University Press, 1986), 171-75.

28 See the case of the Shon Yee Benevolent Association in *Jianada wenhua tiecheng chongyi zonghui chengli di qishi zhounian jinian tekan* [Souvenir Publication of the Seventieth Anniversary of the Shon Yee Benevolent Association of Canada, Vancouver, 1914-1984] 1984, 24-28 ff.

29 The reorientation of the Chinese Freemasons is best described in Harry Con, *Zhongguo hongmen zai jianada* [The Chinese Freemasons in Canada] (Vancouver: Chinese Freemasons Canadian Headquarters, 1989), 84.

30 Larry Chu, 'A Review of the Activities and Special Events Committees,' in *Zhonghua wenhua zhongxin chengli shi zhounian jinian tekan*, 28-31, offers a useful summary of these CCC functions.

31   To be exact, Wah Leung was born in Jiangmen, Guangdong, in 1918. He came with his mother and elder brother to Canada in 1927 to join his father, who was then serving as a minister in Edmonton. Wah was thus one of a handful of Chinese entering Canada during the exclusion era. His background fits my description of the older first generation of Canadian-born Chinese. Leung's recollections of the early years of the CCC are available in 'The First Ten Years: A Rocky Road to Success,' in *Zhonghua wenhua zhongxin chengli shi zhounian jinian tekan*, 18-20; and 'Random Reflections,' in *Zhonghua wenhua zhongxin chengli shiwu zhounian tekan* [Chinese Cultural Centre Fifteenth Anniversary Souvenir Publication, 1973-1988] 1988, 8-10. Sophia Leung and Paul Robertson, eds., *S. Wah Leung: Celebration of a Splendid Life* (Vancouver: Faculty of Dentistry, University of British Columbia, 1992) contains useful biographical materials. His personal papers, in the custody of Mrs. Sophia Leung, were invaluable to my research.

32   The perspectives of this generation are available in 'Interview with Bing Thom on China, the Chinese Canadian Movement, and the Vancouver Chinese Cultural Centre,' in *Inalienable Rice: A Chinese and Japanese Anthology*, ed. Garrick Chu et al. (Vancouver: Powell Street Revue and the Chinese Canadian Writers Workshop, 1979), 33-38; and Paul Yee, 'Where Do We Go From Here?' in *Zhonghua wenhua zhongxin chengli shi zhounian jinian tekan*, 39-41.

33   This point is noteworthy because 'ethnic' organizations are often thought of as being for cultural retention and against integration. I owe this observation to Edgar Wickberg, 'Some Comparative Perspectives on Contemporary Chinese Ethnicity in the Philippines,' *Asian Culture* 14 (1990): 29-30; 'Notes on Some Contemporary Social Organizations in Manila Chinese Society,' in *China, Across the Seas; The Chinese as Filipinos*, ed. Aileen S.P. Baviera and Teresita Ang See (Quezon City: Philippine Association for Chinese Studies, 1992), 143-66; and 'Chinese Organizations and Ethnicity in Southeast Asia and North America since 1945: A Comparative Analysis,' in *Changing Identities of the Southeast Asian Chinese since World War II*, ed. Jennifer Cushman and Wang Gungwu (Hong Kong: Hong Kong University Press, 1988), 312 and note 36.

34   Chu, 'A Review of the Activities and Special Events Committees.' See also a brief essay by Gordon Chang, 'Ethnic History: A Case for Chinese Canadians,' *Mainstream* 1.3 (December 1979): 18.

35   *Chinese Cultural Centre Report*, January 1978. On the planning of this trip to China, see *Minutes of Meetings, Board of Directors of the CCC*, 3 March 1976, in S. Wah Leung Papers.

36   'CCC Workers Conference, January 17-18, 1976,' in S. Wah Leung Papers. Perhaps it should be pointed out that, among these various models, the mass culture of Hong Kong began to gain considerable popularity, ultimately at the others' expense. Especially noteworthy was the new generation of Hong Kong-produced kung fu movies by Bruce Lee during the 1970s.

37   Chu, 'A Review of the Activities and Special Events Committees,' 30.

38   Joe Wai and Chu Cheong, 'The Building and Planning Committee Report,' in *Zhonghua wenhua zhongxin chengli shi zhounian jinian tekan*, 21-26; *Chinatown News*, 18 February 1973; and Chu, 'A Review of the Activities and Special Events Committee,' 31.

39   'U.N. Habitat Conference, May-June 1976,' and a news release by the CCC, 28 July 1976, on Vancouver City Council's decision. These two items, as well as the organizational details of other similar events, can be found in S. Wah Leung Papers.

40   Stasiulis, 'The Political Structuring of Ethnic Community Action,' especially 35 and note 23.

41   See the open letter of Sammy Kee, co-chairperson of the Chinese Canadian Activity Centre Society, *New Republic*, 28 February 1977; and *Chinatown News*, 3 March 1977. My account of the entire episode draws heavily on the reports in the ethnic press as well as on leaflets and propaganda materials distributed by the contenders. Some of these items, including newspaper clippings from the mainstream media, are from the subject file, 'CBA Reform,' file nos. 84-21 and 84-22, in the Chinese Community History Room. The S. Wah Leung Papers contain the best information on the CCC's perspectives. My interviews with individuals from both sides were also helpful in ensuring some balance in this assessment. John Wong, interview by author, 30 November 1990; Wong Kung Wai, interview by author, 18 January 1991.

42 An open letter by S. Wah Leung, 9 February 1977. The original is in S. Wah Leung Papers. Printed in the *Chinese Times* and the *Chinese Voice*, 16 February 1977, and the *Chinatown News*, 3 March 1977. See also a special issue of the *Chinese Cultural Centre Report* September 1977, 'CCC, CBA, and [the] Chinese Community.'

43 Years later, S. Wah Leung commented regretfully on that situation but was still unable to offer an explanation. See his 'Random Reflections.'

44 Paul Yee, 'Where Have All the Young People Gone? Vancouver's Chinese Cultural Centre and Its Native-Born,' in *Asian Canadians: Regional Perspectives*, ed. K.V. Ujimoto and G. Hirabayashi (Published Conference Proceedings of the Asian Canadian Symposium V, 1982), 355-56, 364-67.

45 William Wei, *The Asian American Movement* (Philadelphia: Temple University Press, 1993). Three other items I find very useful are: Amy Tachiki et al., *Roots: An Asian American Reader* (Los Angeles: Asian American Studies Center, University of California, 1971); Emma Gee, ed., *Counterpoint: Perspectives on Asian America* (Los Angeles: Asian American Studies Center, University of California, 1976); and 'Salute to the 60s and 70s: Legacy of the San Francisco State Strike,' Special Issue of *Amerasia Journal* 15.1 (1989).

46 Yee, 'Where Have All the Young People Gone?' 356-58.

47 'Interview with Bing Thom,' 37-38.

48 Quoted in Yee, 'Where Have All the Young People Gone?' 361. *Gum San Po* lasted for just a few issues. The only copy I have seen is 2.1 (February-March 1974).

49 'A Report on the B.C. Chinese Canadian Youth Conference, UBC, May 16-18, 1975,' in *Pender Guy* Archives.

50 Barry Wong, '*Pender Guy*,' *The Asianadian* 3.2 (1980): 24-25; and 'The Chinese Canadian Communities Research in the Fraser Valley,' a report prepared by Anthony Chung, Summer 1977, in *Pender Guy* Archives. Also active around the same time was the West Coast Chinese Canadian Historical Society, which seems to have been modeled on historical societies founded earlier by the American-born Chinese. See *Chinatown News*, 18 June, 18 October 1977; 3 and 18 May, 18 July 1978. On the historical societies in the United States, see Wing Chung Ng, 'Scholarship on Post-World War II Chinese Societies in North America: A Thematic Discussion,' in *Chinese America: History and Perspectives 1992* (San Francisco: Chinese Historical Society of America and Asian American Studies, San Francisco State University, 1992), 181 and note 9.

51 Bennett Lee, 'Early Casualties, or How to Lose out to the History Books: The Chinese in British Columbia,' in Garrick Chu et al., *Inalienable Rice*, 3-7.

52 Yee, '*Pender Guy*,' 65. Barry Wong, interview by author, 12 March 1993; Ramona Mar, interview by author, 22 March 1993. Both were former members of *Pender Guy*.

53 I want to thank Barry Wong for giving me two cassette tapes of recorded Pender Guy programs.

54 The quotes are from 'Life on *Pender Guy*,' *Co-op Radio: 102.7 FM Program Guide*, November 1980, in *Pender Guy* Archives; *Chinatown News*, 3 July 1978; and Barry Wong, '*Pender Guy*: Street History,' n.d.

55 In the S. Wah Leung Papers there is a file of materials on the CBA-CCC joint campaign to demand the withdrawal of the documentary. The script critique by Patrick Chen and Sean Gunn was published in the *Chinatown News*, 3 August 1979.

56 For a Toronto-centred account of this incident, see Anthony Chan, *Gold Mountain: The Chinese in the New World* (Vancouver: New Star, 1983), 161-86. Materials on the Vancouver campaign against *W-5* are available in the S. Wah Leung Papers. See also *Chinatown News*, 3 March, 3 and 18 April, and 3 May 1980. On the award-winning program, see *Co-op Radio: 102.7 FM Program Guide*, November 1980.

57 Freda Hawkins, *Canada and Immigration: Public Policy and Public Concern* (Montreal and Kingston: McGill-Queen's University Press, 1972), 71-173.

58 *Chinatown News*, 17 September, 3 December 1967; 3 December 1969; 18 June 1970; 3 July 1973; and 3 June 1974.

59 Edgar Wickberg, ed., *From China to Canada: A History of the Chinese Communities in Canada* (Toronto: McClelland and Stewart, 1982), 257.

60 *Chinatown News*, 9 February 1970, 3 December 1971, and 3 May 1974.

61 See the case of the Chinese Baptist Church in *Jianada wengehua huaren jinxinhui chengli shi zhounian jinian tekan* [Vancouver Chinese Baptist Church Tenth Anniversary Souvenir, 1969-1979] 1979. Rev. Jonathan Cheung, interview by author, 26 March 1991. The Chinese Alliance Church and the Evangelical Free Church are two other examples. There are feature articles on the mushrooming of ethnic Chinese churches in Vancouver in the *Chinatown News*, 18 May 1973 and 3 November 1977.

62 Richard C. Nann and Lilian To, 'Experiences of Chinese Immigrants in Canada: (A) Building an Indigenous Support System,' in Richard Nann, ed., *Uprooting and Surviving: Adaptation and Resettlement of Migrant Families and Children* (Dordrecht, Holland: Reidel, 1982), 155-63.

63 'A Presentation on SUCCESS,' May 1980; *Success 1980: A Souvenir Booklet*, and *Annual Reports* 1978-1981. See also Nann and To, 'Experiences of Chinese Immigrants in Canada'; and Yvonne Au-Yeung, 'A Story of SUCCESS,' in *Huasi ji* [The Overseers] by the Chinese Students Association of the University of British Columbia 1981, 16-19.

64 'A Presentation on SUCCESS,' 12; Nann and To, 'Experiences of Chinese Immigrants in Canada,' 155; Jonathan Lau, interview by author, 15 December 1992. A social worker in the Strathcona area since he arrived from Hong Kong in 1968, Lau was the first executive director of SUCCESS.

65 Roy Mah, Harry Con, and Maggie Ip of SUCCESS formed the chairing committee of the national conference. The official organizer of the event was the Vancouver Immigration Policy Action Committee, an ad hoc coalition spearheaded by the CCC after the Green Paper was released in early 1975. Reports on the conference are available in the *Chinatown News*, 3 and 18 August, 3 and 18 September 1975. Here it should be noted that Ip was the first woman leader of a major ethnic Chinese community organization. She and her husband Kelly Ip, both of Hong Kong background, came to Canada in the 1960s as foreign students.

66 *Da Zhong Bao*, 3 November 1979; *Chinatown News*, 3 November 1980. A file on the Vietnamese Refugees Assistance Association, a SUCCESS sub-agency, is in S. Wah Leung Papers. On the award, see *Chinatown News*, 3 July 1980.

Chapter 8: Beyond a Conclusion

1 It is said that the confusion and loss of records created by the San Francisco earthquake of 1906 had allowed many Chinese, otherwise unqualified for naturalization, to claim American citizenship. It is also not uncommon for these 'American citizens,' after a visit to China and upon their return to the United States, to report the birth of a son at home, thereby creating a slot for future use. That ingenious practice, however, did not guarantee the smooth entry of many prospective 'paper sons' under the vigilant eyes of the American immigration authorities, as may be seen in the history of that infamous immigration station on Angel Island. See Him Mark Lai, Genny Lim, and Judy Yung, *Island: Poetry and History of Chinese Immigrants on Angel Island 1910-1940* (San Francisco: Hoc Doi, 1980).

2 The best account of the rise of the American-born Chinese in the early twentieth century is given by Him Mark Lai, *Cong huaqiao dao huaren: ershi shiji meiguo huaren shehui fazhanshi* [From Overseas Chinese to Ethnic Chinese: A History of Chinese Society in the United States in the Twentieth Century] (Hong Kong: Joint Publishing, 1992), 130-73. For autobiographical materials, see Pardee Lowe, *Father and Glorious Descendant: A Story of Chinese Life in America* (Boston: Little, Brown, 1943); and Jade Snow Wong, *Fifth Chinese Daughter* (Seattle: University of Washington Press, 1989). The now classic study by the Nees of the San Francisco Chinatown in the early 1970s offers by far the most complex view of generational divisions, but the tantalizing account is short on group interactions. See Victor G. Nee and Brett de Bary Nee, *Longtime Californ': A Documentary Study of an American Chinatown* (Stanford: Stanford University Press, 1972).

3 Personal communication with Edgar Wickberg, 8 December 1997. On colonial Malaya and Singapore, see Yen Ching-hwang, *A Social History of the Chinese in Singapore and Malaya 1800-1911* (Singapore: Oxford University Press, 1986), 46-48, 146-54. In his field report, Ju-K'ang T'ien shows that the negative connotations of the term 'sinkheh' were still at work as of the 1940s. *The Chinese of Sarawak: A Study of Social Structure* (London: London School of Economic and Political Science, 1953), 39.

4 Skinner, 'Creolized Chinese Societies in Southeast Asia,' in *Sojourners and Settlers: Histories of Southeast Asia and the Chinese*, ed. Anthony Reid (St. Leonards, Australia: Allen and Unwin, 1996), 51-59, 64-85.

5 On the Peranakan Chinese, see the many works of Leo Suryadinata, especially *Peranakan Chinese Politics in Java*, rev. ed. (Singapore: Singapore University Press, 1981); and *Political Thinking of the Indonesian Chinese, 1900-1977* (Singapore: Singapore University Press, 1979). Lea Williams, *Overseas Chinese Nationalism: The Genesis of the Pan-Chinese Movement in Indonesia, 1900-1916* (Glencoe: Free Press, 1960) remains useful on the initial onslaught of rising Chinese nationalist sentiments at the beginning of the twentieth century. On the Chinese Mestizos, see the classic study by Wickberg, *Chinese in Philippine Life 1850-1898* (New Haven: Yale University Press, 1965); and an earlier article, 'The Chinese Mestizo in Philippine History,' *Journal of Southeast Asian History* 5.1 (1964): 62-100. Anthropological understanding of the Baba is well served by the work of Tan Chee Beng, especially his book *Baba of Malaka: Culture and Identity of a Chinese Peranakan Community in Malaysia* (Kuala Lumpur: Pelanduk, 1988), but historical scholarship is relatively lacking. For a most sophisticated analysis of the different cultural trajectories of these three groups in the twentieth century, see Skinner, 'Creolized Chinese Societies in Southeast Asia,' 85-93.

6 Historically, Chinese in Malaya and Singapore had the most elaborate *bang* structure because of the relatively fair distribution of the five major dialect groups: Hokkien, Teochew, Cantonese, Hakka, and Hainanese. See Yen, *A Social History of the Chinese in Singapore and Malaya*, 177-94; and Mak Lau Fong, *Fangyanqun rentong: zaoqi xingma huaren de fenlei faze* [Dialect Group Identity: A Study of Chinese Subethnic Groups in Early Malaya] (Taipei: Academia Sinica, 1985). By the way, *bang* were also fairly common in internal migration within China involving merchant groups and labour gangs.

7 Skinner, *Leadership and Power in the Chinese Community of Thailand* (Ithaca: Cornell University Press, 1958); Maurice Freedman, 'Immigrants and Associations: Chinese in Nineteenth-Century Singapore,' *Comparative Studies in Society and History* 3.1 (1960): 25-48; and Lawrence Crissman, 'The Segmentary Structure of Urban Overseas Chinese Communities,' *Man* (n.s.) 2.2 (1967): 185-204.

8 For yet another good example of the previous research paradigm at work, see Yao Souchou, 'Why Chinese Voluntary Associations: Structure or Function,' *Journal of the South Seas Society* 39.1-2 (1984): 75-88. Note the contrast with the new perspective on social institutions that has shaped the work of some younger scholars in Chinese history and Asian American Studies, such as Bryna Goodman, *Native Place, City, and Nation: Regional Networks and Identities in Shanghai, 1853-1937* (Berkeley: University of California Press, 1995); and Yen Le Espiritu, *Asian American Panethnicity: Bridging Institutions and Identities* (Philadelphia: Temple University Press, 1992), respectively.

9 This is most clearly argued in two of the papers presented at a panel I organized for the *Luodi Sheng'gen* Conference in San Francisco in November 1992. See Wickberg, 'Chinese Organizations in Philippine Cities Since World War II: The Case of Manila'; and Him Mark Lai, 'Development of Organizations among Chinese in America since World War II.'

10 This unique contribution on the part of See Chinben is duly recognized and publicized by Edgar Wickberg, whose latest research promises to carry See's work even further. See his 'Chinese Organizations in Philippine Cities since World War II.'

11 A good example is the Kaisa Para Sa Kaunlaran formed in the early 1970s by a group of young ethnic Chinese university graduates in the Philippines. According to Wickberg, Kaisa 'encourages the understanding and retention of one's Chinese culture while fully identifying oneself with the Philippines and with Filipinos of non-Chinese backgrounds.' See his 'Some Comparative Perspectives on Contemporary Chinese Ethnicity in the Philippines,' *Asian Culture* 14 (1990): 29.

12 Tu Wei-ming's most frequently cited work is 'Cultural China: The Periphery as the Center,' in *The Living Tree: The Changing Meaning of Being Chinese Today*, ed. Tu Wei-ming (Stanford: Stanford University Press, 1994), 1-34. The literature on the rise of South China and its impact on national identity and local consciousness has been steadily expanding since the late 1980s. The following are just the more notable examples: Helen Siu, 'Cultural Identity and the Politics of Difference in South China,' *Daedalus* 122.2 (spring 1993): 19-43; Lynn

White and Li Cheng, 'China Coast Identities: Regional, National, and Global,' in *China's Quest for National Identity*, ed. Lowell Dittmer and Samuel S. Kim (Ithaca: Cornell University Press, 1993), 154-93; David S.G. Goodman and Feng Chongyi, 'Guangdong: Greater Hong Kong and the New Regionalist Future,' in *China Deconstruct: Politics, Trade and Regionalism*, ed. David Goodman and Gerald Segal (London: Routledge, 1994), 177-201; Thomas Gold, 'Go with Your Feelings: Hong Kong and Taiwan Popular Culture in Greater China,' *China Quarterly* 136 (December 1993): 907-25; George Crane, '"Special Things in Special Ways": National Economic Identity and China's Special Economic Zones,' *Australian Journal of Chinese Affairs* 32 (July 1994): 71-92; and Edward Friedman, *National Identity and Democratic Prospects in Socialist China* (Armonk, NY: Sharpe, 1995), especially part 2.

13 While this was generally the case, Wang Gungwu has provided a perceptive and detailed comparative discussion in 'Greater China and the Chinese Overseas,' *China Quarterly* 136 (December 1993): 926-48.

14 As Edgar Wickberg argued long ago, the Chinese Mestizos had taken form as a distinct group in the early Spanish period largely because of the government's desire to create a 'tamed' and acculturated (meaning Catholicized) group with the necessary 'Chinese' economic skills. See Wickberg, 'The Chinese Mestizo in Philippine History,' 67-71. Likewise, William Skinner has observed that the Peranakans were able to hold on to their collective identity against the pressure of re-sinicization in the early twentieth century in part because the Dutch stepped in at that critical juncture to cultivate their loyalty. See Skinner, 'Creolized Chinese Societies in Southeast Asia,' 91-92.

15 This was most clearly the case in Cambodia under French rule, where the system of *congrégation* incorporated the *bang* and its leadership into the colonial governing structure. See William Willmott, *The Political Structure of the Chinese Community in Cambodia* (London: Athlone, 1970), 18-45. Nowhere in colonial Southeast Asia was the system of indirect rule based on *bang* as elaborated and fully institutionalized as it was in Cambodia. For British Malaya, see Yen, *A Social History of the Chinese in Singapore and Malaya*, 177-94.

16 See the reflections of Wang Gungwu during the late 1950s in his 'A Short History of the Nanyang Chinese,' reprinted in his *Community and Nation: China, Southeast Asia and Australia* (St. Leonards, Australia: Allen and Unwin, 1992), especially 35-39. On the 1960s and 1970s, the best account is Leo Suryadinata, *China and the ASEAN States: The Ethnic Chinese Dimension* (Singapore: Singapore University Press, 1985).

17 William Wei, *The Asian American Movement* (Philadelphia: Temple University Press, 1993), 11-43.

18 Espiritu, *Asian American Panethnicity*.

19 David Hollinger, *Postethnic America: Beyond Multiculturalism* (New York: Basic, 1995), 19-50. For an example of earlier probing into pan-Asian ethnicity in Canada, see Anthony Chan, 'Neither French nor British: The Rise of the Asianadian Culture,' *Canadian Ethnic Studies* 10.2 (1978): 37-46.

20 Wei, *The Asian American Movement*, 44-71, 101-61.

21 Graham Johnson, 'Ethnic and Racial Communities in Canada and Problems of Adaptation: Chinese Canadians in the Contemporary Period,' *Ethnic Groups* 9 (1992): 151-74; and 'Hong Kong Immigration and the Chinese Community in Vancouver,' in *Reluctant Exiles: Hong Kong Communities Overseas*, ed. Ronald Skeldon (Armonk, NY: Sharpe, 1994), 120-38. See also Peter Li, 'Chinese Investment and Business in Canada: Ethnic Enterpreneurship Reconsidered,' *Pacific Affairs* 66 (1993): 219-43.

22 See the report by Hugh Tan in *Canada and Hong Kong Update* 5 (Fall 1991), 14-15.

23 Bernard Luk and Fatima Lee, 'The Chinese Communities of Toronto,' manuscript, January 1996. They also make a distinction between the Cantonese-speaking immigrants from the Pearl River Delta (the traditional emigrant districts) and the Mandarin speakers from other parts of Mainland China. This phenomenon of subethnicity is also being recognized by scholars working on contemporary Chinese immigration in the United States. See Peter Kwong, *Forbidden Workers: Illegal Chinese Immigrants and American Labor* (New York: New Press, 1997), for a penetrating analysis of the Fuzhounese (Hokchiu) in New York; and

Bernard Wong's latest San Francisco study, *Ethnicity and Entrepreneurship: The New Chinese Immigrants in the San Francisco Bay Area* (Boston: Allyn and Bacon, 1998).

24 In 1997, immigrants from Taiwan were estimated to have reached some 40,000 to 50,000 in Greater Vancouver. Some of their more high-profile organizations include the Buddhist Tzu Chi Foundation and the Taiwanese Canadian Cultural Society. Their strong presence probably explains why in 1991 the Taiwan government chose the city as the location for its first quasi-diplomatic body (the Taipei Economic and Cultural Office) in Canada.

25 Ethnic Chinese figure prominently in Kotkin's thesis of global tribes, made up of 'globally dispersed ethnic groups' and 'today's quintessential cosmopolitans.' See Joel Kotkin, *Tribes: How Race, Religion, and Identity Determine Success in the New Global Economy* (New York: Random, 1993), 3-4, 166-200. These contemporary trends in Chinese and global migration have prompted Wang Gungwu to refurbish the concept of sojourning in his latest work. See his 'Sojourning: The Chinese Experience in Southeast Asia,' *Asian Culture* 18 (June 1994): 52-61; and 'Migration and Its Enemies,' in *Conceptualizing Global History*, ed. Bruce Mazlish and Ralph Buultjens (Boulder: Westview, 1993), 131-51. Scholars in cultural studies have also attempted to conceptualize the problem of Chinese transnationalism, as in Aihwa Ong, 'On the Edge of Empires: Flexible Citizenship Among Chinese in Diaspora,' *Positions* 1.3 (1993): 745-78; and an important collection of essays in Aihwa Ong and Donald Nonini, eds., *Ungrounded Empires: The Cultural Politics of Modern Chinese Transnationalism* (New York: Routledge, 1997). On the Hong Kong Chinese in Vancouver specifically, see Katharyne Mitchell, 'Transnational Subjects: Constituting the Cultural Citizen in the Era of Pacific Rim Capital,' in Ong and Nononi, *Ungrounded Empires*, 228-56; and 'Flexible Circulation in the Pacific Rim: Capitalisms in Cultural Context,' *Economic Geography* 71.4 (1995): 364-82.

26 Arif Dirlik, 'Asians on the Rim: Transnational Capital and Local Community in the Making of Contemporary Asian America,' *Amerasia Journal* 22.3 (1996): 1-24. No less interesting is Sau-Ling C. Wong, 'Denationalization Reconsidered: Asian American Cultural Criticism at a Theoretical Crossroads,' *Amerasia Journal* 21.1-2 (1995): 1-27.

27 Note, for instance, Arif Dirlik's critique of the new literature on Chinese capitalism and its many assumptions about overseas Chinese culture and identity in his 'Critical Reflections on "Chinese Capitalism" as Paradigm,' in *South China: State, Culture and Social Change during the 20th Century*, ed. Leo Douw and Peter Post (Amsterdam: Royal Netherlands Academy of Arts and Sciences, 1996), 3-17; and 'Confucius in the Borderlands: Global Capitalism and the Reinvention of Confucianism,' *Boundary 2* 22.3 (1995): 229-73. In the same vein is Wang Gungwu's reservation about the term 'Greater China,' often employed in an alarmist fashion with reference to the growing power of ethnic Chinese businesses in the Asia Pacific and their presumed connection with China's latest attempt to achieve capitalism 'Chinese style.' See Wang Guangwu, 'Upgrading the Migrant: Neither *Huaqiao* nor *Huaren*,' in *The Last Half Century of Chinese Overseas*, ed. Elizabeth Sinn (Hong Kong: Hong Kong University Press, 1998), especially 23-24; and 'Greater China and the Chinese Overseas.' More directly, Go Bon Juan, a Chinese Filipino banker and newspaper publisher in Manila, has argued that the global Chinese obsession with 'Chineseness' is an ethnocentric expression of chauvinism. Given the long-term tendency of acculturation and local identification, Go believes that many ethnic Chinese would feel more at home with fellow members of a national and cultural group than with Chinese from other places. See his paper, 'Huaren zuowei shijie xianzhang' [Ethnic Chinese as a global phenomenon], *Si Yu Yan* 31.3 (1993): 143-52. Finally, on some recent attempts to 'resurrect to theoretical respectability the theme of (Chinese) diaspora,' see Ien Ang, 'To Be or Not to Be Chinese: Diaspora, Culture and Postmodern Ethnicity,' *Southeast Asian Journal of Social Science* 21.1 (1993): 1-17; and Ong and Nonini, *Ungrounded Empires*. The phase, immediately above, is from Nonini and Ong's introductory essay to this volume, 'Chinese Transnationalism as Alternative Modernity,' 18.

28 It is worth pointing out that the only scholar working extensively on transnationalism among Chinese in Vancouver is the University of Washington geographer Katharyne Mitchell. For an example of critical reflections by Chinese-Canadian artists and writers,

see the exhibition catalogue edited by Henry Tsang, *Self Not Whole: Cultural Identity and Chinese-Canadian Artists in Vancouver* (Vancouver: Chinese Cultural Centre, 1991).

29 For a recent analysis of this trendy development among ethnic Chinese worldwide, see Hong Liu, 'Old Linkages, New Networks: The Globalization of Overseas Chinese Voluntary Associations and Its Implications,' *China Quarterly* 155 (1998): 582-609.

30 During one of my recent visits to UBC at the time of a spring commencement, a Chinese friend told me, evidently out of annoyance, that because of the large number of Chinese graduates, mostly of Hong Kong background, there was a saying that UBC now stood for 'The University of Brilliant Chinese.'

31 Peter Li, 'Unneighbourly Houses or Unwelcome Chinese: The Social Construction of Race in the Battle over "Monster Homes" in Vancouver, Canada,' *International Journal of Comparative Race and Ethnic Studies* 1.1 (1994): 14-33.

32 Writing in the 1980s, Kay Anderson has argued that multiculturalism allowed the Canadian state to continuously define ethnic Chinese as 'outsiders.' See Kay Anderson, *Vancouver's Chinatown: Racial Discourse in Canada, 1875-1980* (Montreal and Kingston: McGill-Queen's University Press, 1991), 211-44. See also Karin Lee, 'Chinese – Chinese-Canadian – Canadian,' in Tsang, *Self Not Whole*, 24-29, which calls the policy a 'lightly disguised racial and cultural apartheid' (28).

33 Michael Goldberg, *The Chinese Connection: Getting Plugged into Pacific Rim Real Estate, Trade, and Capital Markets* (Vancouver: University of British Columbia, 1985); Victor Ujimoto, 'Multiculturalism and the Global Information Society,' in *Deconstructing A Nation: Immigration, Multiculturalism and Racism in 90s Canada* (Halifax: Fernwood, 1992), 351-57; and Kartharyne Mitchell, 'Multiculturalism, or the United Colors of Capitalism?' *Antipode* 25.4 (1993): 263-94. Notable examples of state patronage of ethnic Chinese include the appointment of David Lam, in 1988, as British Columbia's twentieth-fifth lieutenant-governor and the appointment of Raymond Chan, newly elected MP from Richmond, to a junior ministerial position in charge of Asia-Pacific affairs in 1993.

Glossary

Anti-Communist National Salvation Association　華僑反共救國會

baizi hui　百子會
baizi qiansun　百子千孫
bang　幫
Bo Yi Ju She　博藝劇社
bu touming　不透明
bu wanshan　不完善

Chan Wing Chun Tong　陳穎川堂
Chee Duck Tong　至德堂
Chee Kung Tong　致公堂
Chen Zhong She　晨鐘社
Cheng Wing Yeong Tong　鄭榮陽堂
Chew Luen Society　昭倫公所
Chiang Kai-shek　蔣介石
Chinatown Lions Club　華埠獅子會
Chinatown News　華埠新聞
Chinatown Property Owners Association　華埠業主會
Chinese Anglican Church　華人聖公會
Chinese Benevolent Association　中華會館
Chinese Canadian Citizens Association　中加友誼會
Chinese Canadian Club　同源會
Chinese Catholic Mission in Vancouver (which was renamed
　the Chinese Catholic Centre)　溫哥華聖方濟堂華人公教中心
Chinese Community Enrichment Services Society　中僑互助會
Chinese Community Reading Room (Chinese Community
　Library Services Association)　溫哥華中文圖書館
Chinese Consolidated Benevolent Association　域多利中華會館
Chinese Cultural Centre　中華文化中心

Chinese Elks　華人鹿頭會
Chinese-English Daily News (Huaying ribao)　華英日報
Chinese Literary Society (Huacui wenyi xuehui)　華萃文藝學會
Chinese Merchants Association　中華商會
Chinese Public School　華僑公立學校
Chinese Times (Dahan bao; Dahan gongbao)　大漢報、大漢公報
Chinese United Church　華人協和教會
Chinese Varsity Club　華生會
Chinese Veterans　華裔退伍軍人協會
Chinese Voice (Qiaosheng)　僑聲報
Chinese Youth Association　青年聯誼會
Ching Won　清韻音樂社
Chongyang　重陽
chu kou fei　出口費
chuncui de zuguo feng　純粹的祖國風
Chung Shan Lung Jen Association　中山隆鎮同鄉會

Da Zhong Bao　大衆報
Daily News (Rixin bao)　日新報
David T.H. Lee　李東海
Douglas Jung　鄭天華

Empire Reform Association *(Bao huang hui)*　保皇會
Enping　恩平

fang　房
fangkou　房口
fangong　反共
fanhua　反華
fan renmin　反人民
Father Peter Chow　周若漁神父
Fong Loon Tong　鳳倫堂
Foon Sien Wong　黃文甫
Freemasons　洪門民治黨
Freemasons Athletic Society　洪門體育會

gaodeng yule　高等娛樂
Gee How Oak Tin Association　至孝篤親公所
George D. Wong　黃鼎南
gongchan zai　共產仔

Hai Fung Club　海鋒會
haijian　漢奸

haiwai huaqiao zhi xianfeng　海外華僑之先鋒
Harry Con　簡建平
Harry Fan　范爾銳
Hon Hsing　漢升體育會
Hong Kong Merchants Association　香港僑商會
houtian de qinshan gan　後天的親善感
Hoy Ping District Association　開平會館
Hoy Sun Ning Yung Benevolent Association　台山寧陽會館
huaqiao　華僑
Huaqiao wenhua de luohou　華僑文化的落後

Ing Suey Sun Tong　伍胥山堂

jia aiguo　假愛國
jia zhongli　假中立
Jin Wah Sing　振華聲
jinru yiwu　盡足義務
Jinshan　金山

K. Tong Au　區鏡棠
Kaiping　開平
Kang Youwei　康有爲
Kelly Ip　葉承基
Kong Chow District Association　岡州會館
Kuomintang　國民黨

Lam Fong　林西屏
Lam Sai Ho Tong　林西河堂
Lao huaqiao　老華僑
Lee Clan Association　李氏公所
Li Hongzhang　李鴻章
Liang Qichao　梁啓超
longduan huaqiao wenhua　壟斷華僑文化
Lu Ming Bitsuey　鹿鳴別墅
Lung Kong Kung So　龍岡公所

Mah Fat Sing　馬榮騰
Mah Society　馬氏公所
Majong　麻雀
minzu bailei　民族敗類
minzu zunyan　民族尊嚴
Ming Po　明報
Ming Sing Reading Room　民星閱報社

Mon Keong   文疆學校

Nam Ping Bitsuey   南平別墅
Nam Yeung Tong   南陽堂
Nanhai   南海
New Republic (Xin minguo bao)   新民國報
Ng Tung King   伍冬瓊
Ngai Lum Musical Society   藝林音樂社
Ning Yang   寧陽

Oylin Society   愛蓮公所

Panyu   番禺
Paul Yee   余兆昌

Qiao Ying Qingnian She   僑英青年社
Qingming   清明
Qing Hua She   菁華社
Qing Lian Wen Lian She   青聯文聯社
Qing Yun Cao Tang Shi She   青雲草堂詩社
Qun Qing She   群青社

Reverend Andrew Lam   林恩澤牧師

S. Wah Leung   梁甦華
S. Won Leung   梁甦魂
Sanyi   三邑
Say Yup   四邑
Seto Gock   司徒國
Shek Kip Mei   石硤尾
Shon Yee Benevolent Association   鐵城崇義會
Shunde   順德
Sing Tao   星島日報
Sinkheh   新客
Siyi   四邑
Strathcona Property Owners and Tenants Association
   士達孔拿業主與住客協會
Sue Yuen Tong   溯源堂
Sun Yat-sen   孫中山

Tai Kung   大公義學
Taishan   台山
Tangshan   唐山

Tiankou　天九
Tung Wah Hospital　東華醫院
tusheng　土生
tusheng huayi　土生華裔

Vancouver Chinese Association of Commerce　溫哥華中華總商會

Wang Meng-hsien　王孟顯
Wen Yu Zhi Yao She　文娛之友社
Wong Kung Har Tong　黃江夏堂
Wong Sang　黃生
Wong Wun San Society　黃雲山公所
Wong's Benevolent Association　黃氏宗親會
World Journal　世界日報

Xian Qu Wenyu She　先驅文娛社
Xihua　西化
Xinhui　新會

Yee Fung Toy Tong　余風采堂
Yin Ping District Association　恩平會館
youru guoti　有辱國體
Yue San Association　禺山公所
Yun Qing Hui　雲青會
yundong　運動

Zhongguoren yu zhongwen　中國人與中文
Zhongshan　中山
Zhong qiao　中僑
zuguo qingnian　祖國青年

Bibliography

Newspapers, Periodicals, and Magazines
Chinese Language
Chinese Times 1946-80, various dates.
Chinese Voice 1954-70.
Da Zhong Bao 1965-81.
New Republic 1957-70, various dates.

English Language
Chinatown News 1953-80.
Da Zhong Bao September-December 1970.
Gum San Po 2.1 (February-March 1974).
New Bridge 1.1-7 (February-September 1971).
The New Citizen 1949-52, various issues.

Bilingual
Chinese Bulletin December 1960-May 1981, various issues. Renamed *Chinese Canadian Bulletin* in February 1968.
Mirror: Strathcona Community News 1.1 (10 June 1977)-2.8 (6 March 1978).

Special Publications and Newsletters of Chinese Organizations
'A Brief History of the Parish Church of the Good Shepherd.' In *The Dedication of the Church of the Good Shepherd Souvenir*. 1985.
Chinese Community Library Services Association Twentieth Anniversary Commemorative Special Publication 1972-1992. 1992.
Chinese Cultural Centre Report August 1975-May 1979. Continued thereafter as the *Mainstream*.
Chinese Tennis Club Annals. 1939, 1940, and 1946.
Chongyi qingnian yanjiu she tekan [Special Publication of the Shon Yee Youth Society]. 1952.
Enping zong huiguan nanping bieshu lianhe kenqinhui tekan [Yin Ping District Association Headquarters Nam Ping Bitsuey Joint Convention Special Publication]. 1981.
Haifeng hui jinian kan [Hai Fung Club: A Souvenir Publication]. 1968.
Huang hansheng tiyuhui qi zhounian jinian ji [Chronicle of the Wong Hon Hsing Athletic Club Seventh Anniversary]. 1947.
Huang wenfu xiansheng aisi lu [Memorial Volume of Mr. Foon Sien Wong]. 1971.
Huang yunshang zong gongsuo guozhi louye baogaoshu [Report on the Purchase of Land Properties by the Wong Wun San Society Headquarters]. 1957.
Huang yunshang zong gongsuo shiye gongsi zhangcheng [Constitution of the Real Estate Company of the Wong Wun San Society Headquarters]. 1953.

Huang yunshang zong gongsuo xinzhi luocheng kaimu ji di'er jie kenqin dahui shimoji [An Account of the Official Opening of the New Premises of the Wong Wun San Society Headquarters and the Second National Convention]. 1954.

Huaqiao gongli xuexiao choumu jingfei zhengxinlu [Chinese Public School Fund-Raising Report]. 1962.

Huaxin ji: zhongguo liu jia tongxuehui niankan chuangkanhao [Chinese Overseas Students Association Yearbook, First Issue]. 1962.

Huaxin ji [Chinese Overseas Students Association Yearbooks]. 1965 and 1970.

Huasi ji [The Overseers] by the Chinese Students Association of The University of British Columbia, September 1974, January 1975, January 1976, September 1976, January 1980, and 1981.

Jianada huang jiangxia tong shiye gongsi zhangcheng [Constitution of the Real Estate Company of the Wong Kung Har Tong of Canada]. 1944 and 1950.

Jianada huang jiangxia zongtong di liujie quanjia kenqin dahui shimoji [An Account of the Sixth National Convention of the Wong Kung Har Tong Canadian Headquarters]. 1955.

Jianada huang jiangxia zongtong di wujie quanjia kenqin dahui shimoji [An Account of the Fifth National Convention of the Wong Kung Har Tong Canadian Headquarters]. 1950.

Jianada wengehua chongzheng hui chengli shi zhounian jinian tekan [Vancouver Tsung Tsin Association Tenth Anniversary Souvenir Publication]. 1983.

Jianada wengehua huaren jinxinhui chengli shi zhounian jinian tekan [Vancouver Chinese Baptist Church Tenth Anniversary Souvenir, 1969-1979]. 1979.

Jianada wengehua tiecheng chongyi zonghui chengli di qishi zhounian jinian tekan [Souvenir Publication of the Seventieth Anniversary of the Shon Yee Benevolent Association of Canada, Vancouver, 1914-1984]. 1984.

Jianada wengehua yuemianliao huayi wuzuo lianyihui huikan [Vancouver Indochina Chinese Benevolent Association Publication]. 1985?.

Jianada yungaohua huaren xiehe jiaohui jiushisan zhounian jinian tekan [Ninety-third Anniversary of the Chinese United Church, Vancouver, BC, 1881-1981]. 1981.

Jianada yungaohua zhonghua huiguan juxing zhongxiu luocheng kaimu dianli tekan [Special Publication on the Opening Ceremony of the Chinese Benevolent Association in Vancouver, Canada, at the Completion of its Renovation]. 1952.

Jiayun hansheng tiyuhui chengli ershiwu zhounian jinian tekan [Twenty-Fifth Anniversary Souvenir Issue of the Hon Hsing Athletic Club, Vancouver, Canada]. 1965.

Jiayun hansheng tiyuhui disi zhounian jinian tekan [Fourth Anniversary Souvenir Issue of the Hon Hsing Athletic Club, Vancouver, Canada]. 1944.

Lishi yuekan [Lee's Association of Canada Monthly Magazine] 1.1-12 (October 1960-September 1961).

Lim xihe zongtong qiumu gongsuo hebing jinxi jinian tekan [Special Issue of the Lim Sai Ho Tong Headquarters – Kow Mock Kung So Amalgamation Golden Anniversary]. 1980.

Mainstream 1.1 (August 1979)-2.5 (December, 1980). Succeeded the *Chinese Cultural Centre Report*.

Quanjia lishi disan jie kenqin dahui jinian tekan [Souvenir Publication of the Third National Convention of the Lee Clan Association of Canada]. 1985.

Quanjia lishi disi jie kenqin dahui jinian tekan [Souvenir Publication of the Fourth National Convention of the Lee Clan Association of Canada]. 1988.

Quanjia taishan yiqiao dierjie kenqin dahui tekan [Special Issue of the Second Convention of the Taishan Overseas Chinese in Canada]. 1975.

Quanjia zhonghua zong huiguan gaikuang [Inside the Chinese Benevolent Association: A Report of Some Activities of the Highest Governing Body of the Chinese in Canada]. 1969.

Quanjia zhonghua zong huiguan zhengxinlu [Financial Report of the Chinese Benevolent Association of Canada]. 1952-53.

Quanjia zhonghua zong huiguan zhengxinlu [Financial Report of the Chinese Benevolent Association of Canada]. 1956-59.

Shengfangji tong jinqing jinian [Saint Francis Xavier Parish Golden Jubilee, 1933-1983]. 1983.

Shidakongna qu yezhu zhuke xiehui sannian gongzuo baogao [SPOTA Triennial Report]. November 1971.

The Strathcona Story. 1976.

SUCCESS 1980: A Souvenir Booklet. 1980.

Taishan ningyang huiguan liushi zhounian jinian tekan [Hoy Sun Ning Yung Benevolent Association Sixtieth Anniversary Souvenir Publication]. 1958.

Vancouver Chinatown Lions Club Thirtieth Anniversary 1954-1984. 1984.

Wenjiang xuexiao xiaokan [Mon Keong School, 1925-1985]. 1985.

Yushan zong gongsuo luocheng jinian ce [Commemorative Publication of the New Building of the Yue San Association Headquarters]. 1949.

Yunbu huaren zhanglaohui qishi zhounian jinian ji mingxie [Thanksgiving and Souvenir Publication of the Seventieth Anniversary of the Chinese Presbyterian Church in Vancouver, 1895-1965]. 1965.

Yunbu huaren zhanglaohui jiushi zhounian tangqing [Chinese Presbyterian Church of Vancouver Ninetieth Anniversary Souvenir, 1895-1985]. 1985.

Yunbu taishan huiguan bashi zhounian jinian tekan [Vancouver Hoy Sun Benevolent Association Eightieth Anniversary Souvenir Publication]. 1977.

Zhonghua wenhua zhongxin chengli shi zhounian jinian tekan [Chinese Cultural Centre Tenth Anniversary Souvenir Publication, 1973-1983]. 1983.

Zhonghua wenhua zhongxin chengli shiwu zhounian tekan [Chinese Cultural Centre Fifteenth Anniversary Souvenir Publication, 1973-1988]. 1988.

Zhuyun quanjia kaiping zong huiguan tekan [Special Issue of the Hoy Ping District Association Canadian Headquarters in Vancouver]. 1947.

Zili zhonghua jidu jiaohui qishiwu zhounian gan'en jinian kan [Seventy-fifth Anniversary Thanksgiving Report of the Christ Church of China]. 1986.

Organizational Archives

Unless otherwise stated, the following items remain in the custody of the respective Chinese organizations.

Chinese Cultural Centre. *Minutes of Meetings, Board of Directors* 1975-81. In S. Wah Leung Papers.

–. 'CCC Workers Conference, January 17-18, 1976.' In S. Wah Leung Papers.

–. 'U.N. Habitat Conference, May-June 1976.' In S. Wah Leung Papers.

Chinese United Church of Vancouver. *Annual Reports* 1959-67.

–. *Minutes of the Official Board* 1953-67.

Ing Suey Sun Tong. *Wu xushan tong caoliu bao* [Ing Suey Sun Tong Account Books] 1936-43, 1944-51, and 1952-55.

–. *Wu xushan tong yi'an bao* [Ing Suey Sun Tong Minutes of Meetings] 1927-37, 1938-53, and 1976-92.

Pender Guy Archives, 1975-81. Deposited with the Chinese Community Library Services Association.

–. 'The Chinese Canadian Communities Research in the Fraser Valley.' A report prepared by Anthony Chung, Summer 1977.

–. 'Life on Pender Guy.' *Co-op Radio: 102.7 FM Programme Guide* November 1980.

–. 'A Report on the B.C. Chinese Canadian Youth Conference, UBC, May 16-18, 1975.'

SPOTA Files, City of Vancouver Archives. ADD. MSS. 734.

SUCCESS, *Annual Reports* 1978-81.

–. 'A Presentation on SUCCESS.' May 1980.

Personal Papers and Collections of Research Materials

Chinese Canadian Research Collections, Special Collections Division, University of British Columbia Library.

Chinese Community History Room Collections, Chinese Community Library Services Association, Vancouver.

S. Wah Leung Papers, 1973-88. In possession of Sophia Leung.

Thomas Moore Whaun Papers, 1914-84. Special Collections Division, University of British Columbia Library.

Foon Sien Wong Papers, 1930s-1960s. Special Collections Division, University of British Columbia Library.

Public Archival Materials

'A Brief Concerning Immigration Laws (and Citizenship Act) for Presentation to the Honourable Ellen L. Fairclough, Minister of Citizenship and Immigration, by the Chinese Benevolent Association, June 24, 1959.' In National Archives of Canada, H.W. Herridge Papers, MG 32 C13, vol. 40, file 5.

'A Brief Concerning Immigration Laws Submitted to the Cabinet by the Chinese Benevolent Association, March 24, 1950.' In National Archives of Canada, RG 76, vol. 122, file 23635.

City of Vancouver, Office of the City Clerk, 81 D7, File on Civic Development, Expropriation, Redevelopment Project II A5 A6 A7.

Letter from Andrew Lam to Paul Lacoste, co-secretary, Royal Commission on Bilingualism and Biculturalism, 21 June 1965. In National Archives of Canada, RG 33, series 80, vol. 121, file 679E.

'Memorandum and Petition Submitted to the Honourable, the Premier of British Columbia, John Hart, Esq., and the Honourable Ministers of the Executive Council of the Government of the Province of British Columbia, on February 16, 1945, by a Delegation representing the Chinese Canadian Association.' In National Archives of Canada, Roy Graham Dunlop Papers, MG 30 D 349, vol. 1, II 53-54, BC-1944-61.

'Report: Private Meeting with [a] Chinese Canadian Group, Vancouver.' In National Archives of Canada, RG 33, series 80, Royal Commission on Bilingualism and Biculturalism, vol. 120, file 634E.

Submission by the Chinese Merchants Association. In National Archives of Canada, Chinese Consular Records, MG 10 C2, vol. 4, file 5.

Published Government Documents

Canadian Citizenship Statistics. 1952-80.

Census of Canada. 1951-81.

City of Vancouver, Planning Department. *Chinatown, Vancouver: Design Proposal for Improvement*. 1964.

–. Planning Department. *Chinatown Planning Newsletter*. November 1976.

–. Planning Department for the Housing Research Committee. *Vancouver Redevelopment Study*. 1957.

–. Technical Planning Board. *Redevelopment Project No. 2*. July, 1963.

–. Technical Planning Board. *Strathcona Sub-area Report, Urban Renewal, Scheme 3*. 1968.

Department of Citizenship and Immigration. *Annual Reports*. 1949-56.

Immigration Branch, Department of Mines and Resources. *Annual Reports*. 1946-49.

Immigration Statistics. 1956-80.

Report of the Royal Commission on Chinese and Japanese Immigration. Ottawa: Printed by S.E. Dawson 1902.

Report of the Royal Commission on Chinese Immigration. Ottawa: Printed by Order of the Commission 1885.

Books, Monographs, and Theses

Anderson, Benedict. *Imagined Communities: Reflections on the Origins and Spread of Nationalism*. Rev. ed. London: Verso, 1991.

Anderson, Kay. *Vancouver's Chinatown: Racial Discourse in Canada, 1875-1980*. Montreal and Kingston: McGill-Queen's University Press, 1991.

Bell, Catherine. *Ritual Theory, Ritual Practice*. New York: Oxford University Press, 1992.

Bell, Larry, and Richard Moore. *The Strathcona Rehabilitation Project: Documentation and Analysis*. Vancouver: Social Policy and Research, United Way of Greater Vancouver, 1975.

Benton, Gregor, and Frank N. Pieke, eds. *The Chinese in Europe*. New York: St. Martin's, 1998.

Brown, Melissa J., ed. *Negotiating Ethnicities in China and Taiwan*. Berkeley: Center for Chinese Studies, University of California, 1996.

Burnet, Jean. *Coming Canadians: An Introduction to a History of Canada's Peoples*. Toronto: McClelland and Stewart, 1988.

Chan, Anthony. *Gold Mountain: The Chinese in the New World*. Vancouver: New Star, 1983.

Chen, Chung-min, Chuang Ying-chang, and Huang Shu-min, eds. *Ethnicity in Taiwan: Social, Historical, and Cultural Perspectives*. Taipei: Institute of Ethnology, Academia Sinica, 1994.

Chirot, Daniel, and Anthony Reid, eds. *Essential Outsiders: Chinese and Jews in the Modern Transformation of Southeast Asia and Central Europe*. Seattle: University of Washington Press, 1997.

Chong, Denise. *The Concubine's Children: Portrait of a Family Divided*. Toronto: Viking, 1994.

Chow, Peter. *Jing quan ji* [The Fountain]. Vancouver: Chinese Catholic Publishing Bureau, 1956; 2nd. ed. 1958.

Chow, Rey. *Writing Diaspora: Tactics of Intervention in Contemporary Cultural Studies*. Bloomington: Indiana University Press, 1993.

Chu, Garrick, et al. eds. *Inalienable Rice: A Chinese and Japanese Anthology*. Vancouver: Powell Street Revue and the Chinese Canadian Writers Workshop, 1979.

Cohen, Robin. *Global Diasporas: An Introduction*. Seattle: University of Washington Press, 1997.

Cole, James H. *Shaohsing: Competition and Cooperation in Nineteenth-Century China*. Tucson: University of Arizona Press, 1986.

Con, Harry. *Zhongguo hongmen zai jianada* [The Chinese Freemasons in Canada]. Vancouver: Chinese Freemasons Canadian Headquarters, 1989.

Constable, Nicole. *Christian Souls and Chinese Spirits: A Hakka Community in Hong Kong*. Berkeley: University of California Press, 1994.

–. ed. *Guest People: Hakka Identity in China and Abroad*. Seattle: University of Washington Press, 1996.

Crossley, Pamela. *Orphan Warriors: Three Manchu Generations and the End of the Qing World*. Princeton: Princeton University Press, 1990.

–. *The Manchus*. Cambridge, MA: Blackwell, 1997.

Cushman, Jennifer, and Wang Gungwu, eds. *Changing Identities of the Southeast Asian Chinese since World War II*. Hong Kong: Hong Kong University Press, 1988.

Dou, Jiliang. *Tongxiang zuzhi zhi yanjiu* [Studies on Native Place Organizations]. Chongqing: Zhengzhong, 1943.

Dreisziger, D.F., with M.L. Kovacs, Paul Body, and Bennett Kovrig. *Struggle and Hope: The Hungarian-Canadian Experience*. Toronto: McClelland and Stewart, 1982.

Eisen, Arnold M. *Galut: Modern Jewish Reflection on Homelessness and Homecoming*. Bloomington: Indiana University Press, 1986.

Erickson, B.H. 'Prestige, Power and the Chinese.' MA thesis, University of British Columbia, 1966.

Espiritu, Yen Le. *Asian American Panethnicity: Bridging Institutions and Identities*. Philadelphia: Temple University Press, 1992.

'Ethnicity in Qing China.' Special Issue of *Late Imperial China* 11.1 (1990).

Evans, Paul, and Michael Frolic, eds. *Reluctant Adversaries: Canada and the People's Republic of China, 1949-1971*. Toronto: University of Toronto Press, 1991.

Faure, David, and Helen F. Siu, eds. *Down to Earth: The Territorial Bond in South China*. Stanford: Stanford University Press, 1995.

Fitzgerald, Stephen. *China and the Overseas Chinese: A Study of Peking's Changing Policy, 1949-1970*. Cambridge: Cambridge University Press, 1972.

Friedman, Edward. *National Identity and Democratic Prospects in Socialist China*. Armonk, NY: Sharpe, 1995.

Gee, Emma, ed. *Counterpoint: Perspectives on Asian America*. Los Angeles: Asian American Studies Center, University of California, 1976.

Geertz, Clifford. *The Interpretation of Cultures*. New York: Basic, 1973.

Gilroy, Paul. *The Black Atlantic: Modernity and Double Consciousness*. Cambridge, MA: Harvard University Press, 1993.

Gladney, Dru. *Muslim Chinese: Ethnic Nationalism in the People's Republic*. Cambridge, MA: Council on East Asian Studies, Harvard University Press, 1991.

Godley, Michael. *The Mandarin-Capitalists from Nanyang: Overseas Chinese Enterprise in the Modernization of China, 1893-1911*. Cambridge: Cambridge University Press, 1981.

Goldberg, Michael. *The Chinese Connection: Getting Plugged into Pacific Rim Real Estate, Trade, and Capital Markets*. Vancouver: UBC Press, 1985.

Goodman, Bryna. *Native Place, City, and Nation: Regional Networks and Identities in Shanghai, 1853-1937*. Berkeley: University of California Press, 1995.

'Greater China.' Special Issue of *China Quarterly* 136 (1993).

Gunn, Sean, and Paul Yee, eds. 'A Special Issue on Vancouver.' *Asianadian* 3.2 (1980).

Hambro, Edvard. *The Problem of Chinese Refugees in Hong Kong: Report Submitted to the United Nations High Commissioner for Refugees*. Leyden, Holland: Sijthoff, 1955.

Harrell, Stevan, ed. *Cultural Encounters on China's Ethnic Frontiers*. Seattle: University of Washington Press, 1995.

Hawkins, Freda. *Canada and Immigration: Public Policy and Public Concern*. Montreal and Kingston: McGill-Queen's University Press, 1972.

Ho, Ping-ti. *Zhongguo huiguan shilun* [A Historical Survey of Landsmannschaften in China]. Taipei: Xuesheng, 1966.

Hollinger, David A. *Postethnic America: Beyond Multiculturalism*. New York: Basic, 1995.

Honig, Emily. *Creating Chinese Ethnicity: Subei People in Shanghai, 1850-1980*. New Haven: Yale University Press, 1992.

Hsu, Madeline Yuan-Yin, 'Living Abroad and Faring Well: Migration and Transnationalism in Taishan County, Guangdong 1904-1939.' PhD diss., Yale University, 1996.

Huang, Belinda. 'Gender, Race, and Power: The Chinese in Canada, 1920-1950.' MA thesis, McGill University, 1998.

Huang, Evelyn. *Chinese Canadians: Voices from a Community*. Vancouver: Douglas and McIntyre, 1992.

Jarvie, Ian C., and Joseph Agassi, eds. *Hong Kong: A Society in Transition*. New York: Praeger, 1968.

Kotkin, Joel. *Tribes: How Race, Religion, and Identity Determine Success in the New Global Economy*. New York: Random, 1993.

Kuo, Chia-ling. *Social and Political Change in New York's Chinatown: The Role of Voluntary Associations*. New York: Praeger, 1977.

Kwong, Peter. *The New Chinatown*. New York: Hill and Wang, 1987.

–. *Forbidden Workers: Illegal Chinese Immigrants and American Labor*. New York: New Press, 1997.

Lai, David Chuenyan. *Chinatowns: Towns within Cities in Canada*. Vancouver: UBC Press, 1988.

–. *The Forbidden City Within Victoria: Myth, Symbol and Streetscape of Canada's Earliest Chinatown*. Victoria: Orca, 1991.

Lai, Him Mark. *Cong huaqiao dao huaren: ershi shiji meiguo huaren shehui fazhanshi* [From Overseas Chinese to Ethnic Chinese: A History of Chinese Society in the United States in the Twentieth Century]. Hong Kong: Joint Publishing, 1992.

Lai, Him Mark, Genny Lim, and Judy Yung. *Island: Poetry and History of Chinese Immigrants on Angel Island 1910-1940*. San Francisco: Hoc Doi, 1980.

Lee, David T.H. *Jianada huaqiao shi* [A History of the Chinese in Canada]. Taipei: Canada Free Press, 1967.

Lee, Rose Hum. *The Chinese in the United States of America*. Hong Kong: Hong Kong University Press, 1960.

Leong, Sow-Theng, *Migration and Ethnicity in Chinese History: Hakkas, Pengmin, and Their Neighbors*. Stanford: Stanford University Press, 1997.

Leung, Sophia, and Paul Robertson, eds. *S. Wah Leung: Celebration of a Splendid Life*. Vancouver: Faculty of Dentistry, University of British Columbia, 1992.

Li, Peter S. *The Chinese in Canada.* Toronto: Oxford University Press, 1988.

Lim, Linda Y.C., and L.A. Peter Gosling, eds. *The Chinese in Southeast Asia:* Vol. 1, *Ethnicity and Economic Activity;* Vol. 2, *Identity, Culture and Politics.* Singapore: Maruzen Asia, 1983.

Lin, Sen. *Yimin jianada bidu* [Must-Reading for Emigration to Canada]. Hong Kong: Lin Sen, 1968.

Lipman, Jonathan N. *Familiar Strangers: A History of Muslims in Northwest China.* Seattle: University of Washington Press, 1997.

Liu, Haiming. 'Between China and America: The Trans-Pacific History of the Chang Family.' PhD diss., University of California, Irvine, 1996.

Lowe, Pardee. *Father and Glorious Descendant: A Story of Chinese Life in America.* Boston: Little, Brown, 1943.

Lyman, Stanford. *Chinese Americans.* New York: Random, 1974.

Ma, Eve Armentrout. *Revolutionaries, Monarchists and Chinatowns: Chinese Politics in Americas and the 1911 Revolution.* Honolulu: University of Hawaii Press, 1990.

Mak, Lau Fong. *Fangyanqun rentong: zaoqi xingma huaren de fenlei faze* [Dialect Group Identity: A Study of Chinese Subethnic Groups in Early Malaya]. Taipei: Academia Sinica, 1985.

Makabe, Tomoko. *The Canadian Sansei.* Toronto: University of Toronto Press, 1998.

Marsh, Leonard. *Rebuilding a Neighbourhood: Report on a Demonstration Slum-Clearance and Urban Rehabilitation Project in a Key Central Area in Vancouver.* Research Publications, no. 1. Vancouver: University of British Columbia, 1950.

Morton, James. *In the Sea of Sterile Mountains: The Chinese in British Columbia.* Vancouver: Douglas, 1977.

Nann, Richard. 'Urban Renewal and Relocation of Chinese Community Families.' PhD diss., University of California at Berkeley, 1970.

Nee, Victor G., and Brett de Bary Nee. *Longtime Californ': A Documentary Study of an American Chinatown.* Stanford: Stanford University Press, 1972.

Ong, Aihwa, and Donald Nonini, eds. *Ungrounded Empires: The Cultural Politics of Modern Chinese Transnationalism.* New York: Routledge, 1997.

Otsuka, Chihiro. 'Remaking an Institution and Community: The Vancouver Japanese Language School after the War.' MA thesis, University of British Columbia, 1995.

Overseas Chinese Affairs Commission, comp. *Qiaowu ershiwu nian* [Overseas Chinese Affairs, 1932-57]. Taiwan: Overseas Chinese Affairs Commission, 1958.

Ownby, David, and Mary Somers Heidhues, eds. *'Secret Societies' Reconsidered: Perspectives on the Social History of Modern South China and Southeast Asia.* Armonk, NY: Sharpe, 1993.

Pan, Lynn. *Sons of the Yellow Emperor: The Story of the Overseas Chinese.* London: Secker and Warburg, 1990.

Pendakur, Setty. *Cities, Citizens and Freeways.* Vancouver: Pendakur, 1972.

Poon, Joanne M. 'Miss Queen of Cathay (1954): Chinese Women, Families and Associations in Vancouver.' MA thesis, University of British Columbia, 1995.

Porter, John. *The Vertical Mosaic.* Toronto: University of Toronto Press, 1965.

Rasporich, Anthony W. *For a Better Life: A History of the Croatians in Canada.* Toronto: McClelland and Stewart, 1982.

Rowe, William. *Hankow: Commerce and Society in a Chinese City, 1796-1889.* Stanford: Stanford University Press, 1984.

–. *Hankow: Conflict and Community in a Chinese City 1796-1895.* Stanford: Stanford University Press, 1989.

Roy, Patricia. *A White Man's Province: British Columbia Politicians and Chinese and Japanese Immigrants, 1858-1914.* Vancouver: UBC Press, 1989.

Rudelson, Justin Jon. *Oasis Identities: Uyghur Nationalism Along China's Silk Road.* New York: Columbia University Press, 1997.

'Salute to the 60s and 70s: Legacy of the San Francisco State Strike.' Special Issue of *Amerasia Journal* 15.1 (1989).

Sangren, Steven. *History and Magical Power in a Chinese Community.* Stanford: Stanford University Press, 1987.

Seagrave, Sterling. *Lords of the Rim: The Invisible Empire of the Overseas Chinese.* New York: Putnam, 1995.

Sien Lok Society of Calgary. *National Conference on Urban Renewal as It Affects Chinatown.* Calgary: Sien Lok Society, 1969.

Sinn, Elizabeth. *Power and Charity: The Early History of the Tung Wah Hospital, Hong Kong.* Hong Kong: Oxford University Press, 1990.

–, ed. *The Last Half Century of Chinese Overseas.* Hong Kong: Hong Kong University Press, 1998.

Siu, Paul C.P. *The Chinese Laundryman: A Study of Social Isolation.* New York: New York University Press, 1987.

Skeldon, Ronald, ed. *Reluctant Exiles? Migration from Hong Kong and the New Overseas Chinese.* Armonk, NY: Sharpe, 1994.

–. *Emigration from Hong Kong: Tendencies and Impact.* Hong Kong: Chinese University Press, 1995.

Skinner, William. *Chinese Society in Thailand: An Analytical History.* Ithaca: Cornell University Press, 1957.

–. *Leadership and Power in the Chinese Community of Thailand.* Ithaca: Cornell University Press, 1958.

Spence, Jonathan. *The Search for Modern China.* New York: Norton, 1990.

Stanley, Timothy. 'Defining the Chinese Other: White Supremacy, Schooling and Social Structure in British Columbia before 1923.' PhD diss., University of British Columbia, 1991.

Straaton, K. 'The Political System of the Vancouver Chinese Community: Associations and Leadership in the Early 1960s.' MA thesis, University of British Columbia, 1974.

Suryadinata, Leo, ed. *Political Thinking of Indonesian Chinese, 1900-1977.* Singapore: Singapore University Press, 1979.

–. *Peranakan Chinese Politics in Java.* Rev. ed. Singapore: Singapore University Press, 1981.

–. *China and the ASEAN States: The Ethnic Chinese Dimension.* Singapore: Singapore University Press, 1985.

–. ed. *Ethnic Chinese as Southeast Asians.* New York: St. Martin's, 1997.

Tachiki, Amy, et al. *Roots: An Asian American Reader.* Los Angeles: Asian American Studies Center, University of California, 1971.

Takaki, Ronald. *Strangers from a Different Shore: A History of Asian Americans.* New York: Penguin, 1989.

Tan, Chee Beng, *The Baba of Melaka: Culture and Identity of a Chinese Peranakan Community in Malaysia.* Kuala Lumpur: Pelanduk, 1988.

Tan, Thomas Tsu-wee. 'Singapore Modernization: A Study of Traditional Chinese Voluntary Associations in Social Change.' PhD diss., University of Virginia, 1983.

T'ien, Ju-K'ang. *The Chinese of Sarawak: A Study of Social Structure.* London: London School of Economic and Political Science, 1953.

Tong, Benson. *Unsubmissive Women: Chinese Prostitutes in Nineteenth-Century San Francisco.* Norman: University of Oklahoma Press, 1994.

Tsai, Shih-shan Henry. *The Chinese Experience in America.* Bloomington: Indiana University Press, 1986.

Tsang, Henry, ed. *Self Not Whole: Cultural Identity and Chinese-Canadian Artists in Vancouver.* Vancouver: Chinese Cultural Centre, 1991.

Tseng, Timothy. 'Ministry at Arm's-Length: Asian Americans in the Racial Ideology of American Mainline Protestants, 1882-1952.' PhD diss., Union Theological Seminary, New York, 1994.

Tu, Wei-ming, ed. *The Living Tree: The Changing Meaning of Being Chinese Today.* Stanford: Stanford University Press, 1994.

Turner, Victor. *From Ritual to Theatre: The Human Seriousness of Play.* New York: Performing Arts Journal Publications, 1982.

–, ed. *Celebration: Studies in Festivity and Ritual.* Washington, DC: Smithsonian Institution Press, 1982.

Wai, Hayne Yip. 'The Chinese and the Voluntary Association in British Columbia: A Political Machine Interpretation.' MA thesis, Queen's University, 1970.

Ward, Peter. *White Canada Forever: Popular Attitudes and Public Policy towards Orientals in British Columbia.* 2nd ed. Montreal and Kingston: McGill-Queen's University Press, 1990.

Wasserstrom, Jeffrey. *Student Protests in Twentieth-Century China: The View from Shanghai.* Stanford: Stanford University Press, 1991.

Webber, Jonathan, ed. *Jewish Identities in the New Europe.* London: Littman Library, 1994.

Wei, William. *The Asian American Movement.* Philadelphia: Temple University Press, 1993.

Weiss, Melford S. *Valley City: A Chinese Community in America.* Cambridge, MA: Schenkman, 1974.

Wickberg, Edgar. *The Chinese in Philippine Life 1850-1898.* New Haven: Yale University Press, 1965.

– ed. *From China to Canada: A History of the Chinese Communities in Canada.* Toronto: McClelland and Stewart, 1982.

Williams, Lea E. *Overseas Chinese Nationalism: The Genesis of the Pan-Chinese Movement in Indonesia, 1900-1916.* Glencoe: Free Press, 1960.

Willmott, William E. *The Political Structure of the Chinese Community in Cambodia.* London: Athlone, 1970.

Women's Book Committee, Chinese Canadian National Council. *Jin Guo: Voices of Chinese Canadian Women.* Toronto: Women's Press, 1992.

Wong, Bernard. *Ethnicity and Entrepreneurship: The New Chinese Immigrants in the San Francisco Bay Area.* Boston: Allyn and Bacon, 1998.

Wong, Jade Snow. *Fifth Chinese Daughter.* Seattle: University of Washington Press, 1989.

Woo, Wesley S. 'Protestant Work among the Chinese in the San Francisco Bay Area, 1850-1920,' PhD diss., Graduate Theological Union, Berkeley, 1983.

Woon, Yuen-fong. *The Excluded Wife.* Montreal and Kingston: McGill-Queen's University Press, 1998.

Wynn, Graeme, and Timothy Oke, eds. *Vancouver and Its Region.* Vancouver: UBC Press 1992.

Yang, C.K. *Religion in Chinese Society: A Study of Contemporary Social Functions of Religion and Some of Their Historical Factors.* Berkeley: University of California Press, 1961.

Yee, Paul. 'Chinese Business in Vancouver, 1886-1914.' MA thesis, University of British Columbia, 1983.

–. *Saltwater City: An Illustrated History of the Chinese in Vancouver.* Vancouver: Douglas and McIntyre, 1988.

Yen, Ching-hwang. *A Social History of the Chinese in Singapore and Malaya 1800-1911.* Singapore: Oxford University Press, 1986.

Yip, Quene. *Vancouver Chinatown: Specially Prepared for the Vancouver Golden Jubilee, 1886-1936.* Vancouver: n.p. 1936.

Yung, Judy. *Unbound Feet: A Social History of Chinese Women in San Francisco.* Berkeley: University of California Press, 1995.

Articles

Adilman, Tamara. 'A Preliminary Sketch of Chinese Women and Work in British Columbia, 1858-1950.' In *Not Just Pin Money: Selected Essays on the History of Women's Work in British Columbia*, ed. B. Latham, R. Latham, and R. Pazdro, 53-78. Victoria: Camosun College Press, 1984; reprinted in *British Columbia Reconsidered: Essays on Women*, ed. Gillian Creese and Veronica Strong-Boag, 309-39. Vancouver: Press Gang, 1992.

Ang, Ien. 'To Be or Not to Be Chinese: Diaspora, Culture and Postmodern Ethnicity.' *Southeast Asian Journal of Social Science* 21.1 (1993): 1-17.

Appadurai, Arjun. 'Global Ethnoscapes: Notes and Queries for a Transnational Anthropology.' In *Recapturing Anthropology: Writing in the Present*, ed. Richard G. Fox, 191-210. Santa Fe: School of American Research Press, 1991.

–. 'Sovereignty Without Territoriality: Notes for a Postnational Geography.' In *The Geography of Identity*, ed. Patricia Yaeger, 40-58. Ann Arbor: University of Michigan Press, 1996.

Au-Yeung, Yvonne. 'A Story of SUCCESS.' In *Huasi ji* [The Overseers] by the Chinese Students Association of the University of British Columbia, 16-19. 1981.

Barth, Frederik. 'Introduction.' In *Ethnic Groups and Boundaries*, ed. Frederik Barth, 9-38. Boston: Little, Brown, 1969.

Baureiss, Gunter. 'Ethnic Resilience and Discrimination: Two Chinese Communities in Canada.' *Journal of Ethnic Studies* 10.1 (1982): 69-87.

Bociurkiw, Bohdan. 'The Federal Policy of Multiculturalism and the Ukrainian-Canadian Community.' In *Ukrainian Canadians, Multiculturalism, and Separatism: An Assessment*, ed. Manoly R. Lupul, 98-128. Alberta: Canadian Institute of Ukrainian Studies, University of Alberta Press, 1978.

Boyarin, Daniel, and Jonathan Boyarin. 'Diaspora: Generation and the Ground of Jewish Identity.' In *Identities*, ed. Kwame Anthony Appiah and Henry Louis Gates, Jr., 305-37. Chicago: University of Chicago Press, 1995.

Breton, Raymond. 'Institutional Completeness of Ethnic Communities and the Personal Relations of Immigrants.' *American Journal of Sociology* 70.2 (1964): 193-205.

–. 'The Production and Allocation of Symbolic Resources: An Analysis of the Linguistic and Ethnocultural Fields in Canada.' *Canadian Review of Sociology and Anthropology* 21.2 (1984): 123-44.

Burnet, Jean. 'The Policy of Multiculturalism within a Bilingual Framework: A Stock-Taking.' *Canadian Ethnic Studies* 10.2 (1978): 107-13.

Cannadine, David. 'The Context, Performance, and Meaning of Ritual: The British Monarchy and the "Invention of Tradition," c. 1820-1977.' In *The Invention of Tradition*, ed. Eric Hobsbawm and Terence Ranger, 101-64. Cambridge: Cambridge University Press, 1983.

Chan, Anthony. 'Neither French nor British: The Rise of the Asianadian Culture.' *Canadian Ethnic Studies* 10.2 (1978): 37-46.

–. 'Citizen Aliens: Television and the Hong Kong Chinese as Sojourner.' *Asian Profile* 18.2 (1990): 117-25.

Chan, Ming K. 'All in the Family: The Hong Kong-Guangdong Link in Historical Perspective.' In *The Hong Kong-Guangdong Link: Partnership in Flux*, ed. Reginald Yin-Wang Kwok and Alvin Y. So, 31-63. Armonk, NY: Sharpe, 1995.

Chan, Sucheng. 'Asian American Historiography.' *Pacific Historical Review* 65.3 (1996): 363-99.

Chang, Gordon. 'Ethnic History: A Case for Chinese Canadians.' *Mainstream* 1.3 (December 1979): 18.

Cho, George, and Roger Leigh. 'Patterns of Residence of the Chinese in Vancouver.' In *Peoples of the Living Land*, ed. J. Minghi, 67-84. BC Geographical Series, no. 15. Vancouver: Tantalus, 1972.

Choi, Po-king. 'A Search for Cultural Identity: The Students' Movement of the Early Seventies.' In *Differences and Identities: Education Argument in Late Twentieth Century Hong Kong*, ed. Anthony Sweeting, 81-107. Hong Kong: Faculty of Education, University of Hong Kong, 1990.

–. 'From Dependence to Self-Sufficiency: Rise of the Indigenous Culture of Hong Kong.' *Asian Culture* 14 (1990): 161-77.

Chu, Larry. 'A Review of the Activities and Special Events Committees.' In *Zhonghua wenhua zhongxin chengli shi zhounian jinian tekan* [The Chinese Cultural Centre Tenth Anniversary Souvenir Publication 1973-1983], 28-31, 1983.

Chun, Allen. 'From Nationalism to Nationalizing: Cultural Imagination and State Formation in Postwar Taiwan.' *Australian Journal of Chinese Affairs* 31 (1994): 49-69.

Clifford, James. 'Traveling Cultures.' In *Cultural Studies*, ed. L. Grossberg, C. Nelson, and P. Treichler, 96-116. New York: Routledge, 1992.

–. 'Diasporas.' *Cultural Anthropology* 9.3 (1994): 302-38.

Cole, James H. 'Competition and Cooperation in Late Imperial China as Reflected in Native Place and Ethnicity.' In *Remapping China: Fissures in Historical Terrain*, ed. Gail Hershatter et al., 156-63. Stanford: Stanford University Press, 1996.

Crane, George T. '"Special Things in Special Ways": National Economic Identity and China's Special Economic Zones.' *Australian Journal of Chinese Affairs*, 32 (July 1994): 71-92.

Creese, Gillian. 'Organizing Against Racism in the Workplace: Chinese Workers in Vancouver before the Second World War.' *Canadian Ethnic Studies* 19.3 (1987): 35-46.

Crissman, Lawrence. 'The Segmentary Structure of Urban Overseas Chinese Communities.' *Man* (n.s.) 2.2 (1967): 185-204.

DeGlopper, Donald. 'Religion and Ritual in Lukang.' In *Religion and Ritual in Chinese Society*, ed. Arthur Wolf, 43-69. Stanford: Stanford University Press, 1974.

Dirlik, Arif. 'Confucius in the Borderlands: Global Capitalism and the Reinvention of Confucianism.' *Boundary 2* 22.3 (1995): 229-73.

–. 'Critical Reflections on "Chinese Capitalism" as Paradigm.' In *South China: State, Culture and Social Change during the 20th Century*, ed. Leo Douw and Peter Post, 3-17. Amsterdam: Royal Netherlands Academy of Arts and Sciences, 1996.

–. 'Asians on the Rim: Transnational Capital and Local Community in the Making of Contemporary Asian America.' *Amerasia Journal* 22.3 (1996): 1-24.

Esherick, Joseph, and Jeffrey Wasserstrom. 'Acting Out Democracy: Political Theatre in Modern China.' *Journal of Asian Studies* 49.4 (1990): 835-65.

Evans, Paul, and Daphne Taras. 'Canadian Public Opinion on Relations with China: An Analysis of Existing Survey Research.' Working Paper No. 33. Toronto: Joint Centre on Modern East Asia, March 1985.

–. 'Looking (Far) East: Parliament and Canada-China Relations, 1949-1982.' In *Parliament and Canadian Foreign Policy*, ed. David Taras, 66-100. Toronto: Canadian Institute of International Affairs, 1988.

Freedman, Maurice. 'The Handling of Money: A Note on the Background to the Economic Sophistication of Overseas Chinese.' *Man* 59 (1959): 64-65.

–. 'Immigrants and Associations: Chinese in Nineteenth-Century Singapore.' *Comparative Studies in Society and History* 3.1 (1960): 25-48.

Frolic, Michael. 'Canada and the People's Republic of China: Twenty Years of a Bilateral Relationship, 1970-1990.' In *Canada and the Growing Presence of Asia*, ed. Frank Langdon, 41-62. Occasional Paper No. 9. Vancouver: University of British Columbia, Institute of Asian Research, 1990.

Go, Bon Juan. 'Huaren zuowei shijie xianzhang' [Ethnic Chinese as a Global Phenomenon]. *Si Yu Yan* 31.3 (1993): 143-52.

Gold, Thomas B. 'Go With Your Feelings: Hong Kong and Taiwan Popular Culture in Greater China.' *China Quarterly* 136 (1993): 907-25.

Goodman, Bryna. 'The Locality as Microcosm of the Nation? Native Place Networks and Early Urban Nationalism in China.' *Modern China* 21.4 (1995): 387-419.

Goodman, David S. G., and Feng Chongyi. 'Guangdong: Greater Hong Kong and the New Regionalist Future.' In *China Deconstruct: Politics, Trade and Regionalism*, ed. David Goodman and Gerald Segal, 177-201. London: Routledge, 1994.

Hall, Stuart. 'Cultural Identity and Diaspora.' In *Identity: Community, Culture, and Difference*, ed. Jonathan Rutherford, 222-37. London: Lawrence and Wishart, 1990.

–. 'The Local and the Global: Globalization and Ethnicity.' In *Culture, Globalization and the World System*, ed. Anthony D. King, 19-39. Binghamton: Department of Art and Art History, State University of New York at Binghamton, 1991.

–. 'Old and New Identities, Old and New Ethnicities.' In *Culture, Globalization and the World System*, ed. Anthony D. King, 41-68. Binghamton: Department of Art and Art History, State University of New York at Binghamton, 1991.

–. 'The Question of Cultural Identity.' In *Modernity and Its Futures*, ed. Stuart Hall, David Held, and Tong McGrew, 273-325. Cambridge: Polity, 1992.

Harney, Robert. 'Boarding and Belonging: Thoughts on Sojourning Institutions.' *Urban History Review* 2 (October 1987): 8-37.

–. '"So Great a Heritage as Ours": Immigration and the Survival of the Canadian Polity.' *Daedalus* 117.4 (1988): 51-97.

Hobsbawm, Eric. 'Introduction: Inventing Traditions.' In *The Invention of Tradition*, ed. Eric Hobsbawm and Terence Ranger, 1-14. Cambridge: Cambridge University Press, 1983.

Honig, Emily. 'Migrant Culture in Shanghai: In Search of a Subei Identity.' In *Shanghai Sojourners*, ed. Frederic Wakeman, Jr. and Wen-hsin Yeh, 239-65. Berkeley: Institute of East Asian Studies, University of California at Berkeley, 1992.

–. 'Native Place and the Making of Chinese Ethnicity.' In *Remapping China: Fissures in Historical Terrain*, ed. Gail Hershatter et al., 143-55. Stanford: Stanford University Press, 1996.

Isajiw, Wsevolod. 'Multiculturalism and the Integration of the Canadian Community.' *Canadian Ethnic Studies* 15.2 (1983): 107-17.

Johnson, Graham. 'Chinese Family and Community in Canada: Tradition and Change.' In *Two Nations, Many Cultures*, ed. Jean Elliot, 358-71. Scarborough: Prentice Hall, 1979.

–. 'Chinese-Canadians in the 1970s: New Wine in New Bottles?' In *Two Nations, Many Cultures*, ed. Jean Elliot, 393-411. Scarborough: Prentice Hall, 1983.

–. 'Ethnic and Racial Communities in Canada and Problems of Adaptation: Chinese Canadians in the Contemporary Period.' *Ethnic Groups* 9 (1992): 151-74.

–. 'Hong Kong Immigration and the Chinese Communities in Vancouver.' In *Reluctant Exiles: Hong Kong Communities Overseas*, ed. Ronald Skeldon, 120-38. Armonk, NY: Sharpe, 1994.

Kallen, Evelyn. 'Multiculturalism: Ideology, Policy and Reality.' *Journal of Canadian Studies* 17.1 (1982): 51-63.

Keyes, Charles. 'Towards a New Formulation of the Concept of Ethnic Group.' *Ethnicity* 3 (1976): 202-13.

–. 'The Dialectics of Ethnic Change.' In *Ethnic Change*, ed. Charles Keyes, 3-30. Seattle: University of Washington Press, 1981.

Kim, Hyung-chan, and Nicholas Lai. 'Chinese Community Resistance to Urban Renewal: The Case of Strathcona in Vancouver, Canada.' *Journal of Ethnic Studies* 10.2 (1982): 67-81.

Lai, Him Mark. 'Historical Development of the Chinese Consolidated Benevolent Association/*Huiguan* System.' In *Chinese America: History and Perspectives 1987*, 13-51. San Francisco: Chinese Historical Society of America, 1987.

–. 'Development of Organizations Among Chinese in America Since World War II.' Paper Presented at the Luodi Sheng'gen Conference, San Francisco, November 26-29, 1992.

Lal, Brij. 'The Chinese Benevolent Association of Vancouver, 1889-1960: An Analytical History.' Unpublished paper, 1975.

Lee, Bennett. 'Early Casualties, or How to Lose out to the History Books: The Chinese in British Columbia.' In *Inalienable Rice: A Chinese and Japanese Anthology*, ed. Garrick Chu et al., 3-7. Vancouver: Powell Street Revue and the Chinese Canadian Writers Workshop, 1979.

Lee, Carol. 'The Road to Enfranchisement: Chinese and Japanese in British Columbia.' *BC Studies* 30 (summer 1976): 44-76.

Lee, Karin. 'Chinese – Chinese-Canadian – Canadian.' In *Self Not Whole: Cultural Identity and Chinese-Canadian Artists in Vancouver*, ed. Henry Tsang, 24-29. Vancouver: Chinese Cultural Centre, 1991.

Lee, Leo Ou-fan. 'On the Margins of the Chinese Discourse: Some Personal Thoughts on the Cultural Meaning of the Periphery.' In *The Living Tree: The Changing Meaning of Being Chinese Today*, ed. Tu Wei-ming, 221-38. Stanford: Stanford University Press, 1994.

Leung, S. Wah. 'The First Ten Years – A Rocky Road to Success.' *Zhonghua wenhua zhongxin chengli shi zhounian jinian tekan* [The Chinese Cultural Centre Tenth Anniversary Souvenir Publication 1973-1983], 18-20.

–. 'Random Reflections.' In *Zhonghua wenhua zhongxin chengli shiwu zhounian tekan* [The Chinese Cultural Centre Fifteenth Anniversary Souvenir Publication 1973-1988], 8-10, 1988.

Ley, David. 'Liberal Ideology and the Postindustrial City.' *Annals of the Association of American Geographers* 70.2 (1980): 238-58.

Li, Peter. 'Immigration Laws and Family Patterns: Some Demographic Changes among Chinese Families in Canada, 1885-1971.' *Canadian Ethnic Studies* 12.1 (1980): 58-73.

–. 'The Emergence of the New Middle Class among the Chinese in Canada.' *Asian Culture* 14 (1990): 187-94.

–. 'Chinese Investment and Business in Canada: Ethnic Enterpreneurship Reconsidered.' *Pacific Affairs* 66 (1993): 219-43.

–. 'Unneighbourly Houses or Unwelcome Chinese: The Social Construction of Race in the Battle over "Monster Homes" in Vancouver, Canada.' *International Journal of Comparative Race and Ethnic Studies* 1.1 (1994): 14-33.

Li, Peter, and Singh Bolaria. 'Canadian Immigration Policy and Assimilationist Theories.' In *Economy, Class and Social Reality*, ed. John Fry, 411-22. Scarborough, Ontario: Butterworths, 1979.

Liu, Hong. 'Old Linkages, New Networks: The Globalization of Overseas Chinese Voluntary Associations and Its Implications.' *China Quarterly* 155 (1998): 582-609.

Luk, H.K. Bernard. 'Xianggang lishi yu xianggang wenhua' [Hong Kong History and Hong Kong Culture]. In *Culture and Society in Hong Kong*, ed. Elizabeth Sinn, 64-79. Hong Kong: Centre of Asian Studies, University of Hong Kong, 1995.

Luk. H.K. Bernard, and Fatima W.B. Lee. 'The Chinese Communities of Toronto.' Manuscript. January 1996.

Lum, Janet. 'Recognition and the Toronto Chinese Community.' In *Reluctant Adversaries: Canada and the People's Republic of China, 1949-1971*, ed. Paul Evans and Michael Frolic, 217-40. Toronto: University of Toronto Press, 1991.

Lyman, Stanford. 'Red Guard on Grant Avenue: The Rise of Youthful Rebellion in Chinatown.' In *The Asian in North America*, ed. Stanford M. Lyman, 177-99. Santa Barbara: ABC-Clio, 1977.

Mackie, J.A.C. 'Overseas Chinese Entrepreneurship.' *Asian-Pacific Economic Literature* 6.1 (1992): 41-64.

McEvoy, E.J. '"A Symbol of Racial Discrimination": The Chinese Immigration Act and Canada's Relations with China, 1942-1947,' *Canadian Ethnic Studies* 14.3 (1982): 24-42.

Mitchell, Katharyne. 'Multiculturalism, or the United Colors of Capitalism?' *Antipode* 25.4 (1993): 263-94.

–. 'Flexible Circulation in the Pacific Rim: Capitalisms in Cultural Context.' *Economic Geography* 71.4 (1995): 364-82.

–. 'Transnational Subjects: Constituting the Cultural Citizen in the Era of Pacific Rim Capital.' In *Ungrounded Empires: The Cultural Politics of Modern Chinese Transnationalism*, ed. Aihwa Ong and Donald Nonini, 228-56. New York: Routledge, 1997.

–. 'Reworking Democracy: Contemporary Immigration and Community Politics in Vancouver's Chinatown.' *Political Geography* 17.6 (1998): 729-50.

Molot, Maureen Appel. 'Canada's Relations with China since 1968.' In *A Foremost Nation: Canadian Foreign Policy and a Changing World*, ed. Norman Hillmer and Garth Stevenson, 230-67. Toronto: McClelland and Stewart, 1976.

Moodley, Kogila. 'Canadian Multiculturalism as Ideology.' *Ethnic and Racial Studies* 3.3 (1983): 320-31.

Nagata, Judith. 'What Is a Malay? Situational Selection of Ethnic Identity in a Plural Society.' *American Ethnologist* 1.2 (1974): 331-50.

–. 'Local and International Networks among Overseas Chinese in Southeast Asia and Canada.' In *The Quality of Life in Southeast Asia*, ed. Bruce Matthews, 255-81. Montreal: CCSEAS, 1992.

Nann, Richard C., and Lilian To. 'Experiences of Chinese Immigrants in Canada: (A) Building an Indigenous Support System.' In *Uprooting and Surviving: Adaptation and Resettlement of Migrant Families and Children*, ed. Richard Nann, 155-63. Dordrecht, Holland: Reidel, 1982.

Ng, Wing Chung. 'Taiwan's Overseas Chinese Policy from 1949 to the Early 1980s.' In *East Asia Inquiry: Selected Articles from the Annual Conferences of the Canadian Asian Studies Association, 1988-1990*, Larry Shyu et al., 265-86. Montreal: CASA, 1991.

–. 'Scholarship on Post-World War II Chinese Societies in North America: A Thematic Discussion.' In *Chinese America: History and Perspectives, 1992*, 177-210. San Francisco: Chinese Historical Society of America and Asian American Studies, San Francisco State University, 1992.

–. 'Urban Chinese Social Organization: Some Unexplored Aspects in *Huiguan* Development in Singapore, 1900-1941.' *Modern Asian Studies* 26.3 (1992): 469-94.

–. 'Review of Kay Anderson, *Vancouver's China: Racial Discourse in Canada.' Histoire sociale – Social History* 26 (May 1993): 135-36.

Nonini, Donald, and Aihwa Ong. 'Chinese Transnationalism as an Alternative Modernity.' In *Ungrounded Empires: The Cultural Politics of Modern Chinese Transnationalism*, 3-33. New York: Routledge, 1997.

Ong, Aihwa. 'On the Edge of Empires: Flexible Citizenship Among Chinese in Diaspora.' *Positions* 1.3 (1993): 745-78.

Palmer, Howard. 'Reluctant Hosts: Anglo-Canadian Views of Multiculturalism in the Twentieth Century.' In *Readings in Canadian History: Post-Confederation*, ed. Douglas Francis and Donald Smith, 185-201. 2nd ed. Toronto: Holt, Rinehart, and Winston, 1986.

–. 'Recent Studies in Canadian Immigration and Ethnic History: The 1970s and 1980s.' *Proceedings of the First Tsukuba Seminar on Canadian Studies*, 3-37. University of Tsukuba, 1989.

Perin, Roberto. 'Clio as an Ethnic: The Third Force in Canadian Historiography.' *Canadian Historical Review* 64.4 (1983): 441-67.

Peter, Karl. 'The Myth of Multiculturalism and Political Fables.' In *Ethnicity, Power and Politics in Canada*, ed. Jorgen Dahlie and Tissa Fernando, 56-67. Toronto: Methuen, 1981.

Peterson, Glen. 'Socialist China and the Huaqiao: The Transition to Socialism in the Overseas Chinese Areas of Rural Guangdong, 1949-1956.' *Modern China* 14.3 (1988): 309-35.

Phillips, Alan. 'The Criminal Society that Dominates the Chinese in Canada.' *Maclean's Magazine* 75.7 (April 7, 1962): 11, 40-48.

Pizanias, Caterina. 'Centering on Changing Communities: Multiculturalism as Meaning and Message.' *Canadian Ethnic Studies* 24.3 (1992): 87-98.

Rawski, Evelyn. 'A Historian's Approach to Chinese Death Ritual.' In *Death Ritual in Late Imperial and Modern China*, ed. James Watson and Evelyn Rawski, 20-34. Berkeley: University of California Press, 1988.

Roy, Patricia E. '"Active Voices": A Third Generation of Studies of the Chinese and Japanese in British Columbia.' *BC Studies* 117 (spring 1998): 51-61.

Safran, William. 'Diasporas in Modern Societies: Myths of Homeland and Return.' *Diaspora* 1.1 (spring 1991): 83-99.

Sedgwick, Charles, and William Willmott. 'External Influences and Emerging Identity: The Evolution of Community Structure among Chinese Canadians.' *Canadian Forum* (September 1974): 8-12.

See, Chinben. 'Feilubin huaren wenhua de zhixu' [Persistence and Preservation of Chinese Culture in the Philippines]. *Bulletin of the Institute of Ethnology, Academia Sinica* 42 (1976): 119-206.

Sharp, Robin. 'A Study in the Voting Behaviour of the Chinese in Vancouver Centre.' Undergraduate essay in Political Science, University of British Columbia, 1956.

Shils, Edward. 'Roots – A Sense of Place and Past: The Cultural Gains and Losses of Migration.' In *Human Migration: Patterns and Policies*, ed. W.H. McNeill and R.S. Adams, 404-26. Bloomington: Indiana University Press, 1978.

Sinn, Elizabeth. 'Challenges and Responses: The Development of Hong Kong's Regional Associations, 1945-1990.' Paper presented at the Twelfth Conference of the International Association of Historians of Asia, 24-28 June 1991, University of Hong Kong.

–. 'Xin Xi Guxiang: A Study of Regional Associations as a Bonding Mechanism in the Chinese Diaspora. The Hong Kong Experience.' *Modern Asian Studies* 31.2 (1997): 375-97.

Siu, Helen F. 'Recycling Tradition: Culture, History, and the Political Economy in the Chrysanthemum Festivals of South China.' *Comparative Studies in Society and History* 32.4 (1990): 765-94.

–. 'Cultural Identity and the Politics of Difference in South China.' *Daedalus* 122.2 (spring 1993): 19-43.

Skinner, William. 'Mobility Strategies in Late Imperial China: A Regional Systems Analysis.' In *Regional Analysis:* Vol. 1, ed. Carol Smith, 327-64. New York: Academic Press, 1976.

–. 'Introduction: Urban Social Structure in Ch'ing China.' In *The City in Late Imperial China*, ed. William Skinner, 521-54. Stanford: Stanford University Press, 1977.

–. 'Creolized Chinese Societies in Southeast Asia.' In *Sojourners and Settlers: Histories of Southeast Asia and the Chinese*, ed. Anthony Reid, 51-93. St. Leonards, Australia: Allen and Unwin, 1996.

Smith, Allan. 'Metaphor and Nationality in North America.' *Canadian Historical Review* 51 (1970): 247-75.

Song, Ping. 'Feilubin huaren zongqinhui de jiangzhu xuejin zhidu' [The System of Scholarship and Bursary in the Chinese Clansmen Associations in the Philippines]. In *Overseas Chinese Historical Studies* (Beijing) 27 (1994): 16-21.

Stanley, Timothy. 'White Supremacy and the Rhetoric of Educational Indoctrination: A Canadian Case Study.' In *Making Imperial Mentalities: Socialization and British Imperialism*, ed. J.A. Mangan, 144-62. Manchester: Manchester University Press, 1990.

–. 'Schooling, White Supremacy and the Formation of a Chinese Merchant Public in British Columbia.' *BC Studies* 107 (autumn 1995): 3-29.

–. '"Chinamen, Wherever We Go": Chinese Nationalism and Guangdong Merchants in British Columbia, 1871-1911.' *Canadian Historical Review*. 77.4 (1996): 475-503.

Stasiulis, Daiva. 'The Political Structuring of Ethnic Community Action: A Reformulation.' *Canadian Ethnic Studies* 12.3 (1980): 19-44.

Sugimoto, Howard. 'The Vancouver Riots of 1907: A Canadian Episode.' In *East Across the Pacific*, ed. Hilary Conroy and Scott Miyakawa, 92-126. Honolulu: University of Hawaii Press, 1972.

Suryadinata, Leo. 'The Ethnic Chinese in the ASEAN States.' In *The Ethnic Chinese in the ASEAN States: Bibliographical Essays*, ed. Suryadinata, 4-42. Singapore: Institute of Southeast Asian Studies, 1989.

Takaki, Ronald. 'Teaching American History through a Different Mirror.' *Perspectives* (American Historical Association Newsletter) 32.7 (1994): 1, 9-12.

Thom, Bing. 'Interview with Bing Thom on China, the Chinese Canadian Movement, and the Vancouver Chinese Cultural Centre.' In *Inalienable Rice: A Chinese and Japanese Anthology*, ed. Garrick Chu et al., 33-38. Vancouver: Powell Street Revue and the Chinese Canadian Writers Workshop, 1979.

Thompson, Richard. 'Ethnicity Versus Class: An Analysis of Conflict in a North American Chinese Community.' *Ethnicity* 4.4 (1979): 306-26.

Tu, Wei-ming. 'Cultural China: The Periphery as the Center.' In *The Living Tree: The Changing Meaning of Being Chinese Today*, ed. Tu Wei-ming, 1-34. Stanford: Stanford University Press, 1994.

Turner, Victor. 'Social Drama and Ritual Metaphor.' In *Ritual, Play, and Performance: Readings in the Social Sciences/Theatre*, ed. Richard Schechner and Mady Schuman, 97-120. New York: Seabury, 1976.

Ujimoto, K. Victor. 'Multiculturalism and the Global Information Society.' In *Deconstructing A Nation: Immigration, Multiculturalism and Racism in 90s Canada*, 351-57. Halifax: Fernwood, 1992.

Wai, Hayne. 'Strathcona – Chinatown ... Twenty Years Ago.' In *Chinese Community Library Services Association Twentieth Anniversary Commemorative Special Publication 1972-1992*, 13-15.

Wai, Joe, and Chu Cheong. 'The Building and Planning Committee Report.' In *Zhonghua wenhua zhongxin chengli shi zhounian jinian tekan* [The Chinese Cultural Centre Tenth Anniversary Souvenir Publication 1973-1983], 21-26.

Wang, Gungwu. 'A Note on the Origins of *Hua-ch'iao*.' In *Community and Nation: Essays on Southeast Asia and the Chinese*, 118-27. Singapore: Heinemenn, 1981.

–. 'The Study of Chinese Identities in Southeast Asia.' In *Changing Identities of the Southeast Asian Chinese since World War II*, ed. Jennifer Cushman and Wang Gungwu, 1-21. Hong Kong: Hong Kong University Press, 1988.

–. 'A Short History of the Nanyang Chinese.' In *Community and Nation: China, Southeast Asia and Australia*, 11-39. St. Leonards, Australia: Allen and Unwin, 1992.

–. 'Chinese Politics in Malaya.' In *Community and Nation: China, Southeast Asia and Australia*, 251-80.

–. 'Migration and Its Enemies.' In *Conceptualizing Global History*, ed. Bruce Mazlish and Ralph Buultjens, 131-51. Boulder: Westview, 1993.

–. 'Greater China and the Chinese Overseas.' *China Quarterly* 136 (December 1993): 926-48.

–. 'Among Non-Chinese.' In *The Living Tree: The Changing Meaning of Being Chinese Today*, ed. Tu Wei-ming, 127-46. Stanford: Stanford University Press, 1994.

–. 'Sojourning: The Chinese Experience in Southeast Asia.' *Asian Culture* 18 (June 1994): 52-61.

–. 'Upgrading the Migrant: Neither *Huaqiao* nor *Huaren*.' In *The Last Half Century of Chinese Overseas*, ed. Elizabeth Sinn, 15-33. Hong Kong: Hong Kong University Press, 1998.

Wang, L. Ling-chi. 'Roots and the Changing Identity of the Chinese in the United States.' In *The Living Tree: The Changing Meaning of Being Chinese Today*, ed. Tu Wei-ming, 185-212. Stanford: Stanford University Press, 1994.

Ward, Peter. 'Class and Race in the Social Structure of British Columbia, 1870-1939.' *BC Studies* 45 (spring 1980): 17-35.

Watson, James L. 'Standardizing the Gods: The Promotion of T'ien Hou (Empress of Heaven) along the South China Coast, 960-1960.' In *Popular Culture in Late Imperial China*, ed. David Johnson, Andrew J. Nathan, and Evelyn S. Rawski, 292-324. Berkeley: University of California Press, 1985.

–. 'The Structure of Chinese Funerary Rites: Elementary Sequence, and the Primacy of Performance.' In *Death Ritual in Late Imperial and Modern China*, ed. James Watson and Evelyn Rawski, 3-19. Berkeley: University of California Press, 1988.

–. 'Rites or Beliefs? The Construction of a Unified Culture in Late Imperial China.' In *China's Quest for National Identity*, ed. Lowell Dittmer and Samuel S. Kim, 80-103. Ithaca: Cornell University Press, 1993.

Webber, Jonathan. 'Modern Jewish Identities: The Ethnographic Complexities.' *Journal of Jewish Studies* 43.2 (1992): 246-67.

White, Lynn, and Li Cheng. 'China Coast Identities: Regional, National, and Global.' In *China's Quest for National Identity*, ed. Lowell Dittmer and Samuel S. Kim, 154-93. Ithaca: Cornell University Press, 1993.

Wickberg, Edgar. 'The Chinese Mestizo in Philippine History.' *Journal of Southeast Asian History* 5.1 (1964): 62-100.

–. 'Chinese Organizations and the Canadian Political Process: Two Case Studies.' In *Ethnicity, Power and Politics in Canada*, ed. Jorgen Dahlie and Tissa Fernando, 172-76. Toronto: Methuen, 1981.

–. 'Chinese Organizations and Ethnicity in Southeast Asia and North America since 1945: A Comparative Analysis.' In *Changing Identities of the Southeast Asian Chinese since World War II*, ed. Jennifer Cushman and Wang Gungwu, 303-18. Hong Kong: Hong Kong University Press, 1988.

–. 'Some Comparative Perspectives on Contemporary Chinese Ethnicity in the Philippines.' *Asian Culture* 14 (1990): 23-37.

–. 'Notes on Some Contemporary Social Organizations in Manila Chinese Society.' In *China, Across the Seas; The Chinese as Filipinos*, ed. Aileen S.P. Baviera and Teresita Ang See, 43-66. Quezon City: Philippine Association for Chinese Studies, 1992.

–. 'Chinese Organizations in Philippine Cities Since World War II: The Case of Manila.' Paper Presented at the Luodi Sheng'gen Conference, San Francisco, November 26-29, 1992.

–. 'Overseas Chinese Adaptive Organizations, Past and Present.' In *Reluctant Exiles? Migration from Hong Kong and the New Overseas Chinese*, ed. Ronald Skeldon, 69-84. Armonk, NY: Sharpe, 1994.

Willmott, William. 'A Study of the Chinese Community in Vancouver: [A] Preliminary Report.' N.d., Chinese Canadian Research Collections, Special Collections, UBC.

–. 'Chinese Clan Associations in Vancouver.' *Man* 64 (1964): 33-37.

–. 'Some Aspects of Chinese Communities in British Columbia Towns.' *BC Studies* 1 (winter 1968-69): 27-36.

–. 'Approaches to the Study of the Chinese in British Columbia.' *BC Studies* 4 (spring 1970): 38-52.

Wong, Barry. 'Pender Guy.' *The Asianadian* 3.2 (1980): 24-25.

–. 'Pender Guy: Street History.' N.d.

Wong, Bernard. 'Elites and Ethnic Boundary Maintenance: A Study of the Roles of Elites in Chinatown, New York City.' *Urban Anthropology* 6.1 (1977): 1-22.

Wong, John. 'A Brief History of the Chinese Cultural Centre.' In *Zhonghua wenhua zhongxin shi zhounian jinian tekan* [The Chinese Cultural Centre Tenth Anniversary Souvenir Publication 1973-1983], 11-17.

Wong, Sau-Ling C. 'Denationalization Reconsidered: Asian American Cultural Criticism at a Theoretical Crossroads.' *Amerasia Journal* 21.1-2 (1995): 1-27.

Wong, Shue Tuck. 'Urban Redevelopment and Rehabilitation in the Strathcona Area: A Case Study of an East Vancouver Community.' In *Vancouver: Western Metropolis*, ed. L. Evenden, 255-69. Victoria: University of Victoria, 1978.

Wong, Paul, et al. 'From Despotism to Pluralism: The Evolution of Voluntary Organizations in Chinese American Communities.' *Ethnic Groups* 8 (1990): 15-33.

Wu, David Yen-ho. 'To Kill Three Birds with One Stone: The Rotating Credit Associations of the Papua New Guinea Chinese.' *American Ethnologist* 1.3 (1974): 565-84.

Yao, Souchou. 'Why Chinese Voluntary Associations: Structure or Function,' *Journal of the South Seas Society* 39.1-2 (1984): 75-88.

Yee, Donald. 'Pender Guy: Are You Listening?' In *Inalienable Rice: A Chinese and Japanese Anthology*, ed. Garrick Chu et al. 65-67. Vancouver: Powell Street Revue and the Chinese Canadian Writers Workshop, 1979.

Yee, Paul. 'Where Have All the Young People Gone? Vancouver's Chinese Cultural Centre and Its Native-Born.' In *Asian Canadians: Regional Perspectives*, ed. K.V. Ujimoto and G. Hirabayashi, 355-68. Published Conference Proceedings of the Asian Canadian Symposium V, 1982.

–. 'Where Do We Go From Here?' In *Zhonghua wenhua zhongxin chengli shi zhounian jinian tekan* [The Chinese Cultural Centre Tenth Anniversary Souvenir Publication 1973-1983], 39-41.

Interviews

I interviewed forty individuals of Chinese background between September 1990 and May 1993. These people included members of various generations of immigrant and local-born Chinese. The interviews did not follow any standard procedure and I did not use a questionnaire. In general, I first asked informants, in a non-threatening and non-intrusive manner, for personal information and then encouraged them to elaborate upon their views of Chinatown events, personalities, and organizations. I did not use a tape recorder.

Index

Set in Stone by Artegraphica Design Co. Ltd.

Printed and bound in Canada by Friesens

Copy editor: Joanne Richardson

Proofreader: Ron Phillips